Introductory Guide

Contents

Foreword	3
Acknowledgements	4
Chapter 1: Introduction and Purpose	5
Chapter 2: NHS Finance Background and Context – how we got to where we are today	7
Chapter 3: NHS Finance – Who Does What: The Role of Government, Ministers, the Department of Health (including its ALBs) and NHS Property Services Ltd	17
Chapter 4: NHS Finance – Who Does What: The Role of NHS England	27
Chapter 5: NHS Finance – Who Does What: The Role of Clinical Commissioning Groups	33
Chapter 6: NHS Finance – Who Does What: The Role of Primary Care	39
Chapter 7: NHS Finance – Who Does What: The Role of Community, Secondary and Tertiary Care Providers	45
Chapter 8: NHS Finance – Who Does What: The Role of Local Authorities, Health and Wellbeing Boards and HealthWatch	53
Chapter 9: NHS Finance – Who Does What: The Role of the Regulators	63
Chapter 10: How the NHS is Financed	71
Chapter 11: How NHS Bodies Demonstrate Financial Accountability	79
Chapter 12: How the NHS is Regulated	91
Chapter 13: Governance – How NHS Organisations are Structured and Run	103
Chapter 14: Revenue Planning and Budgeting	121
Chapter 15: Capital Funding, Planning and Accounting	129
Chapter 16: Commissioning	145

Chapter 17: Costing	155
Chapter 18: How NHS Services are paid for	161
Chapter 19: NHS Charitable Funds	169
Chapter 20: Health and Social Care in Northern Ireland	181
Chapter 21: The NHS in Scotland	191
Chapter 22: The NHS in Wales	201
Appendix: Glossary of Terms	213

Foreword

Welcome to the twelfth edition of the HFMA's *Introductory Guide – NHS Finance*.

This version follows the same structure that we introduced in 2013 but has been updated to reflect policy and organisational changes that have taken place since then. In particular, it sets out the responsibilities and accountabilities of each of the key players in the NHS and explains what their role is in relation to NHS finance.

As with earlier editions, each chapter has been written with the help of practitioners and has been reviewed by experts in the relevant field. Although the main body of the Guide focuses on the policy and organisational framework for the NHS in England, there are separate chapters dedicated to Northern Ireland, Scotland and Wales.

As always, the Guide is designed to give readers a solid grounding in – and practical understanding of – all key aspects of NHS finance. It also provides some contextual background that helps explain how the NHS has developed over the years. As well as appealing to its traditional audience (which ranges from executive and non-executive directors, governors and managers to clinicians, accounts assistants and budget holders), the Guide is an excellent reference source for anyone embarking on a career in NHS finance. It will also be invaluable to anyone who is thinking of undertaking the HFMA's e-learning programme and/or qualifications in healthcare business and finance.

The intention is that the Guide is written in simple, straightforward and accessible language with references at the end of chapters so that readers can delve into subjects in more detail if they wish. Bullet point listings of 'key learning points' are included for the later, subject-based chapters and there is also a glossary of terms in an appendix.

The HFMA is committed to improving the awareness of finance and financial management across the NHS and beyond and we trust that this Guide will further this objective. Above all we hope that you will find it useful, informative and a 'good read'.

If you have any comments, the HFMA team would like to hear from you – please email: publications@hfma.org.uk

Ian Moston
Chair, HFMA Policy and Research Committee.

Acknowledgements

The *Introductory Guide – NHS Finance* is developed under the direction of the HFMA's Policy and Research Committee and with the help of a wide range of practitioners, all of whom give their time and expertise free of charge. The HFMA is extremely grateful to everyone who has been involved in the Guide's production. The main contributors to this edition are:

Andrew Baigent	**Richard Mellor**
Sarah Bence	**Catherine Mitchell**
Phil Bradley	**Charlotte Moar**
Keith Brooks	**Keith Morton**
Mark Collis	**Ian Moston**
Simon Crowther	**Lee Outhwaite**
Jason Dorsett	**Debbie Paterson**
Maureen Edwards	**Tracey Paton**
Steve Elliot	**Alan Payne**
Jon Evans	**Wendy Thompson**
Janice Fawell	**Andrew Treherne**
Nigel Foster	**Simon Sheppard**
Nick Gerrard	**Karl Simkins**
Kavita Gnanaolivu	**Mike Wade**
Anna Green	**Robert White**
John Guggenheim	**Paul Williams**
Emma Knowles	**Steve Wilson**
Craig Marriott	**Keith Wood**
Colin Martin	

Editorial work was carried out by **Anna Green** and **Sarah Bence**.

Chapter 1
Introduction and Purpose

About the Guide

For more than twenty five years, the *Introductory Guide – NHS Finance* has provided an easy to read, accessible overview of the workings and language of NHS finance for the benefit of practitioners and observers. The Guide is produced by The Healthcare Financial Management Association (HFMA), a charity established over 60 years ago to support those working within the NHS finance function. By improving financial literacy both within and outside NHS finance, the HFMA hopes it can inform and improve the debate on healthcare finance issues.

The Guide has been developed to provide a self-contained source of advice and guidance for readers from an array of backgrounds. There are many aspects of NHS finance that are unique to the service, and a language laden with jargon, abbreviations and acronyms has developed that can appear impenetrable to many outsiders or newcomers. Indeed, as the terminology develops with each set of reforms, even the most experienced NHS finance professionals can find themselves in unfamiliar territory!

The Guide aims to provide advice to all levels of finance staff from finance directors (who often use it as an aide memoir to more recent changes) to governors and lay members; non-executive and executive directors (who may not be finance specialists but still have shared corporate responsibility for understanding and managing the financial position); clinicians; budget holders; service managers; accounts assistants and those who need an understanding of NHS finance for academic study purposes.

Over the years the Guide has grown in size as it tries to provide an overview of both the current finance regime along with a sense of how the approach has developed over the years. Nevertheless, it remains (as its title suggests) an introductory guide that gives a reasonably straightforward but comprehensive description of NHS structures and processes.

Approach and Format

This version of the Introductory Guide follows the approach readers will be familiar with – namely that each chapter treats its topic in a largely self-contained way. Cross-references are included where they are helpful and sources of further advice and technical guidance are listed at the end of each chapter. For the later chapters, there are also lists of 'key learning points'.

The bulk of the Guide concentrates on the financial arrangements for the NHS in England but there are also chapters dedicated to highlighting key differences in Northern Ireland, Scotland and Wales.

The Guide ends with a glossary of terms.

HFMA E-learning and the Introductory Award in Healthcare Finance

In addition to the Introductory Guide, the HFMA produces a series of e-learning courses that allow individuals to address their NHS finance training needs in a tailored way. The e-learning modules are aimed primarily at non-finance professionals including governors, lay members, non-executive directors, clinical staff, general practice staff and finance staff that are new to the NHS. They can also be used as 'refreshers' for existing staff.

Although modules can be studied individually, there is an Introductory Award that involves learners selecting five modules from a wide range of topics. These cover both the structure of the NHS (for example, NHS finance, primary care finance and governance) and processes (for example, commissioning, budgeting and costing). Each training session takes between two and three hours to complete and includes an assessment test. On successful completion of the fifth module, an Introductory Award in Healthcare Finance is awarded – this is fast becoming an industry standard; a means of assessing an individual's basic competence in NHS finance. Further details are available from the HFMA website at www.hfma.org.uk

HFMA Qualifications in Healthcare Business and Finance

The HFMA is also designing and developing a set of masters level qualifications that provide a pathway to study for an MBA in healthcare business and finance. The qualifications are due to be launched in 2017.

Each qualification is open to a wide range of learners, including finance staff, general managers, clinicians and other healthcare professionals. There will be two qualifications – the HFMA Diploma and the HFMA Higher Diploma. These are split into modules covering the following topics:

- how finance works in the NHS
- managing the healthcare business
- personal effectiveness and leadership
- tools to support decision-making
- creating and delivering value in healthcare
- comparative healthcare systems.

For further details contact: selma.naden@hfma.org.uk

Chapter 2
NHS Finance Background and Context – how we got to where we are today

> This chapter looks back over the past few decades to chart the development of the NHS so that we can see how we have reached where we are in 2016. It also looks briefly at the origins of the NHS and its guiding principles.

The Introduction of the NHS

The NHS was established by the *NHS Act 1946*. This Act specified that, it was `the duty of the Minister ... to promote the establishment in England and Wales of a comprehensive Health Service designed to secure the improvement of the physical and mental health of the people of England and Wales and the prevention, diagnosis and treatment of illness'. The services provided to meet these aims were to be free of charge, based on clinical need, not the ability to pay.

The NHS was launched and the first patients treated on 5 July 1948.

Underpinning Principles of the NHS

Although there have been many structural and policy developments since 1948, the underlying principles have not changed. These are that NHS services are:

- available to everyone
- free at the point of need (or use)
- based on clinical need, not the ability to pay.

All of the major political parties remain committed to these core principles.

Other enduring characteristics of the NHS are that:

- it is funded through taxation
- it manages within overall resource limits determined by the Government each year
- finite resources have to be matched with infinite demand for health services with tough choices over priorities needed as a result
- there is an expectation that 'efficiency savings' can be made, often as a result of structural or technical developments
- there is intense political, public and media interest in, and scrutiny of, the NHS.

The NHS is also Europe's largest employer with over 1.7 million employees across the UK in 2015[1]. However, although it is usually referred to as if it were a single organisation, it actually comprises a wide range of different bodies with specific responsibilities – we will be looking at many of these later on in the Guide.

Key Policy Developments that have shaped the NHS since the 1980s

The internal market, 1980s

In the late 1980s it was decided that the NHS should be reconfigured to operate a 'quasi-market', known as the internal market, with many treatments commissioned on a 'cost per case' or 'extra contractual referral' basis. A key feature of this approach was the separation

---

[1] The world's biggest employers 2015, Forbes.

of the provision of hospital and community services from the commissioning or purchasing function – the so-called 'purchaser/provider split'. Hospitals were encouraged to apply for self-governing trust status, creating organisations quite separate from the health authorities from which they were devolved. To achieve trust status, and formally separate from the health authorities, provider organisations had to follow an application process that assessed viability and robustness.

There was also an optional scheme to give general practitioners (GPs) the ability to hold budgets for the purchase of hospital services for their patients (known as GP fund holding). At the same time, trusts were encouraged to invest in and develop services and to compete with each other to win patient service contracts with purchasers.

The New NHS – Modern, Dependable, 1997

In 1997, the White Paper *The New NHS – Modern, Dependable* set out a programme for reform of the NHS. These proposals became law with the *Health Act 1999* (since superseded by the *NHS Act 2006* and the *Health and Social Care Act 2012*) and the focus shifted away from competition to a collaborative model, where NHS organisations worked together and with local authorities to re-focus healthcare on the patient. By removing the competitive nature of the internal market, the changes in policy sought to ensure the seamless delivery of services.

Key changes were an end to GP fund holding and the introduction of new organisations for primary care. Primary care organisations (either 'groups' or 'trusts') were formed from groups of local GP practices, or 'natural communities'. Boundaries were encouraged to coincide where possible with local authority borders to simplify the integration of health and social care. In their initial stages these groups were sub-committees of health authorities, used to inform the commissioning process. As they found their feet, they were able to apply for trust status, creating bodies independent from the health authority and managing increasingly significant portions of former health authority budgets.

The *Health Act 1999* also established the Commission for Health Improvement (to be succeeded by the Commission for Healthcare Audit and Inspection, then by the Healthcare Commission and now the Care Quality Commission) and the National Institute for Health and Clinical Excellence or NICE – now the National Institute for Health and Care Excellence.

There was also a renewed emphasis on cutting management costs – a challenging objective given the increase in the number of NHS organisations, and greater involvement of management at a local level. The 'shared services initiative' was, at least to an extent, an attempt to mitigate the pressure on management costs by reducing the cost of providing support services (particularly 'back office' functions). National shared service centre pilots were established, run as a joint venture between the Department of Health and Steria known as NHS Shared Business Services (NHS SBS) and there are now a number of shared business services centres around the country.

The purchaser/provider split created by the internal market was retained. Initially health authorities remained and continued to purchase healthcare using 'service and financial framework agreements'. These health authorities were subsequently abolished (see below) but the division between commissioning and provision continued with primary care trusts (PCTs) taking over responsibility for commissioning hospital services. At their inception, many PCTs also had a provider role in relation to community services.

The 1997 White Paper also heralded a move towards longer planning time frames, promising the replacement of annual contract negotiations with three-year resource announcements.

The NHS was encouraged to form partnerships with both private and public sector partners, including local authority social services. The *Health Act 1999* also broadened the scope for pooling of health and social services budgets. Partnership working with the private sector was formalised in a 'concordat' agreement, which highlighted scope for joint working in elective, critical and intermediate care. New independently run diagnosis and treatment centres or 'independent sector treatment centres' (ISTCs) were established so extending the role of the private sector in the NHS.

The NHS Plan: a Plan for Investment, a Plan for Reform, 2000

In July 2000 the *NHS Plan* was presented to Parliament. The plan consisted of a vision of the NHS first outlined in the 1997 White Paper – modernised, structurally reformed, efficient and properly funded. Much of the document was dedicated to identifying new targets and milestones on wide ranging issues (from waiting lists to implementation of electronic patient records) and measures that needed to be taken to facilitate the achievement of those targets.

The Health Act 2002

In April 2002, a further tranche of changes came into effect. At the end of March 2002, the 95 health authorities in England were abolished and replaced by 28 strategic health authorities (SHAs). At the same time the eight regional offices were replaced by four directorates of health and social care which were themselves dissolved in 2003. The changes, first outlined in April 2001 in the policy paper *Shifting the Balance of Power*, were designed to transfer management resource and control closer to the locality, and hence to the patient.

The establishment of PCTs was also completed in 2002 – a key change here was the fact that PCTs were allowed to expand primary care services beyond those traditionally provided by GPs. This prompted a growth in 'GPs with special interests' and in services provided in the community by PCTs where previously they had been delivered in an acute hospital setting.

Many of the monitoring and planning processes were devolved from the old regional offices to the new SHAs, while commissioning functions were transferred to PCTs.

Payment by results

A key element of the Labour Government's modernisation plans involved reforming the financial framework and the way funding flowed around the NHS. The proposal for bringing about this change was set out in 2002 in *Delivering the NHS Improvement Plan* and introduced a system of payment by results (PBR). This was designed to ensure that money flowed with patients.

The main driver behind this initiative was patient choice – by introducing nationally-set standard prices for treatments, the need for local negotiation on price was removed and instead the focus was shifted to quality and responsiveness, the things that are important to the patient. The combination of patient choice and PBR was expected to drive an increase in healthcare capacity and deliver shorter patient waiting times.

Both patient choice and PBR were phased in over a period of years. Key milestones in the development of patient choice included:

- providing patients waiting for elective surgery for over six months with the choice of an alternative provider (summer 2004)
- patients requiring a routine elective referral offered a choice of four or five providers (including one private sector provider) at the point of referral (i.e. at their GP) by the end of December 2005
- patients needing to see a specialist able to choose to go to any hospital in England, including many private and independent sector hospitals (from April 2008).

The first steps to introduce the PBR financial framework were taken in 2003/04. Chapter 18 looks in more detail at changes in the way that NHS services are reimbursed.

NHS foundation trusts

NHS foundation trusts (FTs) were created as new legal entities in the form of public benefit corporations by the *Health and Social Care (Community Health and Standards) Act 2003*

– now consolidated in the *NHS Act 2006*. They were introduced to help implement the Labour Government's 10-year *NHS Plan* – by creating a new form of NHS trust that had greater freedoms and more extensive powers, it was hoped that services would improve more quickly.

Initially, applications for foundation status were restricted to a number of 'three-star' trusts with the first wave of FTs coming into being in April 2004. Since then there has been a steady growth in the number of FTs although the pace has slowed as organisations struggle to demonstrate their long-term financial viability in the light of difficult economic circumstances and increased expectations in relation to efficiency. The application process for FT status has also changed with an increased focus on clinical quality in the light of high profile governance failures, such as that at Mid-Staffordshire NHS Foundation Trust. NHS Improvement[2] continues to support those organisations keen to pursue foundation status.

Commissioning a Patient-led NHS, 2005

Following a consultation process in 2005, a reconfiguration of SHAs, PCTs and ambulance trusts was launched by the Department of Health with a significant reduction in their overall numbers. The aim was to reduce management overheads and generate cost savings that could be re-invested in the provision of healthcare.

The reduction in PCT numbers was consistent with the simplification of the commissioning process inherent in the patient choice and PBR initiatives. Increasingly patients were able to select their preferred healthcare provider, thereby refocusing the commissioning role on assessing overall supply levels, negotiating provider standards and managing demand.

SHAs also reduced from 28 to 10 to reflect the geographical span of the government offices for the regions, and so make working with other public sector partners easier.

Ambulance trust merger was designed to achieve purchasing and management economies of scale and to allow them to develop greater resilience than was possible with smaller scale operations.

Practice based commissioning

Practice based commissioning (PBC) was introduced in 2005/06 with a view to enabling primary care clinicians to take commissioning decisions themselves, thereby providing patients with higher quality services that better suited their needs and circumstances. The underlying presumption was that primary care professionals were in the best position to decide what services their patients needed and to redesign them accordingly. Unlike GP fund holding, which was a feature of the original purchaser/provider split of the 1990s, PBC covered both emergency services and elective activity.

Under PBC, responsibility for commissioning along with an associated budget from the PCT was allocated to primary care clinicians. However, because PCTs remained legally responsible for managing the money and negotiating and managing all contracts with providers, the budget was notional or 'indicative'. In practice this meant that although primary care clinicians determined the range of services to be provided for their population, the PCT acted as their agent to undertake any required procurements and to carry out the administrative tasks that underpinned these processes.

The Darzi Review – High Quality Care for All, 2007

In July 2007, the Government asked the then health minister Lord Darzi to carry out a wide ranging review of the NHS. An interim report was issued in October 2007 and recommended

---

[2] NHS Improvement (NHSI) is the sector regulator for health and social care. It brings together two separate arm's length bodies (ALBs), Monitor and the NHS Trust Development Authority (NHS TDA), with patient safety and improvement functions from across the NHS under a single leadership and operating model. See chapter 9 for more about NHSI's role.

a number of changes to the provision of healthcare services within the primary and secondary care sectors, including the development of 'poly-clinics' where appropriate – a primary healthcare equivalent of the 'one-stop shop'. The final report – *High Quality Care for All* – was issued in June 2008 (in time for the 60th anniversary of the NHS on 5 July 2008) and set out a vision of an NHS that 'gives patients and the public more information and choice, works in partnership and has quality of care at its heart'.

The NHS Constitution, 2010

In January 2010, the first ever *NHS Constitution* came into effect. All NHS bodies along with private and third sector organisations that provide NHS services are required by law to take account of the Constitution in their decisions and actions.

Equity and Excellence: Liberating the NHS, 2010 and the Health and Social Care Act 2012

In July 2010, following the formation of the Coalition Government, the then Secretary of State for Health issued a series of consultation papers that signalled far-reaching changes for the NHS in England. These proposals (amended in places) were enacted in the *Health and Social Care Act 2012* resulting in a new structure and approach for the NHS from April 2013.

The NHS now

The structure introduced by the 2012 Act is shown in the diagram below and came into effect in April 2013. The one key change since then is the introduction from April 2016 of NHS Improvement (NHSI) – an integrated management structure enabling Monitor and the NHS Trust Development Authority (NHS TDA) to work together closely and support all NHS foundation and non-foundation trusts.

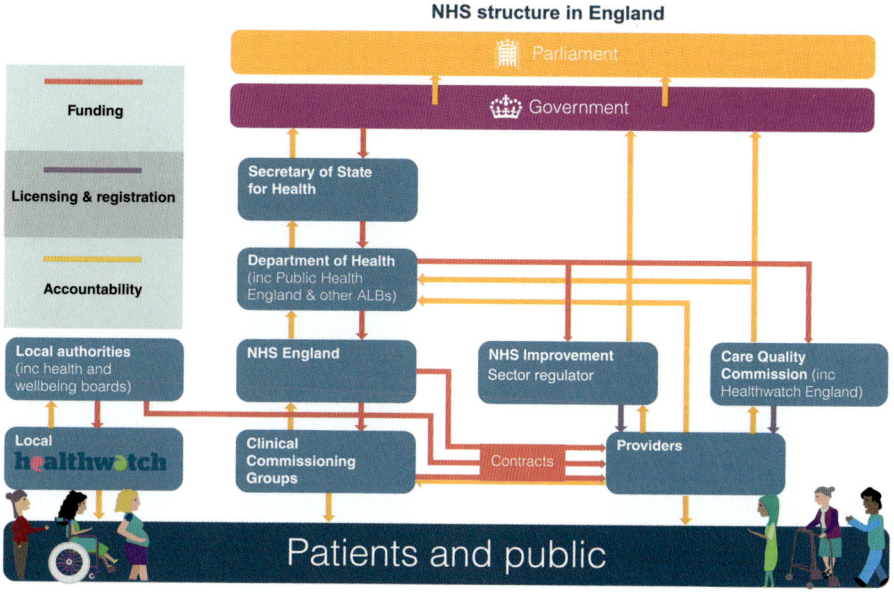

NHS structure in England

The roles and responsibilities of all the key players are discussed in later chapters of this Guide but the table below summarises the key changes introduced by the 2012 Act.

Key Changes introduced by the 2012 Act

- abolishing SHAs and PCTs from April 2013
- introducing NHS England to authorise clinical commissioning groups (CCGs), allocate funding to them and commission some services itself
- handing the majority of NHS commissioning to CCGs that are authorised by (and accountable to) NHS England
- extending Monitor's role to that of sector regulator (now operating as part of NHS Improvement) for the health and social care sectors with responsibility for licensing healthcare providers, setting and regulating prices and (with NHS England) ensuring continuity of services
- strengthening the role of the Care Quality Commission (CQC)
- setting up the NHS Trust Development Authority within the Department of Health to oversee NHS trusts (now operating as part of NHS Improvement)
- allowing commissioners to pay quality increments and impose contractual penalties
- giving FTs greater freedom on income, governance and mergers
- handing responsibility for public health to local authorities with Public Health England set up within the Department of Health
- setting up 'health and wellbeing boards' in every upper tier local authority to 'join up commissioning across the NHS, social care, public health and other services ... directly related to health and wellbeing'
- developing local HealthWatch organisations from existing local involvement networks to ensure that the views of patients, carers and the public are taken into account
- setting up HealthWatch England as an independent committee within the CQC to support and lead local HealthWatch.

Five Year Forward View

In October 2014, the *Five Year Forward View* was published. This sets out the transformational changes needed by the NHS in order to meet the anticipated £30bn funding gap by 2020/21 arising from the difference between existing funding and that needed to meet expected demand. It set out the reasons for transformational change and the way that change may be achieved. The report stated that action was needed on four fronts:

- tackling the root causes of ill health, including obesity and drinking too much alcohol
- giving patients more control over their care
- breaking down barriers between GPs and hospitals, health and social care and physical and mental health
- introducing new models of care as well as investing in workforce, innovation and technology.

The new models of care (in addition to those already operating in the NHS) outlined in the *Five Year Forward View* draw on international experiences and include:

- multispecialty community providers (MCPs)
- primary and acute care systems (PACs)
- urgent and emergency care networks
- viable smaller hospitals
- specialised care
- modern maternity services
- enhanced health in care homes.

The new care models are expected to provide better networks of care with increased out of hospital care and services better integrated around the patient. In January 2015, NHS England invited individual organisations and partnerships to apply to become 'vanguard' sites for the new care models programme. In March 2015 the first 29 sites were chosen comprising integrated primary and acute care systems, enhanced health in care homes and multispecialty community provider vanguards.

In July 2015 eight urgent and emergency care vanguards were chosen followed by thirteen acute care collaborations in September 2015. The latter included viable smaller hospitals, specialised care and modern maternity services. Each vanguard site will develop a new care model that it is anticipated can be replicated elsewhere in England.

The Five Year Forward View for Mental Health

Following the publication of the *Five Year Forward View*, the chief executive of NHS England commissioned an independent review of mental health services. Led by the chief executive of MIND, the Mental Health Taskforce published its final report in February 2016. It set out an assessment of the state of mental health services in England, a long term view of improvements needed along with a series of recommendations for NHS organisations, the Department's arm's length bodies (ALBs), the Government and other partners involved in the commissioning and provision of mental health services. The report concluded that £1 billion of additional investment in mental health services is needed by 2020/21.

Delivering the Five Year Forward View

For the first time, a single set of planning guidance was made available to the NHS in December 2015. Produced by all the Department's ALBs, (NHS England, NHS Improvement (Monitor and the NHS Trust Development Authority), the Care Quality Commission, Health Education England, the National Institute for Health and Care Excellence and Public Health England), *Delivering the Forward View: NHS Shared Planning Guidance 2016/17 to 2020/21* sets out the national priorities for 2016/17 and longer-term challenges for local systems, together with financial assumptions and business rules. In 2016/17, planning for health and its integration with social care took place on a local geographical basis. It is anticipated that this approach will result in better, more cost effective services for patients. More details can be found in chapter 14.

Comprehensive spending reviews and budgets

In terms of overall funding levels, the Labour Government made a commitment in 1997 to increase NHS funding to a level that would bring the UK's health spending in line with the average for the rest of Europe. The first step toward this target was taken in the 2000 budget, with a further significant increase in 2001. However, it was the 2002 budget that gave the first indication of the substantial and long-term increases required if that promise was to be delivered. Funding for these increases was achieved by the introduction of employer and employee national insurance surcharges at a rate of 1%, and from the release of funds from other sources, enabled by the Government's comprehensive spending review (CSR). The CSR process is designed to assess critically the spending of government departments in the light of changing priorities.

Successive budgets maintained the commitment to longer-term funding increases. However, the 2007 CSR process led to more modest increases for the three year period from 2008/09 compared with the preceding period, averaging 3.9% growth in real terms, compared with 7.5% for the previous CSR period.

The impact of the economic downturn following the banking crisis in 2008 led to warnings about the future funding of the NHS. The *Pre-Budget Report 2009*, the 2010/11 *Operating Framework* and the *Budget 2010 – Securing the Recovery* began to highlight the extent of the challenge.

In preparation for tighter times ahead, efficiency savings targets steadily moved upwards. To help achieve these targets and in line with a renewed emphasis on quality, the Department of Health expected NHS organisations to meet the 'quality, innovation, productivity and prevention (QIPP) challenge'. In practice, this meant organisations had to follow 'lean management principles' of avoiding duplication, preventing errors that then need to be corrected, and stopping ineffective practices. Inevitably this involved a focus on reducing back office functions and (from a finance perspective) re-ignited the debate about the relative advantages and disadvantages of shared services.

The most recent spending review took place in November 2015 and focused on the need to reduce the public sector borrowing requirement whilst investing in key services notably the NHS in order to support the delivery of the *Five Year Forward View*. As a result the health budget will increase by £10 billion by 2020 over and above that for 2014/15 (see chapter 10 for more about the financing of the NHS). This will take the projected NHS budget to £119.6 billion. However, over the same period, health and social care are expected to integrate across England, '…joining up services between social care providers and hospitals.'

References and Further Reading

For details of legislation: www.legislation.gov.uk/

The New NHS: Modern, Dependable (1997 White Paper) – Department of Health: https://www.gov.uk/government/publications/the-new-nhs

Care Quality Commission: www.cqc.org.uk/

National Institute for Health and Care Excellence (NICE): www.nice.org.uk

NHS Shared Business Services: www.sbs.nhs.uk/

The NHS Plan: a Plan for Investment, a Plan for Reform, Department of Health, 2000 (archived web pages): http://webarchive.nationalarchives.gov.uk/+/www.dh.gov.uk/en/publicationsandstatistics/publications/publicationspolicyandguidance/dh_4002960

Shifting the Balance of Power, Department of Health, 2001 (archived web pages): http://webarchive.nationalarchives.gov.uk/+/www.dh.gov.uk/en/publicationsandstatistics/publications/publicationspolicyandguidance/dh_4009844

Delivering the NHS Improvement Plan, Department of Health, 2002 (archived web pages): http://webarchive.nationalarchives.gov.uk/+/www.dh.gov.uk/en/publicationsandstatistics/publications/annualreports/browsable/DH_5277178

Practice Based Commissioning – Department of Health (archived web pages): http://webarchive.nationalarchives.gov.uk/+/www.dh.gov.uk/en/Managingyourorganisation/Commissioning/Practice-basedcommissioning/index.htm

High Quality Care for All: NHS Next Stage Review final report, Department of Health, 2008 (archived web pages): http://webarchive.nationalarchives.gov.uk/+/www.dh.gov.uk/en/Publicationsandstatistics/Publications/PublicationsPolicyandGuidance/DH_085825

The NHS Constitution for England, Department of Health, 2016:
https://www.gov.uk/government/publications/the-nhs-constitution-for-england

The Five Year Forward View, NHS England, 2014:
https://www.england.nhs.uk/ourwork/futurenhs/

The Five Year Forward View for Mental Health, Mental Health Taskforce, 2016:
https://www.england.nhs.uk/mentalhealth/taskforce/

Delivering the Forward View: NHS Shared Planning Guidance 2016/17 – 2020/21,
NHS England, 2015: https://www.england.nhs.uk/ourwork/futurenhs/deliver-forward-view/

HM Treasury – Comprehensive Spending Reviews and Budget Reports:
https://www.gov.uk/search?q=spending+review

Chapter 3

NHS Finance – Who Does What: The Role of Government, Ministers, the Department of Health (including its ALBs) and NHS Property Services Ltd

This chapter focuses on the role of the 'centre' in relation to NHS finance and governance – we will look in turn at:

- Parliament
- health ministers
- the Department of Health and its associated arm's length bodies (ALBs)
- Public Health England
- Health Education England
- NHS Property Services Limited.

For each element, the chapter looks at its status; accountabilities; roles and financing. To remind yourself of the overall structure of the NHS and where 'the centre' fits, look back at the diagram on page 11.

Parliament

What it is – status and accountabilities

Parliament is the highest legislative body in the land and so sits at the top of the 'accountability tree'. In relation to the NHS, Parliament holds the Secretary of State for Health to account for its functioning and use of resources.

What Parliament does – roles and responsibilities

As well as holding the Secretary of State to account, the cross party House of Commons Health Committee examines the expenditure, administration and policy of the Department of Health and its associated bodies. The members of this committee are appointed by the House of Commons and its constitution and powers are set out in *House of Commons Standing Order No.152*.

The Health Committee has a maximum of eleven members and the quorum for any formal proceedings is three. As the members of the committee are appointed by the House they remain on the committee until the next dissolution of Parliament, unless discharged.

Within its remit, the committee has complete discretion to decide which areas to investigate and has the power to require the submission of written evidence and documents, and to send for and examine witnesses. The committee's oral evidence sessions are usually open to the public and are often televised. Deliberative meetings are held in private.

When an inquiry ends, a report is agreed by the committee and then published by Her Majesty's Stationery Office. The report is usually published in two volumes: the findings of the committee and the background (memoranda and oral) evidence. The Government is committed to responding to such reports within two months of publication.

The committee is supported in its work by a team of staff and by part-time specialists, usually academics or experts from professions relevant to its inquiries.

Two other Parliamentary committees scrutinise the Department of Health and the NHS:

- the Public Accounts Committee (PAC)
- the Public Administration and Constitutional Affairs Committee (PACAC).

The PAC keeps a check on all public expenditure including money spent on health. Its remit takes it far wider than a view on the annual accounts, with the results of National Audit Office value for money studies usually being considered. In these instances, the PAC takes evidence, usually questioning Accounting Officers, chief executives and director generals from relevant organisations (such as the Department of Health and NHS England), before publishing its own report and making recommendations.

The PACAC examines the reports of the Parliamentary and Health Service Ombudsmen and considers matters relating to the quality and standards of civil service administration.

Other select committees may from time to time conduct inquiries into Government policies that impact upon the Department of Health.

How Parliament is financed

Parliament is funded by public money (i.e. by taxpayers).

Secretary of State for Health

What the role is – status and accountabilities

The Secretary of State for Health is a Cabinet minister with 'ultimate responsibility for ensuring the whole [health and care] system works together to meet the needs of patients and the public and reflect their experiences[1]'. The Secretary of State is accountable to Parliament.

What the Secretary of State does – roles and responsibilities

The NHS was established under the *National Health Service Act, 1946*. This and other subsequent Acts of Parliament relating to the NHS set out the duty of the Secretary of State for Health to provide a comprehensive health service in England.

The Secretary of State is politically accountable for the NHS and for the resources allocated to the health and social care system and also has a duty to 'maximise the autonomy' of commissioners and providers by 'limiting his general powers of direction'.

He or she is also responsible for:

- system design
- the legislative framework
- overall strategic direction
- progress against national outcomes.

Health Ministers

What they are – status and accountabilities

The Secretary of State is supported by a team of health ministers who are appointed by the Government. These ministers are either MPs elected by the public or members of the House of Lords. They are accountable to the Secretary of State.

What ministers do – roles and responsibilities

Health ministers each have individual responsibility for different aspects of the Department of Health's work. The portfolios attached to the ministerial posts often change, depending on

[1] *The Health and Care System Explained*, March 2013, gov.uk website.

the priorities at that point in time and the personal interests of the individuals. For the latest information on ministerial portfolios see the Department's website.

The Department of Health

What it is – status and accountabilities

The Department of Health is the Department of State responsible for the NHS, public health and adult social care in England and is accountable via its 'Principal Accounting Officer' (the permanent secretary) to Parliament 'for the proper use of the resources allocated to the Department'[2].

The Department supports the Secretary of State and ministers in carrying out their ministerial responsibilities including:

- accounting to Parliament and the public for the way money is spent and what is achieved with it
- answering Parliamentary questions and dealing with other Parliamentary business such as debates and enquiries
- responding to communications from the public and MPs
- communicating with the public.

There is a Departmental Board chaired by the Secretary of State which includes non-executives from outside Government. This Board 'scrutinises reports on performance, and challenges the Department on how well it is achieving its objectives[3]'.

To give you an idea of the Department's size, it employs around 2,100 people[4], with headquarters staff based in Leeds and London.

What the Department of Health does – roles and responsibilities

The Department's website states that its overarching purpose is to help people to live better for longer by leading, shaping and funding health and care in England, 'making sure people have the support, care and treatment they need, with the compassion, respect and dignity they deserve'. The website identifies the Department's responsibilities as being to:

- create national policies and legislation, providing the long-term vision and ambition to meet current and future challenges, putting health and care at the heart of Government, and being a global leader in health and care policy
- support the integrity of the health and care system by providing funding, assuring the delivery and continuity of services, and accounting to Parliament in a way that represents the best interests of the patient, public and taxpayer
- champion innovation and improvement by supporting research and technology, promoting honesty, openness and transparency, and instilling an organisational culture that values compassion, dignity and the highest quality of care above everything
- encourage staff in every health and care organisation to understand and learn from people's experience of health and care and apply it to everything they do.

The Department of Health's website also lists ten key priorities that are shared with its arm's length bodies (ALBs)[5]:

---

[2] *Accounting Officer System Statement*, Department of Health, October 2014.
[3] *Accounting Officer System Statement* (as above).
[4] *Annual Report and Accounts 2014/15*, Department of Health, July 2015.
[5] *Shared Delivery Plan 2015 to 2020*, Department of Health, February 2016.

The Department's Priorities 2015 to 2020

- improving out-of-hospital care
- creating the safest, highest quality healthcare services
- maintaining and improving performance against core standards while achieving financial balance
- improving efficiency and productivity of the health and care system
- preventing ill health and supporting people to live healthier lives
- supporting research, innovation and growth
- enabling people and communities to make decisions about their own health and care
- building and developing the workforce
- improving services through the use of digital technology, information and transparency
- supporting the system more efficiently.

Linked to these responsibilities and priorities, the Department has a number of key roles including:

- providing leadership for the NHS, adult social care and public health services (including for example, health promotion, health protection against infectious diseases, the safety of medicines and ethical issues) and setting the strategic framework within which they operate
- developing policy and legislation relating to the NHS, adult social care and public health
- supporting the delivery of improvements in the health and adult social care system via performance monitoring and evaluation; managerial and professional leadership of external groups; building capacity and capability and ensuring value for money
- leading on the integration of health and wellbeing into wider Government policy
- allocating the funding received from the Treasury
- setting healthcare standards, targets and outcome measures – there are separate 'outcomes frameworks' for the NHS, public health and adult social care
- agreeing an annual mandate with NHS England based on these outcomes frameworks
- reviewing the performance of its ALBs (see below) and intervening (by direction) if necessary
- managing performance against its statutory responsibilities and holding the NHS to account – this includes ensuring that the NHS lives within its allocated resources and achieves required efficiency savings.

These roles are translated into a number of specific 'deliverables' for the NHS by NHS England which is responsible for the day-to-day operational management of the NHS and operates at arm's length from the Department (see chapter 4).

How the Department of Health is financed

The Treasury sets the Department of Health's budget for a five-year period in a budgetary exercise known as the spending review, which takes place across Government. The Department submits evidence to the Treasury setting out its proposals for expenditure plans covering the five-year period. These plans are then discussed and challenged over several months before being finalised. The outcome of the most recent spending review was released in November 2015 and covers the years 2016/17 to 2020/21. The next spending review takes place in 2020.

Once the Treasury has set the overall budget total, the Department determines how this should be allocated. The vast majority of funding is allocated to NHS England but some is retained in central budgets. For example, for 2016/17, the total revenue budget for the NHS is around £115.6 billion of which £106.5 billion is allocated to NHS England. The Department of Health's funding also finances its associated ALBs (see below).

Once resources have been allocated, the Department of Health has an on-going responsibility to ensure that the NHS lives within them, and that its objectives are achieved as efficiently as possible. This includes monitoring performance against national targets.

Arm's Length Bodies

What they are – status and accountabilities

Arm's length bodies (ALBs) are stand-alone national organisations sponsored by the Department of Health to undertake activities to help deliver its agenda. They range in size but tend to have boards, employ staff and publish accounts. In constitutional terms, there are three types of ALB[6].

Types of ALB

Executive agencies – these are part of the Department (and are accountable to it) but have greater operational independence than a division or section of the Department.

Special health authorities – these are independent bodies (although they are subject to ministerial direction) that are created by order.

Executive non-departmental public bodies (ENDPBs) – these are established by primary legislation and have their own statutory functions. Their relationship with the Department is defined in legislation and some have greater independence than others. They all play important roles but are not part of the Department.

Regardless of their status, every ALB has a 'framework agreement' which sets out its relationship with the Department – in particular, these agreements cover:

- lines of accountability
- working arrangements
- core financial requirements
- relationships with other ALBs and organisations in the system
- how the ALB is held to account for delivering its objectives and outcomes and for the use of public money.

Each ALB must also submit a business plan to the Department for approval each year indicating how its objectives will be achieved and forecasting its financial performance. Every ALB must lay its annual report and accounts before Parliament.

---

[6] The Department of Health also works with a number of 'advisory non-departmental bodies' such as the NHS Pay Review Body and the Advisory Committee on Clinical Excellence Awards as well as other bodies such as NHS Property Services Ltd and Community Health Partnerships Ltd.

The Department has a duty to keep the performance of ALBs under review and the Secretary of State can intervene in the event of 'significant failure'.

What ALBs do – roles and responsibilities

ALBs can be categorised by function as follows.

ALBs Categorised by Function

Regulatory – ALBs that hold the health and social care system to account:
- NHS England (ENDPB)
- Monitor* (ENDPB)
- NHS Trust Development Authority* (special health authority)
- Care Quality Commission (CQC) (ENDPB)
- Medicines and Healthcare Products Regulatory Agency (executive agency)
- Human Fertilisation and Embryology Authority (ENDPB)
- Human Tissue Authority (ENDPB).

*While they are separate statutory bodies, Monitor and the NHS Trust Development Authority work as a single organisation, with the same management team, under the name of NHS Improvement. The role of NHS Improvement is covered in chapter 9.

Public welfare – ALBs that focus primarily on safety and the protection of public and patients:
- Public Health England (PHE) (executive agency)
- Health Research Authority (ENDPB).

Standards – ALBs that focus primarily on establishing national standards and best practice:
- National Institute for Health and Care Excellence (NICE) (ENDPB).

Central services to the NHS – ALBs that provide cost-effective services and focused expertise across the health and social care system:
- Health and Social Care Information Centre (ENDPB)
- Health Education England (ENDPB)
- NHS Blood and Transplant (special health authority)
- NHS Business Services Authority (special health authority)
- NHS Litigation Authority (special health authority).

We will look more closely at the roles of NHS England, the CQC and NHS Improvement later in the Guide. Some of the other ALBs that have a particular bearing on NHS finance and governance are considered later in this chapter.

How ALBs are financed

ALBs are financed primarily out of the settlement received by the Department of Health (as 'grant in aid') although some levy fees for services provided (for example, the CQC charges a registration fee) and others are financed largely via charges to users of their services – for example, in the case of NHS Blood and Transplant, hospitals (both NHS and private) pay for each unit of blood supplied.

Public Health England

What it is – status and accountabilities

As we have seen earlier in this chapter, the Department of Health has overall responsibility for setting the policy and legal framework in relation to public health. To help it discharge this responsibility, Public Health England (PHE) was established under the *Health and Social Care Act 2012* (the 2012 Act) as an executive agency of the Department of Health. This means that PHE is accountable to the Department.

PHE employs 5,600 staff, most of whom are scientists, researchers and public health professionals. It is organised into 4 regions and 9 centres.

What PHE does – roles and responsibilities

PHE's role is to protect and improve the health and wellbeing of the population and reduce health inequalities. It does this by working closely with the health and social care system and other public services. Although PHE provides leadership, local authorities are responsible for health improvement and reducing health inequalities at local level (see chapter 8).

PHE has four core functions:

- protecting the public's health from infectious diseases and other public health hazards
- improving the public's health and wellbeing
- improving population health through sustainable health and care services
- building the capacity and capability of the public health system.

How PHE is financed

PHE is financed out of the Department of Health's allocation.

Health Education England and Local Education and Training Boards

What it is – status and accountabilities

Health Education England (HEE) was originally established by the 2012 Act as a special health authority within the Department of Health. In April 2015 it became an ENDPB. It has 2,500 members of staff.

What HEE does – roles and responsibilities

HEE provides 'national leadership and oversight on strategic planning and development of the health and public health workforce' and allocates education and training resources. In other words, HEE ensures that the healthcare workforce has the right skills and is available in the right numbers.

HEE has the following key functions:

- providing national leadership on planning and developing the healthcare and public health workforce
- promoting high quality education and training that is responsive to the changing needs of patients and local communities
- ensuring the supply of the health and public health workforce
- allocating and accounting for NHS education and training resources and the outcomes achieved.

One other key area that HEE is responsible for is working with 'Local Education and Training Boards' (LETBs) to improve the quality of education and training outcomes so that they meet the needs of providers, the public and patients. LETBs are statutory committees of HEE. They are based in local offices and have taken on the workforce planning and education and training functions previously carried out by strategic health authorities. There are thirteen LETBs which are accountable to HEE.

How HEE is financed

HEE is financed out of the Department of Health's allocation.

NHS Property Services Ltd

What it is – status and accountabilities

NHS Property Services Limited was set up in 2012 to take over the residual estate left by strategic health authorities and primary care trusts (PCTs) after their abolition. In terms of its constitution, it is a company wholly owned by the Government and is also known as PropCo. It has 3,000 staff.

What it does

NHS Property Services Limited's role is to maintain, manage and develop around 3,500 NHS properties and facilities worth over £3bn. This represents 10% of the English NHS estate. Most of these buildings are used to provide patient care, such as GP surgeries and community hospitals. They do not have responsibility for hospital estates run by NHS trusts and NHS foundation trusts. It has two main roles:

- strategic estates management – acting as a landlord, modernising facilities, buying new facilities and selling facilities the NHS no longer needs
- provider of support services such as cleaning and catering.

How NHS Property Services Ltd is financed

Although NHS Property Services is a company, it is 'wholly owned by the Secretary of State for Health'[7] and is financed from the Department's allocation.

References and Further Reading

For details of legislation including Health Acts: www.legislation.gov.uk/

Select Committees: www.parliament.uk/business/committees/

The Health and Care System Explained, March 2013:
https://www.gov.uk/government/publications/the-health-and-care-system-explained

Department of Health website – for details of how the Department works and ministerial roles:
www.gov.uk/government/organisations/department-of-health

Accounting Officer System Statement, Department of Health, October 2014:
www.gov.uk/government/publications/dh-accounting-officer-responsibilities-statement

Annual Report and Accounts 2014/15, Department of Health, July 2015: www.gov.uk/government/publications/department-of-health-annual-report-and-accounts-2014-to-2015

Shared Delivery Plan 2015 to 2020, Department of Health, February 2016: www.gov.uk/government/publications/department-of-health-shared-delivery-plan-2015-to-2020

Spending reviews and budgets – details available from HM Treasury's website:
https://www.gov.uk/government/topical-events/autumn-statement-and-spending-review-2015

---

[7] NHS Property Services Letter to the System, November 2012.

Department of Health Arm's Length Bodies (includes links to all those referred to in the chapter): https://www.gov.uk/government/publications/how-to-contact-department-of-health-arms-length-bodies

Public Health England: https://www.gov.uk/government/organisations/public-health-england

Health Education England: http://hee.nhs.uk/

NHS Property Services Ltd: www.property.nhs.uk/

NHS Property Services Ltd Letter to the System, November 2012:
www.property.nhs.uk/nhs-property-services-ltd-letter-to-the-system/

Chapter 4
NHS Finance – Who Does What: The Role of NHS England

> This chapter looks what NHS England is, how it is structured and the role it plays in relation to NHS finance and governance. To remind yourself of where NHS England fits into the NHS structure, look back at the diagram on page 11.

What is NHS England?

NHS England was set up under section 9 of the *Health and Social Care Act 2012* and became fully operational on 1 April 2013. Until March 2013 it was called the NHS Commissioning Board (this remains its statutory name).

In constitutional terms, NHS England is an executive non-departmental body working at arm's length from the Department of Health (i.e. it is a Department of Health arm's length body or ALB). NHS England has a board, central department, 4 regional teams and 12 clinical senates. The regions act as the local offices of NHS England with functions that include commissioning primary care and specialised services (see later in the chapter). NHS England's headquarters are in Leeds but it also has a London office. Although it has a regional presence, NHS England's website makes it clear that it is 'one single organisation operating to a common model with one Board'.

NHS England is accountable to the Secretary of State for Health and the Department of Health for meeting its legal duties and fulfilling its 'mandate'. In formal terms, the line of accountability runs from NHS England's Accountable Officer (the chief executive, as designated in the 2012 Act) to the Department of Health's Accountable Officer (the permanent secretary) to the Secretary of State and Parliament.

The mandate is a multi-year document that is updated and published each year. It sets out the objectives that NHS England is expected to deliver in the forthcoming year along with its financial allocation. In response to the mandate, NHS England publishes an annual business plan that shows how it will achieve the objectives it has been set and an annual report showing how it performed. For the first time since its introduction, the mandate for 2016/17 '…sets the objectives for the NHS as a whole.'

As with all ALBs, there is also a 'framework agreement' that sets out the working relationship and lines of accountability between the Department and NHS England along with financial requirements and relationships with other organisations (see chapter 3 for more about ALBs).

NHS England is accountable to the Department for staying within its allocated resources (the 'commissioning revenue limit' allocated to it by the Department) as well as delivering a wide range of improvements to healthcare through a number of 'outcomes frameworks'. NHS England is also responsible for the functioning of the entire commissioning system and the associated budget and for reporting the consolidated financial position of itself and clinical commissioning groups (CCGs).

What NHS England does – Roles and Responsibilities

Alongside the Secretary of State, NHS England has an overriding statutory responsibility for promoting a comprehensive health service that will 'secure improvements in the physical and mental health of the people of England and in the prevention, diagnosis and treatment of physical and mental illness'[1]. As well as general duties (for example, having regard to the *NHS Constitution*; exercising its functions economically, efficiently and effectively; securing continuous improvement and promoting innovation), NHS England has a number of specific

---
[1] NHS England's legal duties and powers are set out in sections 9 and 23 and schedule A1 of the 2012 Act.

statutory duties relating to:

- establishing and holding CCGs to account (for example, ensuring that there is a comprehensive system of CCGs in place and that each GP practice is a member of a CCG; authorising CCGs; providing continuous assessment of CCG plans; reviewing the performance and governance arrangements of CCGs and intervening where necessary to protect the public interest)
- commissioning of services (for example, NHS England must commission directly those services specified in regulations – see below)
- partnership working/co-operation (for example, a duty to co-operate with the Department, NHS Improvement, the Care Quality Commission (CQC), the National Institute for Health and Care Excellence (NICE) and the Health and Social Care Information Centre; meeting safeguarding duties for children and vulnerable groups)
- emergencies – to ensure that it and CCGs are properly prepared and resilient. In the event of a major incident, NHS England assumes responsibility for coordinating the input of all healthcare organisations
- finance – to manage overall expenditure on commissioning and administration and produce accounts that include the consolidated accounts of all CCGs. This is facilitated by the mandated use of a single financial ledger system called the integrated single financial environment (ISFE) that is designed to ensure consistency of reporting and simplify consolidation.

NHS England allocates funding to CCGs and holds them to account for the management of these public funds. It is also responsible for managing financial risk across CCGs.

As mentioned above, NHS England commissions some services itself (referred to as 'direct commissioning') – specifically:

- primary care services provided by GPs (this may be delegated to some CCGs via a co-commissioning arrangement – see chapter 5 for more details), dentists, opticians and community pharmacists
- specialised services – these account for around 15% or £15.7bn of the annual NHS budget and are defined on NHS England's website as 'those services provided in relatively few hospitals, accessed by comparatively small numbers of patients, but with catchment populations of more than one million. These services tend to be located in specialist hospital trusts that can recruit staff with the appropriate expertise and enable them to develop their skills'. A good example is transplant surgery
- offender healthcare (which includes high security psychiatric facilities)
- some services for members of the armed forces.

These services are commissioned by the relevant regional team using common 'single operating models' and reporting to a single board within NHS England. These models have been designed to ensure that all patients are offered consistent, accessible, high quality services across the country.

In addition, although Public Health England (PHE) and local authorities are responsible for commissioning some public health services, many of which are delivered by NHS providers, NHS England has responsibility (under a separate agreement with the Department of Health) for commissioning preventive public health services through a model developed with stakeholders and including:

- the national immunisation programmes
- the national screening programmes

- public health services for offenders in custody
- sexual assault referral centres
- child health information systems.

NHS England is also required to carry out a number of other roles, including those set out below:

NHS England's 'other' Roles

- setting commissioning guidelines
- allocating funding for the purchase of healthcare to CCGs
- developing model care pathways
- establishing model contracts for CCGs to use when commissioning services
- supporting CCGs as they develop their skills and capacity including promoting good practice
- determining the structure of future payment systems
- promoting and extending choice
- the roll-out of personal health budgets (see chapter 5 for more details)
- championing patient and carer involvement
- hosting 'clinical senates' (doctors, nurses and other professionals who advise NHS England, CCGs and health and wellbeing boards on 'strategic clinical decision making to support commissioners') and strategic clinical networks (to advise on specific areas of care such as cancer)
- overseeing the cancer drugs fund.

Commissioning support units

At present, NHS England also hosts a number of commissioning support units (CSUs) for which a hosting charge is levied. CSUs provide both transactional and transformational support and services to many CCGs, helping them to deliver their commissioning role. This may be in the form of business support functions such as finance and human resources; providing data analysis and storage; developing the health needs assessment or handling media enquiries.

Arrangements between CSUs and CCGs are covered by service level agreements (SLAs) that set out the expectations and requirements of each party.

Each CSU is led by a managing director and operates with a governing body (but not a legal board) – as they are part of NHS England, all hosted CSUs fall within NHS England's own governance arrangements.

Each CSU operates under an agreed NHS England operating framework which sets out the powers delegated by NHS England and reflects any additional conditions under which the CSU must operate. CSUs are required to break even with any profits reinvested into the business.

NHS England will host CSUs until they become independent, commercial organisations. In April 2013 there were 23 CSUs in operation. The number of operational CSUs has now reduced to 6 as a result of organisational mergers and some closures. All six operational CSUs along with three private sector providers are accredited to provide support services to CCGs and the wider health system via the 'lead provider framework' that was put in place in 2015 by NHS England.

Regional teams

As noted earlier, there are 4 regions – North of England, Midlands and East, London and South of England. Their core functions are focussed on:

- healthcare commissioning and delivery across their geographical areas
- professional leadership of finance, nursing and medical staff
- specialised commissioning
- patients and information
- human resources
- organisational development
- assurance and delivery.

The regional teams also commission GP, dental and pharmacy services and certain aspects of optical services, although following the roll out of the primary care co-commissioning initiative some CCGs may commission GP services themselves through joint or delegated arrangements (see chapter 5 for more details).

Regional teams are supported by local professional networks (LPNs) that work in partnership with CCGs to help provide clinical leadership and support the implementation of national strategies and policies at local level. See NHS England's guide *Securing Excellence in Commissioning Primary Care* for more details.

Clinical senates and strategic clinical networks

NHS England hosts 12 clinical senates. Their role is to help CCGs, health and wellbeing boards and NHS England to make the best possible decisions about healthcare for the population they serve.

There are also a number of strategic clinical networks that are hosted by NHS England – these advise on specific areas of care such as cancer.

How NHS England is Financed

NHS England's budget is allocated to it by the Department of Health. Most of this budget is then allocated to CCGs and used by them to commission services. To give you an idea of the amount of money involved, the total revenue budget that NHS England oversees in 2016/17 is £106.5bn with £71.9bn of this allocated to CCGs including monies for CCG running costs. NHS England's own running costs amount to around £533m and its direct commissioning accounts for £29.1bn. See chapter 10 for more details and a full breakdown of the 2016/17 budget.

NHS England also has a capital budget for 2016/17 of £305m.

References and Further Reading

Health and Social Care Act 2012: www.legislation.gov.uk/ukpga/2012/7/contents/enacted

NHS England: www.england.nhs.uk/

NHS Mandate, 2016/17: www.gov.uk/government/publications/nhs-mandate-2016-to-2017

Delivering the Forward View: NHS Planning Guidance 2016/17 to 2020/21, NHS England, 2015: www.england.nhs.uk/wp-content/uploads/2015/12/planning-guid-16-17-20-21.pdf

NHS England Operating Models for direct commissioning:
www.england.nhs.uk/resources/d-com/

Information about personal health budgets: www.england.nhs.uk/healthbudgets/

SLAs for CCGs and CSUs – see the CCG resources page of NHS England's website:
www.england.nhs.uk/resources/resources-for-ccgs/

Lead Provider Framework, NHS England, 2015: www.england.nhs.uk/lpf/

NHS Outcomes Framework: www.england.nhs.uk/resources/resources-for-ccgs/out-frwrk/

Securing Excellence in Commissioning Primary Care, NHS England, June 2012:
www.england.nhs.uk/wp-content/uploads/2012/06/ex-comm-pc.pdf

Next Steps Towards Primary Care Co-commissioning, NHS England, 2014:
www.england.nhs.uk/commissioning/wp-content/uploads/sites/12/2014/11/nxt-steps-pc-cocomms.pdf

Chapter 5
NHS Finance – Who Does What: The Role of Clinical Commissioning Groups

> This chapter looks at what clinical commissioning groups (CCGs) are, how they are structured and what they do with a focus on accountability, governance and finance. To remind yourself of where CCGs sit in the NHS structure, look back at the diagram on page 11.

What are CCGs?

Constitution

CCGs are statutory bodies created by the *Health and Social Care Act 2012* that cover the whole of England. They took over their statutory roles from 1 April 2013. To exist, a CCG must be authorised by NHS England and continue to comply with the terms of its authorisation.

In April 2016, there were 209 CCGs across England covering areas that are largely in line with upper tier or unitary local authority boundaries. Where this is not the case and a CCG straddles more than one local authority it must be for 'patient interest reasons'. Legislation[1] allows for CCGs to merge or dissolve subject to NHS England approval.

Structure

In terms of their structure, each CCG is made up of members that are the GP practices within its area. They have a 'Council of Members' (on which all the constituent GP practices are represented) and a governing body, a Chair, lay members, an 'Accountable Officer' (see below) and a chief finance officer (CFO). The Council of Members delegates functions to the governing body (or to its members/employees, committees or sub-committees).

The governing body is statutorily responsible for:

- 'ensuring that the group has appropriate arrangements in place to exercise its functions effectively, efficiently and economically and in accordance with the group's principles of good governance (its main function)
- determining the remuneration, fees and other allowances payable to employees or other persons providing services to the group and the allowances payable under any pension scheme...
- approving any functions of the group that are specified in regulations
- other functions delegated to it by the CCG.[2]'

Although the Accountable Officer in a CCG is a senior leadership role, it is not the same as the chief executive in other NHS organisations and will often be filled by a clinical leader. It is for the CCG to nominate its Accountable Officer but he or she is formally appointed by NHS England. The role of the Accountable Officer is set out in NHS England guidance[3] as:

- being responsible for ensuring that the CCG fulfils its duties to exercise its functions effectively, efficiently and economically thus ensuring improvement in the quality of services and the health of the local population whilst maintaining value for money

---

[1] Section 25 *Health and Social Care Act 2012*.
[2] *Model Constitution for CCGs*, NHS England.
[3] *Clinical Commissioning Group Governing Body Members: Role Outlines, Attributes and Skills*, NHS England, 2012.

- ensuring that the regularity and propriety of expenditure is discharged at all times, and that arrangements are put in place to ensure that good practice is embodied and that safeguarding of funds is ensured through effective financial and management systems
- working closely with the Chair of the governing body, ensuring that proper constitutional, governance and development arrangements are put in place to assure the members (through the governing body) of the organisation's on-going capability and capacity to meet its duties and responsibilities (including arrangements for the on-going development of its members and staff).

In the same guidance, the chief finance officer's role is described as:

- being the governing body's professional expert on finance and ensuring, through robust systems and processes, the regularity and propriety of expenditure is fully discharged
- making appropriate arrangements to support, monitor and report on the CCG's finances
- overseeing robust audit and governance arrangements leading to propriety in the use of the CCG's resources
- being able to advise the governing body on the effective, efficient and economic use of the group's allocation, to remain within that allocation and deliver required financial targets and duties
- producing the financial statements for audit and publication in accordance with the statutory requirements to demonstrate effective stewardship of public money and accountability to NHS England.

Accountabilities

CCGs are accountable to NHS England (for improving outcomes to patients and for getting the best possible value for money from the money they receive) and to the public and patients. The formal accountability link is from the CCG's Accountable Officer to NHS England's Accountable Officer but from the public/patient viewpoint the key document is the CCG's written constitution. This document is a statutory requirement and must be available to the public.

A CCG's constitution sets out how it will meet its responsibilities and describes its governing principles, rules and procedures.

As well as being a public document, the constitution must be adhered to by:

- the group's member practices
- the CCG's employees
- individuals working on behalf of the CCG
- anyone who is a member of the CCG's governing body or any committees/sub-committees established by the governing body.

A CCG's constitution must meet the requirements set out in the 2012 Act. CCGs must also adhere to the *Commissioning Outcomes Indicator Set* developed by the National Institute for Health and Care Excellence (NICE). This provides clear, comparative information about the quality of health services and associated health outcomes. NHS England uses this as part of its ongoing assessment process for CCGs – it will look at performance against the outcomes indicators and also assess how well CCGs are meeting their financial duties. NHS England uses an *Improvement and Assessment Framework (IAF)* to assess a CCG's overall performance. This comprises a range of indicators across four domains:

- better health – including addressing personalisation, choice and health inequalities
- better care – including the availability of seven day services and the provision of high quality mental health services

- sustainability – including financial sustainability and new models of care
- leadership – including governance arrangements and the management of conflicts of interest.

If a CCG is unable to fulfill its duties effectively or there is a significant risk of failure, NHS England has powers to intervene. These powers range from telling a CCG how it should discharge its functions, known as 'direction', through to dissolving a CCG completely if it is failing over a period of time. See chapter 12 for more details.

What CCGs do – Roles and Responsibilities

Commissioning

CCGs are responsible for agreeing the care that patients registered with their constituent practices need, negotiating contracts with healthcare providers and monitoring their implementation. CCGs commission the majority of NHS services for their patients[4] and in 2016/17 were allocated £71.9bn of the £106.5bn NHS revenue budget. Commissioning can take a number of forms:

Services Commissioned Directly by CCGs

- planned hospital care
- rehabilitative care
- maternity services
- urgent and emergency services including ambulance and out-of-hours services (CCGs must also commission these services for anyone in their area although for some patients the costs will subsequently be charged to the CCG with which they are registered)
- community health services
- mental health services
- learning disabilities services
- abortion services
- infertility services
- continuing healthcare

Personal health budgets

CCGs also have a role in the implementation, promotion and expansion of personal health budgets or PHBs. Patients eligible for continuing healthcare have the right to a PHB – an amount of money used to support a person's health and wellbeing needs, planned and agreed between the person and their local NHS team. PHBs allow individual patients to decide how to use the money that they are entitled to, to deliver the care they need. By enabling individuals to undertake the commissioning role themselves, they have more choice and control over how their long-term healthcare needs and outcomes are met.

Integrated personal commissioning

A CCG may also be involved in integrated personal commissioning (IPC). This combines a PHB with a social care budget to provide individuals with an integrated 'year of care' budget. This combined budget can be managed by individuals or on their behalf by local authorities,

---

[4] CCG patient numbers vary from fewer than 100,000 to 900,000.

the NHS or a voluntary organisation. It is particularly suitable for someone with complex needs. At present this covers:

- older people with long term conditions
- children with disabilities and their families
- people with learning disabilities
- people living with serious mental illness.

Co-commissioning

CCGs may also be responsible for commissioning services provided by GPs. Since April 2015, CCGs working with NHS England have been able to adopt one of the following 'co-commissioning' models:

- involvement – allowing CCGs to collaborate with local NHS England teams in terms of discussions prior to decision-making
- joint commissioning – '… enables one or more CCGs to jointly commission general practice services with NHS England through a joint committee'[5]
- delegated responsibility – the CCG assumes full delegated responsibility for primary care – for example, by designing new enhanced services[6].

It is anticipated that co-commissioning will be extended to other areas of primary care in the future. However, it is important to note that NHS England retains its statutory responsibilities in relation to commissioning primary care even where a CCG is operating under full delegated responsibility.

At present, CCGs are *not* responsible for commissioning other core primary care (i.e. services provided by dentists, community pharmacists and holders of ophthalmic contracts), national and regional specialised services and a number of other prescribed services including offender healthcare – these are commissioned by NHS England (see chapter 4).

However, CCGs are responsible for managing GP prescribing – they meet the costs of prescriptions written by their member practices but not the associated dispensing fees.

Statutory duties

CCGs must fulfil a number of other statutory duties which are grouped under four headings in the Department of Health's guide *The Functions of Clinical Commissioning Groups*:

CCG Statutory Duties

General – for example, to co-operate with other NHS bodies; to have regard to the NHS Constitution and guidance on commissioning issued by NHS England; to promote innovation in health service provision; to promote the involvement of patients.

Planning, agreeing, monitoring services – for example, to contribute to the JSNA (joint strategic needs assessment) and JHWS (joint health and wellbeing strategy) and to have regard to them; to prepare and publish a commissioning plan before the start of each financial year which sets out how the CCG will secure improvements in services and outcomes, reduce inequalities, involve patients and fulfil its financial duties; to comply with regulations relating to best practice in procurement/patient choice and anti-competitive conduct.

---

[5] Primary care co-commissioning pages of the NHS England website:
https://www.england.nhs.uk/commissioning/pc-co-comms/
[6] Services provided over and above those required by the GMS contract.

> NHS England issues financial planning guidance each year that establishes the 'business rules' for the financial position. For 2016/17, each CCG must plan to achieve a 1% cumulative surplus, a 1% uncommitted non-recurrent investment reserve, 0.5% contingency and meet its 'parity of esteem' commitment to mental health services.
>
> **Finance** – for example, to ensure the annual budget, revenue and capital limits and running cost allowance are not exceeded; to provide financial information to NHS England; to keep proper accounts and records; to use the prescribed banking service.
>
> **Governance** – for example, to have a governing body and Accountable Officer; to have a published constitution; to publish an annual report; to maintain one or more publicly accessible registers of interest; to make arrangements for managing conflicts of interest.

The same guidance identifies CCG powers under the same headings. In relation to finance and governance notable powers include the ability to:

- enter into partnership arrangements with local authorities (for example, pooled budgets and lead commissioning)
- enter into contracts to provide services
- act jointly with other CCGs, including pooling commissioning funds for lead/joint commissioning
- make direct payments to patients (subject to regulations)[7]
- enter into externally financed development arrangements
- pay governing body members remuneration and travelling or other allowances.

For full details of a CCG's functions, duties and powers refer to the Department of Health guide.

Commissioning support units (CSUs)

Initially all CCGs had the option to obtain business support services – notably payroll, HR, finance, IT and communications services, from commissioning support units (CSUs) hosted by NHS England. Service level agreements (SLAs) set out what each party to the agreement expected and/or required. Initial SLAs were in place until October 2014. NHS England subsequently ran a national procurement process to make commissioning support services available to CCGs and other commissioners of health and social care. This resulted in a number of CSUs and 3 private sector providers being accredited via the Lead Provider Framework (LPF). If CSU-style services are sourced from 'non-accredited' organisations, a far lengthier procurement process is likely to be necessary. See chapter 4 for more about CSUs.

How CCGs are financed

CCGs receive funding for commissioning NHS services from NHS England. The main allocation is based on a formula that supports the aim of improving health outcomes and reducing inequalities. It takes account of the number of people registered with each GP as well as the sparsity of the local population (see chapter 10 for more details). Part of a CCG's allocation must be put into a pooled budget with the relevant local authority designated as the better care fund (BCF). As CCGs are required to work collaboratively with local authorities 'to make the most efficient and effective use of health and social care funding', the size and scale of pooled funds is set to increase over the spending review period (to 2020).

CCGs may also receive a 'quality premium' payment. The '… scheme is about rewarding (CCGs) for improvements in the quality of the services they commission. The scheme also

---

[7] See personal health budgets above.

incentivises CCGs to improve patient health outcomes and reduce inequalities in health outcomes and improve access to services.'[8] The requirements change each year and are designed to support the NHS's key priorities for the coming period. For 2016/17, 70% of the quality premium is based on the achievement of national priorities (cancer, GP patient survey, electronic referrals and antibiotic prescribing) with the balance tied to the achievement of local priorities. The maximum payment is set at £5 per head for each CCG.

There is also a separate running cost allowance that is based on the population served by each CCG's constituent practices adjusted to take account of inaccurate lists and unregistered people. In 2016/17, the allowance is set at a maximum of £22.07 per head. This allowance must cover all CCG management costs including the costs of commissioning support services. CCGs are free to decide how best to use this allowance to carry out commissioning support activities and may choose to undertake some or all of these roles themselves. They also have the flexibility to use the money to buy in the services needed (for example, data analysis and contract monitoring) from external sources. As well as covering the costs directly associated with commissioning, the allowance covers the costs of the Accountable Officer, chief finance officer, internal and external audit and counter fraud services.

References and Further Reading

Clinical Commissioning Group Governing Body Members: Role Outlines, Attributes and Skills, NHS England, 2012:
www.england.nhs.uk/wp-content/uploads/2012/09/ccg-members-roles.pdf

CCG Outcomes Indicator Set, NHS England: www.england.nhs.uk/ccg-ois/

CCG Improvement and Assessment Framework 2016/17, NHS England, 2016: https://www.england.nhs.uk/commissioning/wp-content/uploads/sites/12/2016/03/ccg-iaf-mar16.pdf

Information about personal health budgets: www.england.nhs.uk/healthbudgets/

Next Steps Towards Primary Care Co-commissioning, NHS England, 2014:
https://www.england.nhs.uk/commissioning/pc-co-comms/

The Functions of Clinical Commissioning Groups, Department of Health, 2012:
https://www.gov.uk/government/publications/the-functions-of-clinical-commissioning-groups-updated-to-reflect-the-final-health-and-social-care-act-2012

Lead Provider Framework, NHS England, 2015: https://www.england.nhs.uk/lpf/

Quality Premium: 2016/17: Guidance for CCGs, NHS England, 2016:
https://www.england.nhs.uk/resources/resources-for-ccgs/ccg-out-tool/ccg-ois/qual-prem/

---

[8] *Quality Premium Guidance for 2016/17*, NHS England, March 2016

Chapter 6
NHS Finance – Who Does What: The Role of Primary Care

> This chapter looks at the main primary care services in the NHS with a focus on what they do and how they are financed. In terms of their position in the NHS structure, primary care services fall within the 'providers' box in the diagram on page 11.

What is Primary Care and Who Provides it?

Primary care is where people normally go when they first develop a health problem – usually this will be a GP but there are many other health professionals in this front line team including nurses, health visitors, dentists, opticians and pharmacists.

In this chapter we are going to focus on providers of primary care services and will also look at prescribing (a significant cost to the NHS).

It is worth noting at the outset that, although they are an essential part of the NHS, most family doctors, dentists, opticians and pharmacists are independent contractors or businesses – i.e. they are not NHS employees.

Accountability

Primary care service providers are accountable to:

- the patients to whom they provide services
- NHS England and/or the clinical commissioning group (CCG) that agrees signed contracts with them for the services provided and outcomes achieved
- (in the case of GP practices) the CCG of which they are members
- their own professional bodies
- the Care Quality Commission (CQC) for meeting fundamental standards of quality care – i.e. the standards below which care must never fall.

What Primary Care Providers do

Primary care health providers play a central role in the community. All of us will have some contact with NHS primary care during our lives. General practitioners (GPs) or 'family doctors', pharmacists, dentists and opticians all provide health services to the public. They also act as a gateway to other services. For example, the vast majority of referrals to secondary care in hospitals will come from a primary care practitioner, usually a GP.

How Primary Care is Financed

Primary care services are commissioned by NHS England and financed via contracts that it holds. These contracts are agreed nationally and refreshed each year. In the case of GPs, services may now be 'co-commissioned' by NHS England working with the relevant CCG or commissioned directly by the CCG where the responsibility is formally delegated. However, even where a CCG has a role, NHS England remains statutorily responsible (see chapter 5 for more about the role of CCGs)[1].

Each primary care services contract is discussed in turn below.

---

[1] 'CCGs can discuss dental, eye health and community pharmacy commissioning with NHS England but have no decision making role', *Eye Health Policy Book*, NHS England, 2016: https://www.england.nhs.uk/eye-heath/

GP services

At present, there are three main contract types for GP services – General Medical Services (GMS), Personal Medical Services (PMS) and Alternative Provider Medical Services (APMS). From April 2017, there will also be an option to move to a new voluntary Multispecialty Community Provider (MCP) contract to 'integrate general practice services with community services and wider healthcare services'[2].

General Medical Services (GMS)

The GMS contract (also known as the GP contract) came into effect in April 2004 and is agreed nationally. This practice-based contract has three main income streams:

GMS Contract – Main Income Streams

A **global sum** to cover running costs and the provision of 'essential' and 'additional' services – this is calculated through a resource allocation formula based on the age/sex of the practice's population, additional needs, list turnover, nursing home patients and rurality. In addition to general running costs (for example, practice staff, heating, lighting and consumables), this global sum covers the provision of essential and additional services. Essential services, which have to be provided by every practice, cover the care of patients during an episode of illness, the general management of chronic disease and care for the terminally ill. Additional services, such as contraceptive services, minor surgery, child health surveillance and out of hours services are voluntary. Practices that opt out of providing additional services have their global sum reduced by a nationally agreed percentage rate.

The **Quality and Outcomes Framework (QOF)** to reward practices for the provision of 'quality care' and improving standards. The QOF sets out a range of standards across two domains – clinical and public health. Practices are awarded points for achieving these standards, set out in a range of indicators, and receive a payment per point, dependent upon the number of registered patients. Although participation in QOF is voluntary, most GP practices take part.

Enhanced service payments to meet the costs of extra services or essential services that are delivered to a higher standard than is required under the core GMS contract. There are two types of enhanced services and GP practices can choose whether they want to participate in each one:

- Directed Enhanced Services (DES) that must be commissioned (for example, schemes for extended hours access, to avoid unplanned admissions, childhood immunisation, dementia and learning disabilities health checks). These schemes are nationally specified and payments are agreed at a national level.

- Local Enhanced Services (LES) that are optional and are commissioned by local negotiation to meet specific local needs (for example, enhanced medical care for asylum seekers or non-English speakers). Commissioners agree these schemes locally and payments vary accordingly.

Since April 2013, NHS England has been responsible for commissioning enhanced services nationally (equivalent to DES) although it devolves responsibility for managing some of them to CCGs. Although NHS England retains the ability to commission LES, it is unlikely to do so. Instead, CCGs are expected to decide how best to use local resources to invest in community based services that are beyond the scope of the GP contract.

---

[2] *General Practice Forward View*, NHS England, April 2016: https://www.england.nhs.uk/ourwork/gpfv/

There are also funding streams for GP practices to cover:

- premises: under the terms of the GMS contract, practices are reimbursed for their premises costs. This includes rent and rates charges incurred. A notional rent payment is made to practices that own their premises
- seniority pay: this is paid at nationally agreed rates and is dependent upon the number of years a GP has worked in the NHS. Since April 2004 there have been no new entrants to this scheme and it will cease altogether on 31st March 2020
- dispensing doctors: GP practices (usually in rural areas) that provide dispensing services to patients receive a fee for each item that they dispense in line with an agreed fee scale
- locum cover: practices may receive a contribution towards the costs of employing a locum to cover maternity, paternity and sickness of a partner
- information communications and technology (ICT): responsibility for the delivery of primary care information services rests with NHS England. However, it has delegated responsibility (and the associated funding) for the operational management of GP IT services to CCGs. CCGs can commission these services from any provider that meets a set of quality standards that have been set by NHS England in conjunction with CCGs.

The GMS contract tends to be adjusted annually with the payment provisions set out in detail in the 'Statement of Financial Entitlements (SFE)'. At present around 55% of practices have GMS contracts.

Personal Medical Services (PMS)

PMS contracts were introduced in 1998 and allow a GP practice to negotiate a local agreement with its commissioner in line with local healthcare needs. This means that GPs are paid contract sums to deliver a defined service. PMS practices are also able to receive QOF payments and are eligible for enhanced services (if these are not already in their PMS contract) plus premises, ICT and seniority payments. Currently around 40% of practices receive their funding under locally agreed PMS contracts. PMS practices can opt to switch into the GMS contract.

Alternative Provider Medical Services (APMS)

APMS contracts are provided under directions of the Secretary of State for Health and can be let to private sector, voluntary and not-for-profit providers of general medical services as well as to traditional GP practices, NHS and foundation trusts. APMS contracts tend to be used in areas of historic under provision or to 're-provide' services where GP practices have opted out. They can also be used to improve access where GP recruitment and retention is a problem. Currently around 5% of GP services are delivered under APMS contracts.

Out of hours services

Since April 2004, GP practices have been able to opt out of providing out of hours services and around 90% of GMS and PMS practices have gone down this route. Since April 2013, CCGs have been responsible for commissioning out of hours services for those practices that have opted out. Where out of hours services are still provided by GP practices under the GMS/PMS contract (i.e. the 10% that did not opt out), NHS England is responsible for their commissioning as in such instances, they remain an integral part of the GMS/PMS contract.

General Practice Forward View

The *General Practice Forward View*, published by NHS England in April 2016 sets out a plan to 'stabilise and transform general practice' with a commitment to invest an additional £2.4 billion a year by 2020/21. As well as plans to introduce a new MCP contract, the *Forward View* includes proposals to upgrade practice premises with new rules to allow NHS England to fund up to 100% of the costs.

Dental services

Most primary dental care (i.e. the main dental care needed to maintain good oral health) is provided by self-employed dentists or corporate bodies that hold contracts with the NHS. At present there are two types of contract.

> **Dental Contracts**
>
> **General dental services (GDS)** – this contract came into force in 2006 and pays dentists a set value for an agreed number of units of dental activity (UDAs). A reform of patients' charges came into effect at the same time with the introduction of three bands based on the type of treatment received.
>
> **Personal dental services (PDS)** – under this contract, practices are paid a set contract value in return for having an agreed number of patients on their list. The contract is designed to give a 10% decrease in working time to allow dentists to use 5% to give access slots to unregistered patients to be seen urgently, and 5% to take them off the 'treadmill' of items of service payments.

Both GDS and PDS contracts are negotiated locally using national regulations. The key difference is that PDS contracts are time limited and GDS contracts are not.

As with GP contracts, payments for GDS and PDS contracts are made in line with a Statement of Financial Entitlements (SFE) that covers reimbursements for services provided and payments related to dentists' employment. All dentists under both GDS and PDS contracts must provide a full range of general dental services plus any agreed additional services. Dentists can provide private dental services from the same premises as their NHS contract but patients must be informed if the services they are offered are being provided privately.

Since April 2013, NHS England has been responsible for commissioning all NHS dental services as part of its direct commissioning responsibilities. This includes primary dental care, dental hospitals and out of hours services.

The Government plans to introduce a new national dental contract based on capitation, activity and quality. This will mean that dentists will be paid on a 'per patient' rather than a 'per treatment' basis and rewarded for continuity and quality of care. A range of different contract models were piloted at 70 sites throughout England up until March 2013 with another 25 sites then 'fine tuning' different elements. In 2015, the Department of Health invited dentists to take part in testing contract 'prototypes' with a view to introducing a reformed contract in 2018/19.

Pharmacy services

In April 2005, a 'new' community pharmacy contract came into effect which has since been re-negotiated annually. This contract specifies three levels of service.

> **Pharmacy Services – the Three Levels of Service**
>
> 1. **Essential services and clinical governance** – services that must be provided by all pharmacies. For example, dispensing and repeat dispensing; disposal of unwanted medicines; promoting healthy lifestyles; signposting and support for self-care
> 2. **Advanced services** – services that may be provided by accredited pharmacists and pharmacies. There are five advanced services: medicine use reviews (MURs), appliance use reviews (AURs); the new medicine service (NMS); flu vaccination and stoma appliance customisation (SAC)
> 3. **Enhanced (or 'locally commissioned') services** – services that may be commissioned to meet local needs, including stop smoking schemes, emergency hormonal contraception and minor ailments.

Since April 2013, NHS England has been responsible for commissioning essential and advanced community pharmacy services as part of its direct commissioning activities. Enhanced (or locally commissioned) services that are not covered by the pharmacy contract can be commissioned directly from community pharmacists by a range of different commissioners including CCGs, local authorities and local NHS England teams. Where this happens, the specification and payment terms are agreed locally.

In relation to the supply and dispensing of drugs, NHS Prescriptions Services (part of the NHS Business Services Authority) receives details of all prescriptions dispensed in England, and then calculates the amounts payable, allowing for the drug and container cost and a service fee.

An electronic prescription service (EPS) is also in use – this allows prescribers (such as GPs and practice nurses) to send prescriptions electronically to a dispenser of the patient's choice, thus making the prescribing and dispensing process safer and more convenient. Community pharmacies receive payments for signing up to the scheme and updating their systems. They also receive monthly payments for using the system.

The cost of drugs dispensed is charged to CCGs' prescribing budgets, based on the GP practice that issued the prescription (see prescribing section below for more information).

Ophthalmic services

The basis on which payments are made for optical services is set out in the *NHS Act 2006* which introduced three tiers of service.

Ophthalmic Services – the Three Tiers of Service

1. **Mandatory (or 'essential')** – services that all commissioners must commission and which any eligible contractor can provide (i.e. the provision of NHS sight tests)
2. **Additional** – services that all commissioners must commission but not all contractors are obliged to provide. For example, the provision of sight tests in alternative settings such as a nursing home
3. **Enhanced** – services that a commissioner may choose to commission and fund to meet local needs.

Payments for NHS sight tests for 'eligible patients' (patients who meet set criteria – for example, children under 16 and adults over 60) are made in accordance with the Department of Health's 'general ophthalmic services' (GOS) regulations. Only fees for eligible patients are met from the NHS budget – all other patients pay privately for these services. In addition, opticians are able to issue a 'voucher' in certain circumstances to help eligible patients with the cost of glasses. Patients can top up the value of this voucher in order to buy more expensive glasses if they wish.

Since April 2013, NHS England has been responsible for commissioning mandatory and additional services as part of its direct commissioning function and is able to commission enhanced services. CCGs can also commission enhanced services directly from providers on a locally agreed basis (i.e. they are outside the GOS contract).

Prescribing

The rising cost of primary care prescribing (over £9 billion each year) is a significant cost pressure with drug inflation regularly outstripping inflation on other budgets. Prescribing costs have generally risen faster than general inflation as new, more effective (and often more expensive) drugs become available. However, this has become even more pronounced in recent years partly as a result of guidance from the National Institute for Health and Care Excellence (NICE). One of NICE's roles is to assess the clinical and cost-effectiveness of new drugs and technologies and this has an impact on both prescription volume and cost. The effects are mitigated to an extent by securing efficiencies from improvements in prescribing practice.

From a financing viewpoint, prescribing is not covered in GPs or dentists contracts. Instead, as mentioned earlier, the costs of drugs prescribed are calculated by NHS Prescription Services and charged to the relevant CCG (for GP prescriptions) and to NHS England (for dentists). The associated dispensing fees are met by NHS England.

References and Further Reading

NHS primary care commissioning information – NHS England:
www.england.nhs.uk/resources/resource-primary/

GMS contract information:
http://www.nhsemployers.org/your-workforce/primary-care-contacts/general-medical-services

Quality and Outcomes Framework: http://www.nhsemployers.org/your-workforce/primary-care-contacts/general-medical-services/quality-and-outcomes-framework

Enhanced Services information: http://www.nhsemployers.org/your-workforce/primary-care-contacts/general-medical-services/enhanced-services

GP IT Services: Operating Model, NHS England, 2014: www.england.nhs.uk/2012/12/04/gp-it/

Statements of Financial Entitlements for GPs: https://www.gov.uk/government/publications/nhs-primary-medical-services-directions-2013

General Practice Forward View, NHS England, April 2016:
https://www.england.nhs.uk/ourwork/gpfv/

Dental contract information, NHS England, 2016: https://www.england.nhs.uk/dental/

Statements of Financial Entitlements for dentists, NHS Business Services Authority:
http://www.nhsbsa.nhs.uk/860.aspx

Dental contract pilots – information and background:
www.gov.uk/government/publications/extension-to-dental-contract-pilot-scheme

Dental contract prototypes information: https://www.gov.uk/government/publications/dental-reform-next-step

British Dental Association: https://www.bda.org/contractreform

For information about general ophthalmic services regulations and contracts the Local Optical Committee Support Unit's website is helpful: www.locsu.co.uk/regulation/

Pharmacy contract information:
http://www.nhsemployers.org/your-workforce/primary-care-contacts/community-pharmacy

NHS Prescription Services: www.nhsbsa.nhs.uk/prescriptionservices.aspx

Information on prescribing and the electronic prescription service, Health and Social Care Information Centre: www.hscic.gov.uk/prescribingt

Chapter 7

NHS Finance – Who Does What: The Role of Community, Secondary and Tertiary Care Providers

> This chapter looks at the main providers of community, secondary and tertiary care in the NHS with a focus on their roles, responsibilities, financing and governance. To remind yourself of where providers fit into the NHS structure, look back at the diagram on page 11. The chapter also refers to the new ways in which care is being organised.

What is Community Care?

Community care – as its name suggests – is the term used for those health services provided in community settings such as patients' homes, GP practices and (usually small) community hospitals.

> **Community Care Services – Examples**
>
> - community hospitals including some acute care and community-based care for elderly people needing rehabilitation
> - community health services
> - mental health community based services
> - support for people with learning disabilities
> - services for physically disabled people
> - 'virtual' wards where patients are supported in their own homes by nursing therapy clinicians whilst still under the care of acute clinicians
> - tele health, tele care and tele medicine services.

What is Secondary Care?

Secondary care is healthcare usually provided in a hospital setting – for example, acute clinical services at a district general or more specialist hospital following a referral from a primary care professional or through attendance at and/or admission through emergency pathways.

What is Tertiary Care?

Tertiary care comprises those services provided in more specialist centres usually in larger or teaching hospitals – for example, cardiac surgery. Often these services are accessed by a referral from one consultant to another. However, in larger hospitals that provide tertiary care services themselves, referral can take place directly on admission.

Who Provides Community, Secondary and Tertiary Services?

Community, secondary and tertiary services can be commissioned from any service provider that is registered with the Care Quality Commission (CQC) – in other words from 'any qualified provider' or AQP. The CQC regulates a number of activities that are listed in Schedule 1 of the *Health and Social Care Act (Regulated Activities) Regulations 2014*. Regulated activities include surgical procedures and treatment of disease, disorder or injury. Any organisation in England that provides these activities must register with the CQC.

Service providers include NHS organisations, private sector healthcare providers (for example, Virgin Health and BUPA), voluntary or charitable sector providers and social enterprise organisations (some of which are former NHS community service providers).

This chapter's primary focus is on NHS organisations and in particular community, mental health, acute and ambulance service providers. However, we will also look briefly at the part played by social enterprise organisations.

Non-foundation NHS Trusts and NHS foundation trusts (FTs)

All NHS providers in England are part of a non-foundation NHS trust or an NHS foundation trust (FT) or – there are four main types:

- **acute trusts** run hospitals and employ clinical staff (for example, nurses, doctors, pharmacists and midwives); related therapeutic specialists (for example, physiotherapists, radiographers, podiatrists, speech and language therapists, counsellors, occupational therapists and psychologists) and non-clinical staff (for example, porters, cleaners, managers, engineers, caterers and domestic and security staff)
- **community trusts** specialise in delivering NHS care in patients' homes and in community settings – for example in nursing homes, clinics, community hospitals, minor injury units, walk-in centres and mobile units. These trusts employ a range of staff including community and district nurses, physiotherapists, school nurses, health visitors, rehabilitation and palliative care specialists and dieticians
- **mental health trusts** provide health and social care services for people with mental health problems/illnesses or learning disabilities
- **ambulance trusts** provide emergency access to healthcare and patient transport services.

What Trusts do – Roles and Responsibilities

The principal activity of all trusts (non-foundation and FTs) is to provide goods or services for any purpose related to the provision of services for or in connection with the prevention, diagnosis or treatment of illness, and the promotion of public health. All trusts are required to have regard to the *NHS Constitution*, provide high-quality healthcare and spend their money efficiently. They must also decide how the services they deliver will develop and improve.

The **NHS Constitution** sets out the:

- **rights** to which patients, public and staff are entitled
- **pledges** which the NHS is committed to achieve
- **responsibilities** that the public, patients and staff owe to one another.

How Trusts are Financed

Revenue financing

Both types of trust receive revenue income (to meet the costs of their day-today running) from a number of sources including those set out below:

Revenue Income Sources

- contractual income from NHS England, clinical commissioning groups (CCGs), local authorities and other NHS trusts. Trusts are commissioned to provide services for patients and are paid in line with the standard NHS contract
- specific funding to those trusts providing nursing, medical and non-medical staff education and training services (generally based on the number of people in training)
- allocations/grant funding where trusts are undertaking agreed research and development
- charges made for 'hosted services' for example, internal audit consortia
- charges to staff, visitors or patients for services provided for example, catering, car parking or the provision of private patient facilities
- grants from other Government bodies or charitable organisations
- the NHS injury cost recovery scheme – this allows the NHS to reclaim the cost of treating injured patients in all cases where personal injury compensation is paid.

The levels of income received from these sources will vary between different types of trust – for example, community trusts are unlikely to have income relating to injury costs (unless they run minor injury units).

In addition, a limited number of NHS providers have Ministry of Defence (MOD) hospital units. Where this is the case, the organisation will have two contracts: one for training military medical personnel and one for treating military patients. Income relating to the training contract is paid directly to the organisation by the MOD. The contract for treating military personnel mirrors the NHS standard contract and uses the national tariff (see chapter 18) although it may contain the opportunity for additional payments for treating military personnel more quickly.

FTs also derive income from:

- private patients

    Many FTs generate additional income through treating patients privately: either billing insurance companies or individuals direct. Until 1 October 2012, FTs were restricted in the amount of income they could generate in this way by the 'private patient income cap'. However, this cap has now been removed and instead FTs must 'ensure that their total income from NHS-funded goods and services is greater than their total income from any other sources'. There is also a control on how quickly a trust can increase its private and non-NHS income. An FT which proposes to increase by 5% or more the proportion of its total income in any financial year attributable to activities other than the provision of NHS services may only implement the proposal if more than half of the members of the Council of Governors of the trust approve its implementation. They must also produce separate accounts for NHS and private-funded services.

- other commercial ventures

    Many FTs have other commercial sources of income at home and abroad. For example, Moorfields Eye Hospital NHS Foundation Trust has operated an eye hospital in Dubai since 2006. Private patients in London and Dubai contributed a surplus of £3.5 million in 2014/15 to Moorfields Eye Hospital NHS Trust. Healthcare UK (part of the Department of Health and the UK Trade and Investment Department) helps UK healthcare providers to do more business overseas.

Capital financing

Both types of trust have access to a number of well-established funding sources:

- internally generated resources (via retained surpluses, depreciation and proceeds from the sale of non-current assets)
- borrowing (including public dividend capital)
- public private partnerships
- leases
- donations and grants.

The capital expenditure rules for FTs are subtly different from NHS trusts and FTs have the ability to reinvest within set parameters (see chapter 15 for more details about capital funding, planning and accounting).

Constitution, Structure and Accountabilities

The roles and responsibilities of all trusts are very similar and a patient is unlikely to notice any differences between them. However, there are important distinctions in their constitutions, structure and accountabilities. These are outlined below.

Non-foundation NHS trusts – constitution

NHS trusts were formed from 1991 onwards under the *NHS and Community Care Act 1990*. NHS trusts provide mainly, but not exclusively, hospital-based secondary healthcare services. The most common type is an acute hospital trust but as we have seen, there are also mental health, community and ambulance trusts. Some trusts operate regional or national centres of more specialised care, while others are classed as teaching hospitals as they train healthcare professionals and work closely with universities.

Non-foundation NHS trusts – structure

All NHS trusts have a board of directors with a constitution set out in primary legislation under *The NHS Trusts (Membership and Procedure) Regulations 1990* and amended with effect from 14 April 2014.

Each NHS trust board must have an equal number of executive and non-executive members with the Chairperson as an extra non-executive director (NED). Under the original legislation it was typical to have five executive directors and five non-executive directors excluding the Chairperson.

Since April 2013, the NHS Trust Development Authority (NHS TDA), now operating as part of NHS Improvement, has been responsible for appointing NEDs.

Within the board's executive directors, each trust must have:

- a chief officer (the chief executive who is also the 'Accountable Officer' – see below)
- a chief finance officer or finance director
- a medical or dental practitioner, and
- a registered nurse or midwife (except in the case of ambulance trusts).

Other executive directors may attend board meetings (in addition to the chief executive and chief finance officer) although there must be an equal number of voting executive directors and NEDs; the Chairperson provides the casting vote if necessary. Also, although the medical and nursing professions must be represented at board level, this can be via the chief executive if she or he has a medical or nursing background.

An NHS trust board is collectively responsible for promoting the success of the organisation by directing and supervising its affairs. This involves:

- setting the organisation's values and standards and ensuring that its obligations to patients, the local community and the Secretary of State are understood and met
- providing active leadership of the organisation within a framework of prudent and effective controls that enable risk to be assessed and managed
- setting the organisation's strategic aims
- ensuring that the necessary financial and human resources are in place for the organisation to meet its objectives
- reviewing management performance.

NHS trusts are expected to transition to foundation status as swiftly as they can but there is no deadline. To help them work towards this goal, trusts are monitored and supported by NHS Improvement (see chapter 12). In May 2016 there were 82 NHS trusts[1].

Non-foundation NHS trusts – accountabilities

In terms of accountability, an NHS trust's chief executive is the 'Accountable Officer'. This is a statutory role and means that he or she is accountable to the Department of Health's Accounting Officer (via NHS Improvement's Accounting Officer) and ultimately to Parliament (see chapter 13 for more about the role of the Accountable Officer). As well as this formal accountability line, trusts are accountable to their patients and to the commissioners of their services (via contracts). In addition there is a system of independent inspection and regulation by external organisations such as the CQC (see chapters 9 and 12).

Foundation Trusts

Foundation trusts – constitution

NHS foundation trusts (FTs) were created as new legal entities in the form of public benefit corporations by the *Health and Social Care (Community Health and Standards) Act 2003* – updated by the *Health and Social Care Act 2012*. This model draws on the traditions of mutual organisations established under the Industrial and Provident legislation. In practice this means that every FT has a duty to consult and involve a Council of Governors (comprising staff, patients, members of the public and other key stakeholders) in strategic planning.

The first FTs were authorised in 2004. In May 2016 there were 156[2] licensed NHS FTs. The FT structure represents a model of local management where central Government involvement is reduced. However, it is important to remember that FTs remain part of the NHS with the primary purpose of providing NHS services to NHS patients according to NHS principles and standards. To that end, they are regulated by NHS Improvement (see chapters 9 and 12).

Foundation trusts – structure

Council of governors and members

FTs have members that are representative of the local community and provide a link between the trust and its patients, service users and stakeholders. These members consist of the public, patients and staff. When applying to be a member of an FT, an individual applicant can also confirm an interest in becoming a governor. The Council of Governors is required to hold the FT to account and to represent the interests of the members of the trust as a whole and the interests of the public.

The board of directors

Every FT must have a board of directors that consists of a non-executive Chairperson, executive directors (which must include the chief executive, who is the Accounting Officer

---

[1] NHS Confederation key statistics on the NHS: http://www.nhsconfed.org/resources/key-statistics-on-the-nhs
[2] NHS Confederation key statistics on the NHS: http://www.nhsconfed.org/resources/key-statistics-on-the-nhs

(see below) a finance director, a registered medical practitioner or a registered dentist and a registered nurse or a registered midwife) and NEDs. NEDs should have experience or skills that help the board function well. They are appointed by the Council of Governors based on recommendations made by a 'nominations committee'.

The board of directors is collectively responsible for every decision it takes regardless of individual directors' skills or status. In particular, the board of directors must set the FT's strategic aims (taking account of the views of the Council of Governors) and is responsible for ensuring compliance with the FT's terms of authorisation, its constitution, mandatory guidance (for example, issued by NHS Improvement), relevant statutory requirements and contractual obligations. Meetings of the board of directors must be open to the public.

Foundation trusts – accountabilities

The FT's chief executive is also the 'Accounting Officer' (a role known as the 'Accountable Officer' in other NHS organisations). This is a statutory role originally set out in the 2003 Act which provides the formal accountability link from the FT to Parliament. The Accounting Officer's duties are set out in a memorandum issued by NHS Improvement that states that 'accounting officers are responsible to Parliament for the resources under their control'.

As well as the formal accountability line from the Accounting Officer, FTs (like other trusts) are accountable to both their patients and to the commissioners of their services (via contracts). In addition there is a system of independent inspection and regulation by organisations such as the CQC (see chapters 9 and 12).

Although FTs are not directly accountable to the Department of Health they remain part of the NHS with the primary purpose of providing NHS services to NHS patients according to NHS principles and standards. As with NHS trusts, there are foundation trusts that provide acute, tertiary, mental health, community and ambulance services across England.

Social Enterprise Organisations (SEOs)

What they are – constitution, structure and accountabilities

SEOs are not-for-profit service providers accountable to the organisation commissioning healthcare from them. They are run for the benefit of the community and any financial surplus made is reinvested into patient services, staff and local communities.

In terms of regulation and accountability, SEOs are not part of the NHS – instead they are stand-alone businesses. Any SEO that wishes to provide services to NHS patients must therefore be registered with the CQC and licenced by NHS Improvement.

There is a range of SEO models operating in health and social care including mutual, co-operative or employee owned organisations and community interest companies (CICs). CICs are set up specifically for organisations operating for the benefit of the community.

Many SEOs are single service providers for example, providing speech and language therapy or podiatry. However, around 40 were set up as a result of the 'transforming community services (TCS)' programme that removed provider activities from primary care trusts[3]. These tend to provide a full range of community services including district nursing, health visiting and school nursing. For example, Central Surrey Health is co-owned by its employees and provides community nursing and therapy services.

For an SEO to be constituted as a CIC, it must pass a 'community interest test' that shows the company will benefit the community it was set up to serve. An 'asset lock' exists that means that any surpluses made must be reinvested for the good of the community. CICs are granted their status by the CIC Regulator and registered with Companies House. CIC accounts are submitted in line with Companies House timetables rather than those of the NHS.

---

[3] The Department of Health's national TCS programme was completed on 31 March 2011. The Government required primary care trusts to transfer community care to other organisations. Most chose NHS trusts but some were set up as community interest companies.

For more information visit the CIC regulator's website: www.cicregulator.gov.uk

What SEOs do

SEOs are commissioned to provide services to NHS patients to meet local needs.

How SEOs are financed

For SEOs established under TCS the bulk of their funding comes from NHS commissioner contracts. These are often based on historic amounts and paid as a fixed or block amount over a set period of time (for example, 4 years) at which point they are then subject to a tender process. SEOs can expand the range of services provided, the number of commissioners served and income received – for example, by providing services previously delivered by local authorities or forming subsidiary companies (such as 'charitable arms') to take advantage of tax opportunities and enable the receipt of charitable donations.

A Vision for the Future – New Models of Care

Seen as one of the first steps for delivering the shared vision for the future of the NHS outlined in the *Five Year Forward View* (see chapter 2 for more details), the new care models programme supports the improvement and integration of NHS services through better networks of care, increased out of hospital care and services integrated around the patient. The vision is centred around seven new care models that require existing providers to work in different ways often in new partnership arrangements:

- **multispecialty community providers (MCPs):** a range of traditional community based services are coordinated by the MCP. In addition, outpatient and diagnostic services are moved into the community from a hospital setting

- **primary and acute care systems (PACs):** a single local system of care provision (incorporating primary and secondary healthcare services). This may be supported by a per head or capitated budget for all healthcare (and potentially social care) based on patients registered with GPs in the local area

- **urgent and emergency care networks:** here the focus is on new approaches to improve the coordination of services and reduce pressure on existing A&E departments

- **acute care collaborations (ACC):** formal shared working arrangements to enhance the viability of local hospitals. These can be clinical collaborations between different hospitals and/or back office, administration or management arrangements that aim to improve efficiency

- **enhanced health in care homes:** these arrangements aim to offer older people better joined up health, care and rehabilitation services.

References and Further Reading

The Health and Social Care Act 2008 (Regulated Activities) Regulations 2014
http://www.legislation.gov.uk/uksi/2014/2936/contents/made

NHS and Community Care Act 1990: www.legislation.gov.uk/ukpga/1990/19/contents

The NHS Trusts (Membership and Procedure) Regulations 1990:
www.legislation.gov.uk/uksi/1990/2024/contents/made

NHS Improvement – including Monitor and the NHS TDA:
https://improvement.nhs.uk/about-us/who-we-are/

The NHS Constitution for England, Department of Health, 2015:
www.gov.uk/government/publications/the-nhs-constitution-for-england

Information about types of NHS trust – NHS Choices website:
www.nhs.uk/NHSEngland/thenhs/about/Pages/authoritiesandtrusts.aspx

NHS standard contract information: www.england.nhs.uk/nhs-standard-contract/

The NHS Foundation Trust Code of Governance, Monitor, 2014:
www.gov.uk/government/publications/nhs-foundation-trusts-code-of-governance

Information about transforming community services (archived web pages):
http://healthandcare.dh.gov.uk/category/nhs-providers/tcs/

For more about community interest companies: www.bis.gov.uk/cicregulator/

CIC Regulator: www.cicregulator.gov.uk

The Five Year Forward View, NHS England, 2014:
https://www.england.nhs.uk/ourwork/futurenhs/

Chapter 8
NHS Finance – Who Does What: The Role of Local Authorities, Health and Wellbeing Boards and HealthWatch

> This chapter looks at the role of local authorities with a focus on how they work with (and link to) the NHS. In particular, it looks at the practical implications of the duties placed on local authorities as a result of the *Health and Social Care Act 2012* and at the ways in which local authorities and the NHS work together. To see where they fit into the NHS structure, refer to the diagram on page 11.

Local Authorities – what are they?

Local authorities (also known as councils) provide public services to local communities and are run by democratically elected councillors who are accountable to their electorate. Local authorities work with local partners (including charities, businesses and other public service providers like the police and the NHS) and residents to determine and deliver local priorities. They provide a wide range of services, either directly themselves or by commissioning them from other organisations. They also have responsibility for the economic, social and environmental 'wellbeing' of their area.

Local authorities choose how to organise their operations based on their responsibilities. They are structured in different ways in different areas and fall into one of the following categories:

- **two-tier** – a county council upper or first tier (responsible for county-wide services – for example, education, transport, planning, fire and public safety, social care, libraries, waste management and trading standards) and a district/city/borough council second tier (responsible for rubbish collection, recycling, council tax collection, housing and planning applications in their area). So, in two tier areas, services are provided by two different local authorities
- **unitary** – in some parts of the country there is only one tier of local government (hence the term unitary). The 3 main types of unitary authority are city councils in the 'shires' (for example, Nottingham City Council); London boroughs and metropolitan districts. In a unitary area, a single local authority is responsible for all of the services listed above
- **town, parish and community** – these councils are the smallest and most local. They exist in certain parts of the country for historical reasons. They work to maintain local amenities such as allotments, bus shelters and play areas and may be consulted about planning applications and highway issues.

A two-tier or unitary authority can also be part of a combined authority where all the local authorities in an area come together in a voluntary arrangement – for example, Greater Manchester. This allows local authorities to work more closely together in relation to economic development, regeneration and local transport.

How Local Authorities are Financed

Local authority finance is entirely separate from the NHS and so is not discussed here. However, some NHS money does go to local authorities for two key purposes:

- health improvement – a ring fenced grant for local public health services is allocated to local authorities. In spending this money, local authorities must have regard to the *Public Health Outcomes Framework* and publish a Director of Public Health's annual report on the health of the local population
- social care priorities and to support collaboration/integration.

How Local Authorities Link to the NHS

NHS organisations have long been expected to engage with their local communities to improve health and wellbeing and reduce health inequalities. For many years, this has involved NHS organisations working in partnership with local authorities to manage and deliver services in which both parties have an interest. In addition, although the Department of Health is responsible for setting national policy for adult social care and securing its funding from the Treasury within the spending review process (see chapter 10), local authorities deliver the services.

As a result of the *Health and Social Care Act 2012*, the role of local authorities was strengthened to help fulfil the Government's objective that, through the involvement of elected councillors, local authorities will bring greater local democratic legitimacy to the NHS and have more influence over commissioning, particularly in relation to public health and social care. The Act is also designed to make it easier to 'further integrate health with adult social care, children's services (including education) and wider services, including disability services, housing, and tackling crime and disorder'.

This means that local authorities now have a statutory responsibility to join up commissioning of NHS services, social care, public health and health improvement. Local authorities are also required to:

- jointly appoint a Director of Public Health in conjunction with Public Health England
- jointly commission some services with clinical commissioning groups (CCGs)
- lead joint strategic needs assessments (JSNAs) and joint health and wellbeing strategies (JHWS) to ensure coherent and coordinated commissioning strategies (a role carried out jointly with CCGs via health and wellbeing boards – see below)
- support local voice and the exercise of patient choice
- lead on local health improvement and prevention activity.

In practice, this means that much of the joint working that had gone on prior to 2012 continues but local authorities now have additional statutory responsibilities in relation to health improvement and receive a ring fenced grant from the NHS allocation.

One other development that strengthens the link between local authorities and the NHS is the introduction by NHS Improvement of 44 local health and care footprints. These are designed to support longer term planning in the NHS and involve CCGs, non-foundation NHS trusts and foundation trusts, local authorities, other key partners and arm's length bodies agreeing a business and transformation plan.

Local Authorities' Statutory Roles and Responsibilities in Relation to the NHS

Health scrutiny

Since 2003, local authorities with social care responsibilities have been able to establish committees of councillors to provide overview and scrutiny of local NHS bodies. The *Health and Social Care Act 2012* extended this scrutiny role to cover any provider of NHS funded services. It also gave local authorities the ability to discharge their health scrutiny functions in 'the way they deem most suitable'. The aim of this scrutiny role is to secure health improvement for local communities by encouraging authorities to look beyond their own service responsibilities to issues of wider concern to local people. This is achieved by giving democratically elected representatives the right to scrutinise how local health services are provided and developed for their constituents. Health scrutiny powers and duties of local authorities are summarised below.

Local Authority Health Scrutiny Powers

- the right to scrutinise and review health service matters and make reports and recommendations to NHS bodies
- powers to delegate health scrutiny to other authorities, including district councils
- the ability to co-opt from other authorities and to establish joint health overview and scrutiny committees with other first-tier authorities
- authority to place duties on health trusts to consult health overview and scrutiny committees on substantial developments and variations to health services. In relation to local authority overview and scrutiny of NHS services the 2012 Act:
  - requires officers of all NHS bodies to attend local authority scrutiny committees when requested
  - requires NHS bodies to provide health scrutiny committees with information about the planning, commissioning, provision and operation of health services
  - requires NHS bodies to respond to reports and recommendations of health scrutiny committees
  - empowers health scrutiny committees to refer proposals for substantial developments or variations in health services to the Secretary of State.

Health and wellbeing boards

To reflect local authorities' strengthened role, the *Health and Social Care Act 2012* required every upper tier local authority to establish a health and wellbeing board (HWB) to provide a forum for public accountability and join up commissioning across the NHS, social care, public health and other services relating to health and wellbeing. HWBs assumed their powers and duties as statutory committees of (and therefore financed by) local authorities in April 2013.

Core membership of each HWB must include members of CCGs, the Director of Adult Social Services, the Director of Children's Services, the Director of Public health, local HealthWatch (see later on in this chapter) and at least one democratically elected councillor. HWBs can also require the attendance of NHS England when relevant. It must be noted that there is a wide variation in HWB memberships, voting structures and remit over and above the statutory requirements.

At a practical level, HWBs should:

- make themselves aware of how quality is being monitored locally, and of the priority issues and concerns in their locality
- where necessary, ensure action is taken and reported in relation to these priority issues
- ensure a joined up approach and good information-sharing between agencies
- be aware of the work of the quality surveillance group for their area – these groups coordinate quality assurance activity for the NHS
- identify the priorities for fuller scrutiny (for example, by HealthWatch and/or the overview and scrutiny committee).

HWBs lead the development of the JSNA and the high level JHWS (see below). They also have a duty to involve service users and the public and work with CCGs to ensure that commissioning plans meet local needs. This approach is designed to provide strategic coordination to the commissioning of NHS services, social care and health improvement.

Joint strategic needs assessments (JSNAs)

JSNAs are designed to 'identify the current and future health and wellbeing needs of a local population'[1] and have been in place since their introduction in section 116 of the *Local Government and Public Involvement in Health Act 2007*. The *Health and Social Care Act 2012* retains JSNAs but places the responsibility for producing them jointly on local authorities and CCGs. The Act also requires local authorities and CCGs to undertake the JSNA through the HWB so in practice, it is the HWB that pulls the strategy together with local authorities and CCGs ultimately responsible for them and required to 'have regard to them' when exercising their functions.

Joint health and wellbeing strategies (JHWSs)

In addition, the 2012 Act requires local authorities and CCGs to produce (again via the HWB) a joint health and wellbeing strategy that sets out plans to address the needs of the local population and reduce inequalities identified in the JSNA. NHS and local authority commissioners must then 'have regard to' the JHWS when exercising their functions.

Health improvement

As mentioned above, the 2012 Act introduced a statutory duty on affected local authorities (upper tier and unitary) to improve the health of the local population. The Act also gives the Secretary of State the power to require local authorities to carry out certain health protection functions and to prescribe how they carry out their health improvement activities.

There are also statutory arrangements for local authority leadership in this area, complemented by the creation of Public Health England (PHE) – with local directors of public health being appointed jointly by local authorities and PHE. These local directors have a ring-fenced health improvement grant to deliver national and local priorities (the grant is allocated by PHE). There is direct accountability to both the local authority, and (through PHE) to the Secretary of State. As they are employed by the local authority, local directors of public health advise councillors and are part of the senior management team of the local authority.

At a practical level, local authorities are responsible for commissioning a range of health improvement services. A limited number of these services are mandated by Government via regulations under section 6c of the *NHS Act 2006*. Other services can be commissioned on a discretionary basis guided by the *Public Health Outcomes Framework*, the JSNA and the JHWS.

Mandatory Services – Examples

- to deliver the NHS Health Check
- to provide population based public health advice to NHS commissioners
- to provide comprehensive sexual health services (excluding abortion, contraceptive services and HIV treatment)

---

[1] *Guidance on Joint Strategic Needs Assessment*, Departments of Health and Communities and Local Government, 2007.

Discretionary Services – Examples

- lifestyle interventions (for example, to promote physical activity, improve diet and prevent obesity)
- drug and alcohol misuse services
- stop smoking services
- local initiatives to reduce seasonal mortality

As well as commissioning services themselves, local authorities can also work with CCGs and NHS England to make sure services are integrated.

As with other local services, local authorities are accountable primarily to their electorates for work on improving health.

As far as the NHS money is concerned, there are additional accountability mechanisms – specifically:

- PHE publishes data about national and local performance against the *Public Health Outcomes Framework* so local people can see how their local authority is doing
- each local authority chief finance officer must provide a 'statement of grant' showing how the allocation has been spent
- each Director of Public Health must produce (and each local authority publish) an annual report.

Although the Department of Health can incentivise progress in health improvement via the use of a 'health premium', it does not performance manage local authorities or set targets for them.

HealthWatch England and local HealthWatch

HealthWatch England is the national body that champions people who use health and social care and has a key focus on the design of integrated care. HealthWatch England is established as a committee of the Care Quality Commission (CQC). The Chair of HealthWatch England is appointed by the Secretary of State and has a seat on the CQC's board.

In addition to HealthWatch England, each of the 152 local authority areas has a local HealthWatch; these organisations are separately commissioned by local authorities but 'feed into' the national network. Local HealthWatch powers are designed to be 'more like a 'citizen's advice bureau' for health and social care'. HealthWatch provides leadership and support to enable local HealthWatch to deliver their statutory activities and be a powerful advocate for services that work for people.

Each local HealthWatch is concerned with local engagement – collecting and channelling the views of patients, users and the public to decision-makers. They have powers to scrutinise local services (including local authority, NHS and independent sector services) including visiting and observing their operations. Each local HealthWatch also has responsibilities for supporting people in communities by giving them information or signposting the support they need. Local HealthWatch is required by law to be represented on HWBs.

Local authorities, health services and regulators have a duty in law to respond to issues raised by HealthWatch. Local HealthWatch should:

- keep in touch with local people's experience of services
- channel information from networks, voluntary and community groups, identifying any key themes or trends

- alert commissioners and planning and scrutiny bodies (including the HWB and overview and scrutiny committee) to any significant concerns
- carry out bespoke research into people's experience in priority areas, having consulted about what these priorities are
- report to local providers, commissioners and planning and scrutiny bodies on their findings.

Although CCGs are not accountable formally to their local HealthWatch, they have to think about how best to interact with this service.

Local HealthWatch organisations are financed via contracts with the relevant local authorities and are accountable to them for their ability to operate effectively and provide value for money.

Local strategic partnerships

Section 82 of the *NHS Act 2006* requires NHS bodies and local authorities to co-operate with each other 'to secure and advance the health and welfare of the people of England and Wales'. In England local strategic partnerships (LSPs) have been used to help achieve this aim. Where they are in place, LSPs operate at a strategic level and are led by local authorities. LSPs are non-statutory, non-executive, multi-agency bodies that are designed to bring together at local level different parts of the public sector (including the NHS) as well as the private and voluntary sectors so that initiatives and services can support each other and work together.

Section 75 flexibilities

There are a number of arrangements for joint working between NHS organisations and local authorities included within section 75 of the *NHS Act 2006*. These so-called 'section 75 flexibilities' include:

- pooled budgets
- aligned budgets
- lead commissioning
- Integrated provision.

The 2012 Act allows all these section 75 flexibilities to continue but places a duty on CCGs and local authorities (through the HWB) to consider how to make best use of the flexibilities when drawing up the JSNA and JHWS. To reinforce this duty NHS England has a duty to promote the use of these flexibilities by CCGs.

Section 75 Flexibilities

Pooled budgets

The pooling of budgets involves partner organisations contributing funds to a single pot, to be spent on agreed projects for designated services. They exist where a local authority and an NHS body combine resources and jointly commission or manage an integrated service. The idea is that, once a pooled budget is introduced the public will experience a seamless service with a single point of access for their health and social care needs. There are some areas that are particularly well suited to pooled budgets – for example, services for people with a learning disability.

Where a pooled budget exists, regulations for England and Wales require that the partners have written agreements setting out:

- the functions covered
- the aims agreed
- the funds that each partner will contribute
- which partner will act as the 'host' (i.e. which organisation will manage the budget and take responsibility for the accounts and auditing).

Since 2010/11 the standard national NHS contract for mental health services has allowed for pooled budget services to be incorporated into that contract.

Aligned budgets

Aligned budgets can be either an informal or formal (using section 75 flexibilities) arrangement whereby partners align resources to meet agreed aims but have separate accountability for the respective funding streams. The management arrangements can be separate, joint or led by one partner but with joint performance monitoring arrangements against the objectives. An aligned budget can also be used as an interim stage to operating a pooled budget.

Lead commissioning

Under a lead commissioning arrangement, partners agree to delegate commissioning of a service to one lead organisation. As with pooled budgets, lead commissioning was made possible by section 31 of the *1999 Act* (now section 75 of the *NHS Act 2006*).

Integrated provision

Integrated provision involves partners joining together their staff, resources and management structures so that the service is fully combined (or integrated) from managerial level to the front line. One partner acts as the host for the service to be provided. Again this way of working was made possible by section 31 of the *1999 Act* (now section 75 of the *NHS Act 2006*).

Better Care Fund (BCF)

Launched through the Spending Round in June 2013 and highlighted as a key element of public service reform, the better care fund (the BCF) has a primary aim to '…deliver better services to older and disabled people, keeping them out of hospital and avoiding long hospital stays[2]'. A key theme of the Government's announcement was the need to drive better cooperation and collaboration between local public services notably CCGs and local authorities. BCF plans are jointly developed with local government partners and approved by HWBs. The BCF is intended to:

- deliver better services to older and disabled people who have multiple and complex needs
- keep people out of hospital
- avoid people staying in hospital for long periods.

Once CCGs and local authorities have fulfilled the requirements of the BCF, they will be able to move on to integrate in more significant ways. The current Government's vision is that by 2020, health and social care will be integrated across the country.

---

[2] *Spending round 2013*, HM Treasury, June 2013.

Government grants

Government grants are available to the NHS for community-based projects run in conjunction with local authorities. Typically these grants are linked to regeneration and renewal programmes in deprived communities where a partnership board with representation from many elements of the local community (including NHS bodies) has successfully bid for and then managed the distribution of the grant. In terms of the financial framework for these projects, the structure is fairly straightforward – the grant is paid directly to the participating NHS body to cover the costs incurred.

Grants from the NHS to local authorities

NHS bodies have for many years been able to make grants to local authorities for the provision of health services (under sections 256/257 of the *NHS Act 2006* as amended). This is broadly permissive and allows the transfer of revenue or capital resources for most health related functions (excluding emergency ambulance services, surgery and other similar invasive treatments) and for most social services and housing functions. CCGs and/or NHS England are able to make payments to local authorities (or other bodies) towards expenditure on community services. For example, a local authority operating a unit for people with learning difficulties may receive a grant from the NHS body to cover the provision of healthcare to the clients in the unit. Such grants must pay only for medical care and must not contribute towards the provision of social care. They must not involve the transfer of health functions to a local authority.

Grants from Local Authorities to the NHS

Section 76 of the *NHS Act 2006* (as amended) is a parallel provision to section 256 and allows the local authority to make payments to NHS bodies for the performance of prescribed functions. Local authorities are able to make payments to NHS England or CCGs. Again, this includes most hospital and community health services but not surgery, emergency ambulance services etc.

Delayed Transfers of Care

The delay of patients' discharge from hospital remains a problem for the NHS and the Government is keen to see local public sector and other organisations (including housing organisations, primary care and the independent and voluntary sectors) working together to minimise its impact.

To encourage local authorities to do all they can to make swift discharges possible, the *Care and Support (Discharge of Hospital Patients) Regulations 2014* require the relevant local authority to reimburse the NHS provider concerned if a patient is delayed from being discharged solely because a community care package is not in place. As part of this arrangement, trusts must notify social services departments of patients who may require community care following admission.

In addition, if a patient is deemed to be medically ready for discharge and delayed discharge payments have been imposed on local authorities under the 2014 Regulations, commissioners are not liable for any further long stay payments under the national tariff (see chapter 18 for more on the tariff).

References and Further Reading

General information about local authorities – the Local Government Association:
www.local.gov.uk/

Public Health Outcomes Framework, Department of Health, 2015:
www.gov.uk/government/publications/public-health-outcomes-framework-update

Public Health England: www.gov.uk/government/organisations/public-health-england

Considerations for determining local health and care economies and developing sustainability and transformation plans, Monitor, 2015: https://www.gov.uk/government/publications/considerations-for-determining-local-health-and-care-economies

Sustainability and transformation plan footprints, 2016:
https://www.england.nhs.uk/wp-content/uploads/2016/02/stp-footprints-march-2016.pdf

The Role of Local Authorities in Health Issues, Communities and Local Government Committee Report, March 2013:
www.publications.parliament.uk/pa/cm201213/cmselect/cmcomloc/694/69402.htm

The New Public Health Role of Local Authorities, Department of Health, 2012:
https://www.gov.uk/government/uploads/system/uploads/attachment_data/file/127045/Public-health-role-of-local-authorities-factsheet.pdf.pdf

Statutory guidance on JSNAs and JHWSs, Department of Health, 2013:
http://healthandcare.dh.gov.uk/jsnas-jhwss-guidance-published/

For more on local HealthWatch: http://healthandcare.dh.gov.uk/what-is-healthwatch/

Public health grants to local authorities, Department of Health, 2014: www.gov.uk/government/publications/ring-fenced-public-health-grants-to-local-authorities-2013-14-and-2014-15

Better Care Fund: https://www.england.nhs.uk/ourwork/part-rel/transformation-fund/bcf-plan/

The Care and Support (Discharge of Hospital Patients) Regulations 2014:
http://www.legislation.gov.uk/uksi/2014/2823/made

Chapter 9
NHS Finance – Who Does What: The Role of the Regulators

> This chapter looks at how the key sector wide regulators (NHS Improvement, the Care Quality Commission (CQC) and the National Institute for Health and Care Excellence (NICE)) fit into the NHS, how they are structured, what they do and how they are financed. Please note that the focus is on the place of the regulators in the system, not on their approach to regulation – that is covered in chapter 12.
>
> To see where NHS Improvement and the CQC fit into the NHS structure, look back at the diagram on page 11. NICE is not shown explicitly as it does not have a direct regulatory or funding relationship with healthcare providers – instead it falls within the Department of Health as one of its arm's length bodies (ALBs).

NHS Improvement

What it is – constitution, structure and accountabilities

NHS Improvement (NHSI) came into being on 1 April 2016 and brings together two separate arm's length bodies – Monitor and the NHS Trust Development Authority (NHS TDA) – along with teams from four other patient safety and improvement functions[1] from across the NHS under a single leadership and operating model.

In constitutional terms, NHSI is not a separate legal entity – rather it is an 'integrated management structure' that has been set up to allow Monitor and the NHS TDA to work together closely.

NHSI is led by a 14 strong board that is made up of nine non-executive directors and five executives[2]. The process for making appointments to NHSI's board is led by a nominations committee with recommendations submitted to ministers. The board has also established a number of board committees and is advised by two panels: one made up of current NHS chief executives, the other of current NHS Chairpersons.

NHSI also has an executive team that consists of the executive board members, 'direct reports' to the chief executive and others as required.

NHSI is accountable to the Department of Health. NHSI is also reviewed by the Health Select Committee and provides evidence as required to the Public Accounts Committee.

Monitor and the NHS TDA remain separate statutory bodies and have their own specific accountabilities as set out in later in this chapter. In terms of public reporting, they must each publish their own annual report and accounts every year. NHSI will produce an aggregation of these accounts as its main reporting mechanism.

What NHS Improvement does – roles and responsibilities

NHSI is the sector regulator for health and social care.

Its role is to support all NHS healthcare providers (foundation and non-foundation NHS trusts) to deliver 'better healthcare, transformed care delivery and sustainable finances'. It aims to do this by supporting providers and local health systems to improve.

NHSI also holds the boards of individual NHS providers to account and intervenes when necessary.

---

[1] The Patient Safety Domain and Advancing Change Team from NHS England and the National Reporting and Learning System and Intensive Support teams from NHS Interim Management and Support.
[2] NHS Improvement's website: https://improvement.nhs.uk/about-us/leadership/

During 2016/17, NHSI is developing a 'single oversight framework' that will apply to all NHS trusts. This framework will 'identify where providers may benefit from, or require, improvement support' across five themes – quality of care; finance and use of resources (including a series of 'financial rating metrics' that will focus on financial sustainability, efficiency and controls); operational performance; strategic change and leadership and improvement capability.
The new approach will aim to identify problems (and risks of problems) as they emerge and pinpoint the underlying causes so that support can be tailored to meet each provider's specific needs. Providers will be segmented according to the scale of issues they face.

The proposed new framework combines and builds on the approaches used by Monitor and the NHS TDA, with changes 'intended to be as much as possible incremental in nature'. Details are set out in a consultation document issued at the end of June 2016[3].

Until the new framework is introduced, the existing regulatory approaches used by Monitor (the risk assessment framework) and the NHS TDA (the accountability framework) remain in place and are outlined briefly below.

How NHS Improvement is financed

NHSI is funded via the Department of Health's allocation.

Monitor

What it is – constitution, structure and accountabilities

Monitor came into existence in 2004 as an executive non-departmental public body with a remit to authorise and regulate NHS foundation trusts (FTs). Although it is now operating as part of NHSI, Monitor remains an independent statutory body and is formally one of the Department of Health's 'arms' length bodies' (ALBs). This means that it is independent of central government and directly accountable to Parliament. It is also accountable to the Secretary of State for Health and (via its Accountable Officer) to the Department's Accounting Officer (the permanent secretary).

As it is a separate statutory body (or 'legal entity'), Monitor continues to have its own board that consists of a Chairperson, non-executive directors and executive directors. Since 1 April 2016, this board has identical membership to that of the NHS TDA and they meet as one board[4].

Like other ALBs, Monitor has a 'framework agreement' with the Department of Health which sets out its relationship and lines of accountability. See chapter 3 for more about ALBs.

What Monitor does – roles and responsibilities

Pre 2012 Act

Monitor was established to authorise FTs and then regulate and monitor their performance against their terms of authorisation. Although Monitor's role has changed significantly as a result of the *Health and Social Care Act 2012*, it continues to play the role of independent regulator of FTs, assessing NHS trusts for FT status, and ensuring that FTs are 'well-led so that they can provide quality care on a sustainable basis'[5].

The FT assessment process

Before an NHS trust can apply to Monitor to be assessed, it must work with the NHS TDA to prepare its application. It is the NHS TDA's responsibility (on behalf of the Secretary of State) to make sure that the trust is ready and able to apply to become an FT. When the NHS TDA is satisfied that the trust is ready, its application is submitted to Monitor for its assessment.

---

[3] *The Single Oversight Framework*, NHS Improvement, June 2016.
[4] Regulations passed in October 2015 enabled joint non-executive positions so that they are appointed to both boards: http://www.legislation.gov.uk/uksi/2015/1559/regulation/2/made
[5] Monitor website.

Monitor's assessment process takes approximately 4 months and is based on three assessment criteria:

- is the trust well led so it can deliver quality services to patients on a sustainable basis?
- does the trust have governance arrangements that are effective in practice?
- is the trust legally constituted?

The process involves due diligence, a 'board-to-board meeting' which allows the applicant board to 'demonstrate that it is aware of the risks facing the trust and provide details on how these risks can or have been managed and mitigated. It also gives Monitor the opportunity to question the trust's non-executive directors to find out if they have the skills they need to challenge the executive team effectively.'[6]

Applicants meeting the required standards are granted a licence that establishes them as an FT in the legal form of a public benefit entity. The licence also sets out the conditions under which the FT (and other licenced healthcare providers) must operate.

More information about the application process is available on the gov.uk website.

Monitor's approach to regulation (which remains in place until NHSI introduces its single oversight framework) is based on its risk assessment framework – this is outlined in chapter 12.

Post 2012 Act role

As mentioned above, Monitor's responsibilities expanded as a result of the 2012 Act when it became the 'sector regulator for health'. Its main duty is to 'protect and promote the interests of NHS patients'. In particular, Monitor is required to support patient interests by 'promoting the provision of healthcare services that are economic, efficient and effective, and maintains or improves their quality'.[7]

In practice, this means that Monitor is responsible for licensing all providers of NHS-funded care in England including independent providers. If licence conditions are breached, Monitor steps in to help and (if necessary) take more formal steps to rectify problems. In extreme circumstances, Monitor has the power to remove directors and governors as well as revoke a provider's licence to operate.

In carrying out its licensing role, Monitor co-operates with the CQC which continues to be responsible for registering providers against 'fundamental standards of safety and quality'.

In its role as sector regulator, Monitor's core functions are:

- ensuring the continuity of services
- regulating payments made by commissioners for NHS services
- safeguarding choice and preventing anti-competitive behaviour
- enabling integrated care.

---

[6] Guidance for NHS trusts: Apply for NHS Foundation Trust Status, Monitor, 2014:
https://www.gov.uk/guidance/nhs-trusts-apply-for-nhs-foundation-trust-status
[7] Monitor – About us: https://www.gov.uk/government/organisations/monitor/about

Monitor's Core Functions

Supporting the continuity of services

Monitor is required under the 2012 Act to ensure that if a healthcare provider fails, patients will still be able to access the care they need. This is the so-called 'continuity of service regime'. Although the primary responsibility for ensuring that services are available lies with commissioners (supported by NHS England), Monitor has a duty to 'prevent providers from taking actions that could undermine their continued ability to deliver services'. Monitor can also help providers who are having problems (for example, by requiring them to appoint turnaround experts to help avoid failure). In exceptional circumstances, Monitor can appoint a 'trust special administrator' to take control of the provider's business and work with commissioners to make sure that patients can still access services. Where a provider is in financial difficulty, Monitor has a duty to make available a source of finance to cover the costs of administration, via a risk pool arrangement – a fund that is built up via levies on providers and commissioners. However, there is an overarching principle in the 2012 Act that additional regulation will not apply unless 'commissioners can demonstrate that the loss of a particular service…would result in material damage to patients.'

Regulating payments for NHS-funded services

The 2012 Act requires Monitor and NHS England to assume joint responsibility for the way that providers of NHS services are reimbursed. Monitor's focus is on designing the pricing methodology (based on information it collects from providers as required within the licence conditions) and using it to set prices whereas NHS England specifies the services to be priced and the unit of healthcare concerned (i.e. developing the pricing structure) and agreeing these with Monitor. Once agreed by Monitor and NHS England, prices (where they apply) and the rules underpinning the way that the payment mechanism operates are published in the *National Tariff Document*.

Providers of NHS-funded services and clinical commissioning groups (CCGs) are consulted on the underlying methodology used to set the tariff and can raise objections. If a sufficient number of commissioners and/ or 'relevant providers' object, Monitor cannot publish the national tariff and must undertake a further statutory consultation or make a reference to the Competition and Markets Authority.

Safeguarding choice and preventing anti-competitive behaviour

Although CCGs and NHS England decide where competition is used, Monitor makes sure that it is fair and operates in the interests of patients. To do this, Monitor has powers such as those exercised by OFCOM and OFGEM to apply competition law to prevent anti-competitive behaviour. To enable it to carry out this role, Monitor has 'concurrent powers' with the Competition and Markets Authority to investigate provider practices that might restrict competition. Monitor can also set specific licence conditions if it can demonstrate that this will protect competition; conduct market reviews where competition is not functioning properly and refer markets to the Competition and Markets Authority for investigation.

Monitor also protects patients' ability to choose by tackling specific abuses and restrictions that act against patients' interests and ensuring that (amongst other things) there is a fair playing field for all providers. Monitor can also issue regulations to govern commissioners' procurement activities and 'parties with a legitimate interest' can complain to Monitor if they believe commissioners have broken these rules. Commissioners and providers can seek judicial review if they are dissatisfied with Monitor's decisions.

> **Enabling integrated care**
>
> Monitor has a general duty to consider how it can enable or facilitate better integration of services to help improve quality or provide better access for patients. This includes working with others to remove barriers and encouraging innovation and beneficial change by identifying better ways of working.

How Monitor is financed

Monitor is funded through government grant-in-aid from the Department of Health.

NHS Trust Development Authority (NHS TDA)

What it is – status and accountabilities

The NHS TDA was established by the 2012 Act as a time limited special health authority. Since April 2016, it has operated alongside Monitor as part of NHS Improvement. However, it remains a separate statutory body accountable to the Secretary of State for Health and subject to ministerial direction.

As it is a separate statutory body (or 'legal entity'), the NHS TDA continues to have its own board. However, from 1 April 2016, this board has identical membership to that of Monitor and they meet as one board[8].

What the NHS TDA does – roles and responsibilities

The NHS TDA is responsible for:

- monitoring the performance of (non-foundation) NHS trusts, and providing support to help them improve the quality and sustainability of their services
- providing support to NHS trusts to help them improve the quality and sustainability of services
- supporting the transition of NHS trusts to FT status
- assuring clinical quality, governance and risk in NHS trusts
- making appointments to NHS trusts of Chairs and non-executive members and trustees for NHS charities where the Secretary of State has a power to appoint
- designating of 'Accountable Officers'[9] for NHS trusts
- advising the Secretary of State as to whether or not an NHS trust should be placed into the failure regime
- assessing mergers and acquisitions of NHS trusts by other NHS or foundation trusts
- approving capital investments or significant commercial transactions by NHS trusts.

The NHS TDA's approach to regulation (which remains in place until NHSI introduces its single oversight framework) is based on its accountability framework – this is covered in chapter 12.

How the NHS TDA is financed

The NHS TDA is funded via the Department of Health's allocation.

---

[8] Regulations passed in October 2015 enabled joint non-executive positions so that they are appointed to both boards: http://www.legislation.gov.uk/uksi/2015/1559/regulation/2/made
[9] Every NHS organisation must have an 'Accountable Officer' – see chapter 13 for more details.

Care Quality Commission (CQC)

What it is – constitution, structure and accountabilities

The Care Quality Commission began operating on 1 April 2009 as the independent regulator of health and adult social care in England. It is an executive non-departmental public body and was established to regulate fundamental standards of quality and safety, which were first set out in the *Health and Social Care Act 2008*.

Although (like Monitor and the NHS TDA) it is formally an ALB of the Department of Health, the CQC is independent of central government and directly accountable to Parliament. However (as with all ALBs), the CQC has a 'framework agreement' with the Department of Health which sets out its relationship and lines of accountability. It also submits a business plan to the Department for approval each year indicating how its objectives will be achieved and forecasting its financial performance. See chapter 3 for more about ALBs.

The CQC has a board and an executive team – see its website for details.

What it does – roles and responsibilities

The CQC was given a range of legal powers and duties as part of the 2008 Act, these include:

CQC Powers and Duties (2008 Act)

- registering providers of healthcare and social care to ensure they are meeting the essential standards of quality and safety

- monitoring how providers comply with the standards by gathering information and inspecting them when the CQC thinks it is needed

- using enforcement powers, such as fines and public warnings and closing down services, if services drop below the essential standards and particularly if the CQC thinks that people's rights or safety are at risk

- acting to protect patients whose rights are restricted under the *Mental Health Act*

- promoting improvement in services by conducting regular reviews of how well those who arrange and provide services locally are performing

- carrying out special reviews of particular types of services and pathways of care, or investigations on areas where the CQC has concerns about quality and safety

- seeking the views of people who use services and involving them in the CQC's work

- telling people about the quality of their local care services to help providers and commissioners of services to learn from each other about what works best and where improvement is needed, and help to shape national policy.

As a result of the 2012 Act, the CQC now has additional responsibilities – these include:

> **CQC Responsibilities – 2012 Act**
>
> - HealthWatch England – a new national body established to enable the views of people who use NHS and social care services to influence national policy, advice and guidance. It is constituted as a statutory committee of the CQC and its Chairperson is a CQC non-executive director. Its role is to provide leadership, guidance and support to local HealthWatch organisations (see chapter 8) and advise the Secretary of State, NHS England, NHS Improvement and local authorities. HealthWatch England is funded as part of the Department of Health's grant in aid to the CQC and must make an annual report to Parliament
> - in the longer term the integration of certain functions of the Human Fertilisation and Embryology Authority and the Human Tissue Authority into the CQC.

The CQC has issued its strategy for the next five years from 2016 to 2021. As well as making improvements to its 'core operating model', the CQC will focus on four priorities:

- encouraging improvement and sustainability in care
- delivering an intelligence-driven approach to regulation
- promoting a single shared view of quality
- improving its efficiency and effectiveness.

How the CQC is financed

The CQC is funded through a combination of fee income (i.e. fees charged to health and adult social care providers to cover the costs of registration and compliance[10]) and government grant-in-aid from the Department of Health.

The National Institute for Health and Care Excellence (NICE)

What it is – constitution, structure and accountabilities

NICE was set up in 1999 as the National Institute for Clinical Excellence with the aim of reducing variation in the availability and quality of NHS treatments and care. In 2005, NICE merged with the Health Development Agency and began developing public health guidance – its name changed to the National Institute for Health and Clinical Excellence. In April 2013, NICE took on responsibility for developing guidance and quality standards in social care resulting in a further name change to that currently used.

In constitutional terms NICE is an executive non-departmental public body. This means that it is an ALB of the Department of Health with a framework agreement that sets out its relationship and lines of accountability. It also submits a business plan to the Department for approval each year indicating how its objectives will be achieved and forecasting its financial performance. See chapter 3 for more about ALBs.

NICE has a board comprising non-executive and executive directors and a senior management team.

---

[10] For more details about the fees CQC charges see: http://www.cqc.org.uk/organisations-we-regulate/registered-services/fees

What NICE does – roles and responsibilities

NICE's key role is 'to improve outcomes for people using the NHS and other public health and social care services' [11] This includes providing:

- evidence-based guidance and advice on 'effective, good value healthcare'
- quality standards and performance metrics for those commissioners and providers of health and social care services
- a range of information services for commissioners, practitioners and managers.

NICE also has a library of quality standards and metrics that are used in the *NHS Outcomes Framework*, the *Clinical Commissioning Group Outcomes Indicator Set* and to inform payment mechanisms and incentive schemes such as the Quality and Outcomes Framework (QOF).

These quality standards are 'concise sets of statements, with accompanying metrics designed to drive and measure priority quality improvements within a particular area of care'. Standards already exist for a wide range of conditions and interventions including mental health and respiratory medicine.

How NICE is financed

NICE is funded primarily by grant-in-aid from the Department of Health with small amounts of income from other government departments and NHS bodies.

References and Further Reading

NHS Improvement: https://improvement.nhs.uk/

The Single Oversight Framework, NHS Improvement, June 2016:
https://improvement.nhs.uk/uploads/documents/Single_Oversight_Framework_consultation_-_final_draft_28_06_update_CC.pdf

NHS Improvement (includes links to NHS TDA and Monitor):
https://improvement.nhs.uk/about-us/who-we-are/

Care Quality Commission: www.cqc.org.uk/

HealthWatch England: http://www.healthwatch.co.uk/

National Institute for Health and Care Excellence (NICE): https://www.nice.org.uk/

[11] NICE website.

Chapter 10
How the NHS is Financed

> Health spending has always been a topic of political and public interest and in the last decade spending on health increased at a significantly higher rate than many other government programmes[1]. Even now, in a time of austerity, health funding has been protected.
>
> This chapter focuses on how resources are allocated nationally for the NHS and how they are divided up amongst the different areas of health spending. It also gives an idea of the scale of UK spending on health compared with other countries.

UK Spending Levels

The Organisation for Economic Cooperation and Development (OECD) health data for 2015 shows that during 2013, the United Kingdom spent 8.5% of gross domestic product (GDP)[2] on health. This compared with an average across the 30 OECD countries of 8.9% although this figure is made up of national spending in excess of the average – for example, 10.9% in France and 16.4% in the USA[3]. The data also indicates that 83.0% of total spending on health in the UK came from general government expenditure – well above the average for OECD countries of 73%. Given the constraints on public spending following the economic downturn in 2008/09, spending on healthcare is now plateauing.

The Role of the Treasury

The responsibility for allocating and managing the finances of national government lies with the Chancellor of the Exchequer, who leads the Treasury. To promote better planning of public spending the Treasury undertakes periodic spending reviews to set 'departmental expenditure limits' (DELs) for each government department. DELs usually cover a period of three years.

These spending reviews are themselves reviewed twice a year – in the budget and the pre-budget report, where the Government sets out how it will finance its spending commitments and makes any necessary or technical adjustments to its spending plans. The most recent spending review was in November 2015 and set out the Government's departmental spending plans for the next four years – up until 2020/21.

Public expenditure falls into one of two categories:

- DEL spending, which is planned and controlled on a three year basis in spending reviews
- annually managed expenditure (AME), which is expenditure that cannot reasonably be subject to firm, multi-year limits in the same way as DEL. Examples of such spending are social security benefits which are subject to fluctuation depending on the level of unemployment.

Together, DEL plus AME sum to 'total managed expenditure' (TME).

A key issue for any government is the relative level of public spending compared to national wealth. Relative to GDP (which itself fluctuates from year to year), UK public spending since 1970 has varied from 51.2% in 1981 to 38% in 2000. The predicted position for 2015/16 is 40.2%[4].

---

[1] Between 2011/12 and 2014/15, the revenue departmental expenditure limit for health increased by 8.2% compared with a 5.3% increase for education and a 14% reduction for communities and local government.
[2] GDP is the total money value of all final goods and services produced in an economy during a year.
[3] *Health at a Glance 2015*, Organisation for Economic Cooperation and Development (OECD).
[4] *A Brief Guide to the Public Finances*, Office of Budget Responsibility, March 2016.

The Treasury allocates DELs for revenue and capital spending. Revenue spending is for day-to-day items such as salaries and running costs; capital spending is for buying larger items such as buildings and equipment, which have a usable life of over one year.

The Treasury's 2015 spending review resulted in the following pattern of allocations of revenue and capital DELs to government departments:

Total Department Programme and Administration Budgets – revenue (or 'resource') DEL excluding depreciation and capital

	2016/17	2017/18	2018/19	2019/20
	£bn	£bn	£bn	£bn
NHS (Health)	115.6	118.7	121.3	124.1
Education	54.4	55.5	56.4	57.1
Energy and Climate Change	0.9	1.0	1.0	0.9
Communities and Local Government*	9.6	7.4	6.1	5.4
Defence	27.8	28.5	29.2	30.0
Home Office	10.7	10.6	10.6	10.6
Foreign and Commonwealth Office	1.0	1.0	1.0	1.0
Justice	6.5	6.3	5.8	5.6
Business, Innovation and Skills	13.4	12.3	11.7	11.5
Transport	2.0	2.1	2.2	1.8
International Development	9.1	9.3	10.7	11.0
Work and Pensions	6.1	6.3	5.9	5.4
Scotland	26.1	26.3	26.3	26.5
Wales	13.0	13.1	13.2	13.3
Northern Ireland	9.8	9.9	9.9	9.9
Other Departments and Reserve	14.8	14.7	13.9	14.1
TOTAL DEL	**320.8**	**322.9**	**325.2**	**328.3**

Source: *Spending Review 2015*, HM Treasury.

*Excludes locally financed expenditure that constitutes the majority of local government funding.

Total Department Capital DEL

	2016/17	2017/18	2018/19	2019/20
	£bn	£bn	£bn	£bn
NHS (Health)	4.8	4.8	4.8	4.8
Education	5.2	4.6	4.4	4.4
Energy and Climate Change	2.4	2.5	2.4	2.3
Communities and Local Government	4.0	3.7	4.0	3.6
Defence	7.3	7.5	7.8	8.1
Home Office	0.5	0.5	0.4	0.4
Foreign and Commonwealth Office	0.1	0.1	0.1	0.1
Justice	0.7	0.7	0.7	0.4
Business, Innovation and Skills	3.1	2.2	1.7	1.7
Transport	6.3	7.6	8.9	11.4
International Development	2.7	3.2	2.8	3.1
Work and Pensions	0.3	0.4	0.3	0.2
Scotland	3.2	3.2	3.2	3.2
Wales	1.5	1.5	1.6	1.6
Northern Ireland	1.1	1.1	1.2	1.2
Other Departments and Reserves	2.8	3.4	3.2	3.3
TOTAL Capital DEL	**46.0**	**47.0**	**47.5**	**49.8**

Source: *Spending Review 2015*, HM Treasury.

For the NHS in England the position over the spending review period (including percentage growth rates) is summarised in the table that follows:

The NHS in England

	2016/17	2017/18	2018/19	2019/20
	£bn	£bn	£bn	£bn
DEL Settlement i.e. the sum of resource DEL (excluding depreciation) and capital DEL.				
NHS (Health) revenue	115.6	118.7	121.3	124.1
annual growth	3.6%	2.7%	2.2%	2.3%
NHS (Health) capital	4.8	4.8	4.8	4.8
annual growth	0%	0%	0%	0%
NHS (Health) TOTAL	**120.4**	**123.5**	**126.1**	**128.9**
annual growth	**3.6%**	**2.7%**	**2.2%**	**2.3%**
GDP deflator (to take account of inflation)	1.9%	2.0%	1.9%	2.0%
Real growth	1.7%	0.7%	0.3%	0.3%

Source: *Spending Review 2015*, HM Treasury.

Funding for health services in other UK nations is included in the separate Northern Ireland, Scottish and Welsh block grants. Any changes in planned spending in the NHS in England are matched by relative increases within these block grants. However, the individual administrations may spend less or more than these amounts on health services depending on their own priorities.

The Role of the Department of Health

The Department of Health decides how the funding it receives from the Treasury is allocated in England. Health and social services in Northern Ireland, Scotland and Wales are the responsibility of the devolved administrations (see chapters 20 to 22).

Most of the total NHS settlement (over 80%) is allocated to the NHS England which keeps around 20% for its own commissioning responsibilities and running costs and allocates the rest to clinical commissioning groups (CCGs).

The Department retains part of the allocation to meet:

- its own running costs
- the costs of various central health and miscellaneous services (CHMS) – for example, some centrally administered services and projects managed centrally for the benefit of the NHS (such as clinical negligence); a range of statutory and other arm's length bodies funded centrally (for example, the NHS Business Services Authority and Health Education England – see chapter 3 for details)
- the costs of public health spending – this is covered by a separate ring fenced budget (from the Department of Health's allocation) that is passed to and managed by local authorities and Public Health England (an executive agency within the Department – see chapter 3).

The Role of NHS England

NHS England is responsible for using the funding it receives from the Department to deliver the mandate that it agrees annually. In practice this means that NHS England's allocation has to fund the costs of:

- running NHS England, its regional teams, local professional networks, clinical senates and networks
- its direct commissioning activities – including the primary care services provided by GPs, dentists, community pharmacists and opticians; specialised services; offender and military healthcare
- CCG commissioning
- running CCGs (known as the 'running cost allowance')
- some services that are commissioned by local authorities.

For 2016/17 the total revenue budget allocated to NHS England to deliver the mandate is £106.5 billion[5] with £71.9 billion (just over 67% of the total) allocated to CCGs.

NHS England Revenue Budget Split 2016/17

Recipient	Area of Spend	How Much? (£ billion)
NHS England	See table that follows	34.6
CCGs	Local services commissioned for their populations	71.9
Total		**106.5**

NHS England's own allocation for 2016/17 of £34.6 billion is split as follows:

NHS England Allocation Split 2016/17

Area of Spend	How Much?(£ billion)
Commissioning of specialised healthcare, primary care, military and offender services	28.5
Sustainability fund	1.8
Transformation fund	0.3
Other direct commissioning	0.6
NHS England central budgets (e.g. clinical excellence awards)	2.9
Non-recurrent use of drawdown	0.5
Total	**34.6**

The allocations made to NHS England and by it to CCGs are resource and cash-limited and they have a statutory duty not to exceed these limits (see chapter 11 for more on financial duties).

Sustainability and transformation funds

In 2016/17, £2.1 billion has been ring fenced for sustainability and transformation. The sustainability element of the fund is money set aside to support the return of the NHS provider sector to financial balance and has two elements:

- a general element that will be distributed to relevant providers to support the sustainability of emergency services and the achievement of agreed control totals
- a targeted element that will be used to support relevant providers to make additional efficiency gains.

Funding to providers will be made available on a quarterly basis depending on financial and operational performance.

The transformation element of the fund has been set aside to support NHS organisations implement the new models of care (see chapter 7).

---

[5] NHS England also has a capital budget for 2016/17 of £305m. Source: NHS England's mandate 2016/17.

CCG Allocations

The allocations to CCGs are then used by them to commission the majority of NHS services for their patients including:

- planned hospital care
- rehabilitative care
- urgent and emergency services including out-of-hours services
- community health services
- maternity services
- mental health services
- learning disabilities services.

In practice, this means that CCGs agree contracts with 'any qualified providers' of acute, specialist and mental healthcare – see chapter 5 for more about CCGs.

CCGs received three-year firm allocations with a further two years of indicative allocations effective from 1 April 2016. See chapter 5 for more about how CCGs are financed.

Once a CCG has been notified of its allocation for the forthcoming period, it plans how to use the funding across the full range of services that it commissions with the overall aim of improving the health and wellbeing of its population. A CCG commissions services from a range of providers including NHS trusts and foundation trusts, the private and voluntary sectors (see chapter 16 for more on commissioning).

NHS and Foundation Trusts

Funding secondary care

The majority of community, acute, specialist and mental healthcare in England is provided by NHS trusts or NHS foundation trusts. These trusts meet the costs of providing healthcare services (staff salaries are normally the largest element) and receive income from CCGs (and for some services, from NHS England) via contracts that specify the quantity, quality and price of services to be provided. Each CCG (or NHS England) is responsible for meeting the cost of services provided to its population in line with the contract's terms. CCGs, NHS England and providers are responsible for ensuring that patient treatments are clinically appropriate and provided in a cost effective way.

Additional sources of funding

Trusts also receive some income from other sources such as private patient income, hosting services, car park receipts, leasing of buildings and research and development. For many teaching hospitals, the latter can be significant.

NHS funded research is overseen by the National Institute for Health Research (NIHR). The NIHR is funded by the Department to improve the health and wealth of the nation through research and is headed by the chief medical officer. NIHR funding streams include the following:

- local clinical research networks (LCRN). Each of the 15 LCRNs delivers research across 30 clinical specialties
- collaborations for leadership in applied research and care (CLARHCs). CLARHCs undertake high quality applied health research focused on the needs of patients and support the translation of research evidence into practice in the NHS. They are collaborative partnerships between a university and its surrounding NHS organisations, focused on improving patient outcomes through the conduct and application of applied health research

- clinical research facilities (CRFs) for experimental medicine. CRFs are purpose-built, cutting edge facilities with specialist clinical, research and support staff in locations where universities and NHS organisations can work together on dedicated programmes of patient-orientated experimental medicine research
- biomedical research units (BRUs). BRUs undertake clinical research in priority areas of high disease burden and clinical need
- biomedical research centres (BRCs). BRCs drive progress on innovation and research in biomedicine into NHS practice and receive substantial funding to translate biomedical research into clinical research that benefits patients. BRCs are early adopters of new insights in technologies, techniques and treatments for improving health
- research capability funding is allocated to research-active NHS organisations in proportion to the total amount of other NIHR income they receive and the number of NIHR senior investigators associated with the organisation.

In addition, some trusts get substantial sums from the monies earmarked in the centrally held budgets referred to earlier in this chapter, in particular to cover the education and training of clinical staff. These funding flows are governed by Health Education England (HEE) via a system of education tariffs.

Many trusts also have access to funds donated on a charitable basis – for example, by members of the public. However these can be used only for the purpose for which they were given – for more about charitable funds see chapter 19.

Primary Care Services

The majority of primary care services are provided by independent contractors such as general medical practitioners (GPs), general dental practitioners (GDPs), pharmacists and ophthalmic practitioners. Whilst they are an integral part of the NHS, these contractors operate as small businesses that contract with the NHS to provide primary care services. Contracts are designed to reward the quality of treatment.

NHS England pays primary care service providers according to nationally negotiated contracts – although extensions to the basic contract are negotiated locally. For example, GP practices receive a global sum to cover the provision of core services to their registered practice list and additional 'quality' payments for achieving goals set out in the quality and outcomes framework (QOF).

The interface between primary and secondary care is not always clear and GPs with specialist interests are increasingly playing a significant part in delivering patient care outside of the traditional hospital routes.

See chapter 6 for more on primary care services.

What is the Money Spent on?

The Department of Health publishes consolidated accounts for the whole of the NHS in England each year.

According to the 2014/15 accounts, just over 40% of operating expenditure relates to staff costs. The vast majority of these are employed by NHS provider bodies.

An analysis of NHS England's annual report and accounts 2014/15, supplemented by information from the provider summarisation schedules for that year reveals that approximately 62% of commissioners' expenditure is on secondary care, while 22% is spent on primary care.

In terms of activity, during 2014/15, there were just over 13m referrals from GPs to all secondary care specialties (both NHS and non-NHS providers) and, of these, 11m referrals were seen.

In that same period, there were:

- 8m elective general and acute admissions of which 6.5m were day case admissions
- 5.7m non-elective admissions
- 17.4m first outpatient attendances.

Key Learning Points

- The UK spends 8.5% of GDP on health – just below the OECD average
- The Treasury decides how much money each government department receives based on spending reviews
- Money is allocated for both day-to-day (revenue) and capital spending
- The Department of Health decides how the budget is used with over 80% going to NHS England
- The Department keeps some money for central services and arms' length bodies such as Public Health England and Health Education England
- NHS England allocates the bulk of the money it receives to CCGs but keeps some to fund its own direct commissioning functions and running costs
- CCGs receive allocations for 5 years (3 years firm and 2 years of indicative figures for planning purposes)
- NHS and foundation trusts receive the bulk of their income via contracts with CCGs and NHS England; other sources include income from research and development
- Primary care services are provided predominantly by independent contractors who receive income via contracts.

References and Further Reading

Health Data 2015, Organisation for Economic Cooperation and Development (OECD):
http://www.oecd.org/els/health-systems/health-data.htm

A Brief Guide to the Public Finances, Office of Budget Responsibility, 2016:
http://budgetresponsibility.org.uk/guide/brief-guide-public-finances-2/

Spending Review and Autumn Statement 2015, HM Treasury:
https://www.gov.uk/government/topical-events/autumn-statement-and-spending-review-2015

Budget 2016, HM Treasury:
https://www.gov.uk/government/publications/budget-2016-documents

The NHS Mandate 2016/17:
https://www.gov.uk/government/publications/nhs-mandate-2016-to-2017

Financial Allocations 2016/17 – 2020/21, NHS England, 2016:
https://www.england.nhs.uk/wp-content/uploads/2016/01/allocations-201617-202021.pdf

NHS National Institute for Health Research: http://www.nihr.ac.uk/

Health Education England: http://hee.nhs.uk/

Monthly Hospital Admission statistics: www.england.nhs.uk/statistics/statistical-work-areas/hospital-activity/monthly-hospital-activity/

Chapter 11
How NHS Bodies Demonstrate Financial Accountability

> This chapter looks at the key financial and performance reporting mechanisms that NHS bodies use to demonstrate accountability in financial terms. Its primary focus is on external reporting requirements but there is also a section on reports to budget holders and governing bodies.

External Reporting

Statutory requirements

All NHS bodies have a statutory duty to produce an annual report and accounts[1] with the form and content directed by the Secretary of State for Health (for NHS England and non-foundation NHS trusts); NHS England (for clinical commissioning groups (CCGs)) and the sector regulator, NHS Improvement[2] (for foundation trusts (FTs)).

The production of the annual report and accounts is the principal means by which NHS bodies discharge their accountability to taxpayers and users of services for their stewardship of public money.

Annual report

The annual report is primarily a narrative document similar to the directors' report and the remuneration report described in the *Companies Act*, but with additional information reflecting the NHS body's position in the community. The report gives an account of the body's activities and performance over the last financial year.

Although the overall layout of the annual report is at each NHS body's discretion, there are mandatory items that must be included – these are Companies Act and HM Treasury requirements and NHS specific disclosures. The Department of Health, NHS England and NHS Improvement provide specific guidance to NHS bodies in relation to these requirements.

There are some disclosures which are required by statute. For example, CCGs' annual reports must show how the CCG has contributed to the relevant health and wellbeing strategy, and how it has:

- improved the quality of services
- reduced health inequalities
- involved and consulted with the public.

The annual report must be fair, balanced and understandable. Whilst bearing these requirements in mind, some NHS bodies also use the annual report as an opportunity to set out their achievements in the year and highlight the challenges ahead.

The annual report and accounts is a single document which must be published once it has been approved by the governing body/board and signed by the external auditor.

All NHS bodies must publish their annual report and accounts and then present it at a public meeting. FTs must lay their annual report and accounts before Parliament prior to publication or presentation at a public meeting. It is considered best practice for the public meeting to be

---

[1] For CCGs this duty is set out in the *Health and Social Care Act 2012*, part 1, section 26, sub section 14Z15 and schedule 2, paragraph 17 (2). For NHS trusts, the relevant legislation is section 232 and paragraph 3(1) of schedule 15 of the *NHS Act 2006* as amended by part 4, section 154 of the 2012 Act; for NHS foundation trusts (FTs) the relevant legislation is section 30 and paragraph 25(1) of schedule 7 of the *NHS Act 2006* as amended by part 4, section 154 of the 2012 Act.

[2] This chapter refers to NHS Improvement (NHSI) in relation to FTs' reporting requirements. For 2015/16, these were issued by Monitor but for 2016/17 onwards are issued by NHS Improvement although Monitor remains the statutory body responsible.

held before 30 September following the end of the relevant financial year.

Annual accounts

The format of the annual accounts is specified in each accounts direction and is slightly different depending upon the type of NHS body concerned. However, the main elements are shown below:

The Contents of the Annual Accounts

The four primary statements:

- statement of comprehensive income or statement of comprehensive net expenditure
- statement of financial position
- statement of changes in taxpayers' equity
- statement of cash flows.

Notes to the accounts

Statements and certificates:

- directors' statement of responsibilities
- the Accounting (or Accountable) Officer's statement of responsibilities
- the governance statement[3] (see below)
- the auditors' report.

Accounting framework

In preparing their accounts, NHS bodies must follow international financial reporting standards (IFRS) as issued by the International Accounting Standards Board (IASB). These standards are intended to provide a framework for good practice, the common disclosure of information and a benchmark against which an NHS body's audited accounts are judged.

Although NHS bodies must adhere to IFRSs, the Government has the final say on how these standards are applied to the public sector (including NHS bodies) with details set out in the Treasury's *Financial Reporting Manual*. This is because IFRSs are written with profit making organisations in mind and therefore some interpretation is required to allow them to be applied consistently to public sector bodies where profit making is not as relevant.

For 2016/17 onwards, the Department of Health produces a *Group Accounting Manual* that is consistent with the requirements of the *Financial Reporting Manual*. This manual sets out the particular reporting requirements for NHS bodies. From 2016/17 the parts of this manual which relate to the preparation of the annual accounts will be applicable to all NHS bodies.

The parts of the *Group Accounting Manual* which relate to the annual report will apply to CCGs, non-foundation NHS trusts and the Department's arm's length bodies. NHS Improvement will produce an *Annual Reporting Manual* which will provide guidance on the annual report to FTs.

These manuals are updated each year and include a summary of the relevant accounting standards. However, if an NHS body needs a more detailed understanding of a particular aspect it should refer to the relevant accounting standard in full.

---

[3] This statement is also known as the annual governance statement.

Governance statement

NHS bodies produce a governance statement[4] that forms part of the annual report and accounts. This statement focuses on the stewardship of the body and draws together 'position statements and evidence on both corporate and quality governance, risk management and control, to provide a more coherent and consistent reporting mechanism.[5]' Although there is no prescribed format the statement must cover a number of areas including:

- scope of the NHS body's Accounting (or Accountable) Officer's responsibilities
- information about the NHS body's governance framework (including its committee structure)
- a description of how risk is assessed and managed
- information about how the risk and control framework works
- a review of the effectiveness of risk management and internal control
- any significant control issues and how they are being addressed.

Each year, the relevant regulatory body issues guidance for NHS bodies to use when preparing their governance statement. There is also a useful explanation of what governance statements are designed to achieve in Annex 3.1 of the Treasury's publication *Managing Public Money*.

Quality accounts and quality reports

Since April 2010, all providers of acute care (including all NHS provider bodies as well as commercial providers of NHS services) have been required to produce an annual quality account in line with the statutory requirement set out in the *Health Act 2009* and the associated regulations. The aim is to 'enhance accountability to the public and engage the leaders of an NHS body in their quality improvement agenda' by reporting the continuous improvement in the quality of the services provided.

The required contents of the quality account are set out in the statutory instruments supporting the 2009 Act[6] and guidance issued by the Department[7].

Quality accounts must be shared for comment with the local NHS England team, 'dominant' CCG and local health and wellbeing board. The final agreed quality account must be sent to the Secretary of State and made publically available via the NHS Choices website by 30 June following the financial year end.

Alongside this statutory requirement, FTs are required to produce a quality report. This report is the quality account with additional mandated disclosures determined by NHS Improvement. The quality report must be included in the FT's annual report and accounts. NHS Improvement issues guidance on the contents of the quality report annually.

Parts of the quality accounts are subjected to review by auditors as set out in guidance issued by NHS Improvement (for FTs) and the Department (for non-foundation NHS trusts).

---

[4] Also known as an annual governance statement.
[5] 2015/16 annual governance statement guidance, Department of Health, 2015.
[6] *National Health Service (Quality Accounts) Regulations 2010* (SI 2010/279), *National Health Service (Quality Accounts) Amendment Regulations 2011* (SI 2011/269), *National Health Service (Quality Accounts) Amendment Regulations 2012* (SI 2012/3081).
[7] *Quality Accounts Reporting Arrangements*, Department of Health, 2016.

> **What Quality Accounts Include**
>
> An overall statement by the chief executive on the quality of health services provided or sub-contracted during the year
>
> Three to five priorities for improvement and progress on previous priorities
>
> Statements of assurance from the board as required by the regulations
>
> A review of performance against a set of core indicators and statements in relation to the quality of the data reported
>
> What others say about the provider – these include commissioners, local Healthwatch organisations and overview and scrutiny committees
>
> Any other information that the provider body might want to include (for FTs, this section includes other disclosures mandated by NHS Improvement).

Audit

As mentioned above, the NHS body's annual report and accounts are subject to scrutiny from the external auditor and must be signed off by them prior to its publication. To be able to carry out their audit, auditors must be given a copy of the annual report and accounts and working papers at the start of the audit so that they have sufficient time to carry out the required work before the completion of their work.

The auditors follow *International Standards on Auditing for the UK and Ireland (ISAs (UK&I))* when undertaking their work on the annual report and accounts. They are also required to follow the *Code of Audit Practice* published by the National Audit Office which sets out the particular requirements for an audit of an NHS body.

The *Code of Audit Practice* along with the ISAs (UK&I) set out the various elements that make up the auditor's report on the annual report and accounts:

- an audit opinion on the annual accounts which says whether the financial statements give a 'true and fair' view and whether the financial statements have been properly prepared
- a statement that the auditors have read the annual report to ensure consistency with the annual accounts and their knowledge of the NHS body
- a statement that parts of the remuneration report have been properly prepared
- a statement in relation to the NHS body's use of resources
- a certificate that closes the audit.

All auditors issue a report[8] to the audit committee which summarises their findings at the end of the audit. Auditors of CCGs and non-foundation NHS trusts are also required to issue an annual audit letter which is a clear and understandable commentary on the results of the auditors work for the general public.

After the accounts have been audited and any necessary amendments made, the governing body/board is required to formally adopt the accounts and the certificates are signed to demonstrate that approval. The auditor then signs the audit report.

Timetable

The Department of Health determines the overall timetable for the production of the annual report and accounts. Since 2012/13, the timetable has been set so that the Department,

---

[8] This report is called the ISA260 report or report to those charged with governance.

NHS England and NHS Improvement can produce the appropriate consolidated report and accounts and lay them before Parliament prior to the summer recess.

This means that the timetable has now settled: draft annual report and accounts are submitted for audit in the third week of April and the audits are finished in the last week of May (for FTs and CCGs) or the first week in June (for non-foundation NHS trusts). The exact submission dates vary by a matter of days each year to take account of weekends and bank holidays.

Monitoring reports

As well as preparing the statutory annual report and accounts, non-foundation NHS trusts are required to submit financial monitoring and accounts (FMA) forms to NHS Improvement throughout the year. FMA forms are consistent with the annual accounts, but contain slightly different information and are used by NHS Improvement to monitor financial performance throughout the year and, at the year end, prepare the consolidated annual report and accounts for the Department[9].

Non-foundation NHS trusts are also subject to monthly workforce monitoring which includes an analysis of pay expenditure.

FTs have to complete similar monitoring reports for NHS Improvement throughout the year. At the year end, FTs are required to complete consolidation schedules that are consistent with their annual accounts and provide additional information that is used by NHS Improvement to produce a summary of FT accounts which is then included in the Department's consolidated accounts.

During 2016/17, the monitoring forms prepared by non-foundation NHS trusts and FTs will be different as they will continue to use the forms developed by Monitor and the NHS TDA. It is expected that during the year, these forms will be changed so that all NHS provider bodies complete a similar set of returns to be submitted to NHS Improvement.

NHS Improvement will aggregate the returns as its main internal and external reporting mechanism and will include:

- a report on performance against objectives over the past year and key areas of focus for the coming year
- a governance statement covering the role of the board and executive; key risks and their management and data on performance, HR and remuneration
- annual accounts including the auditors' opinion.

NHS Improvement will continue to produce a separate consolidation of FT annual accounts and a consolidation of non-foundation NHS trust accounts.

All CCGs and NHS England use the same financial ledger, the Integrated Single Financial Environment (ISFE). NHS England therefore has access to CCGs' financial information through ISFE so CCGs do not need to complete consolidation schedules. However, at the end of quarter 3 and at the year-end, CCGs and local NHS England offices are required to provide additional financial information which is not available from ISFE to NHS England to allow them to produce their own consolidated report and accounts.

NHS Improvement and NHS England usually publically report the financial performance of each of the sectors of the NHS on a quarterly basis. The use of FMA forms, consolidation schedules and regular financial information also facilitates the preparation of whole of government accounts (WGA) – the consolidated set of financial statements for the UK public sector.

---

[9] This shows how the money allocated to the Department has been spent.

Financial Performance Targets

As well as the statutory requirement to produce annual reports and accounts, NHS bodies are subject to a range of statutory and departmental financial targets. The targets and their nature vary according to the type of NHS body.

NHS England

NHS England's key statutory financial duty is to ensure that in each financial year total spending on health does not exceed the income received. NHS England must also ensure that:

- the total capital resource used in a financial year does not exceed the amount specified by the Secretary of State (known as the capital resource limit or CRL)
- the total revenue resource used in a financial year does not exceed the amount specified by the Secretary of State (known as the revenue resource limit or RRL).

NHS England is also enabled by the 2012 Act to use some of the funding it receives to establish a contingency fund that can be used to help discharge its functions or to help CCGs discharge their functions.

In relation to revenue and capital resource limits, NHS England's chief executive (the Accounting Officer) is held to account by the Department of Health. NHS England is also required to prepare a consolidated annual report and accounts for itself and all CCGs which is a key element in the Department's overall resource account.

Clinical commissioning groups

To be able to fulfil its statutory requirements, NHS England holds CCGs to account for their stewardship of resources and outcomes achieved.

The key financial duty as set out in section 27 of the 2012 Act is that each CCG must not spend more in a year than it receives. In addition, in relation to both revenue and capital resources, each CCG must not spend more than an amount specified by direction of NHS England. In other words each CCG must not exceed its revenue and capital resource limits.

CCG budgets include a maximum allowance to cover administration or running costs. Although they can choose to undertake some or all of these roles themselves, they have the flexibility to use the money to buy in the services needed from commissioning support services. The running cost allowances have been published for the 5 years from 2016 to 2021; the allowances start at £22.07 per head of population and reduce to £21.46 by 2020/21.

Non-foundation NHS trusts

Non-foundation NHS trusts have a statutory financial duty to achieve a break-even position on revenue and expenditure taking one year with another. Trusts must also remain within a borrowing limit set by the Secretary of State[10].

The requirement to break-even is set out in paragraph 2 of Schedule 5 of the *National Health Service Act 2006* and means that a trust must ensure that its revenue is not less than sufficient, taking one financial year with another, to meet outgoings properly charged to the statement of comprehensive income (SOCI). 'Taking one financial year with another' has been interpreted to mean that over a three or five year period, trusts are required to achieve a break-even position on their SOCI. This is to allow some flexibility where exceptional costs are incurred and when managing the financial recovery of a trust with serious financial difficulties.

There is also an annual break-even requirement that is sometimes referred to as an 'administrative duty'. This is monitored by NHS Improvement. An administrative duty is an additional rule and regulation that clarifies or specifies how a trust will operate. Trusts must report on the achievement of their financial duties in the annual report and accounts.

---

[10] See paragraph 1(6) of Schedule 5 of the *NHS Act 2006*.

Other administrative duties are to:

- pay a public dividend capital (PDC)[11] dividend to the Department each year
- manage within a pre-set external financing limit (EFL)
- meet the capital resource limit (CRL)
- comply with the *Better Payment Practice Code* for the payment of invoices.

Chapter 15 contains further information on the first three of these duties.

Better Payment Practice Code

All NHS bodies must comply with the *Better Payment Practice Code*. A target (currently 95%) is set at the start of each year by the Department of Health for the value and volume of invoices that must be paid within 30 days of receipt.

NHS foundation trusts

FTs' financial targets differ from NHS trusts. They do not have any statutory duties in relation to finance and to date, have not had any financial duties imposed by the Department of Health or NHS Improvement. However, since 2015/16, all providers are required to keep their expenditure within a control total set by NHS Improvement. This is the first time that FTs have had a specified financial target to meet.

Although FTs are allowed to incur deficits and operate on a similar basis to commercial organisations, they must operate effectively, efficiently and economically so that they remain going concerns. In effect this means that FTs' main financial target is to remain solvent. As part of the NHS, FTs are also required to demonstrate high standards of financial stewardship in relation to their use of public funds.

During 2016/17, NHS Improvement is developing a single 'oversight framework' but until this is in place FTs will continue to be subject to the *Risk Assessment Framework*[12] which gives each FT a financial risk rating of 1 (high risk) to 4 (low risk). See chapter 12 for more about how NHS bodies are regulated.

Financial Performance Management

Planning

The Department of Health requires the financial performance of NHS bodies to be monitored on a regular basis. The first element of the financial performance management process is the financial plan. All NHS bodies are required to undertake medium term financial planning and as part of this process, the organisation must plan to achieve its financial duties. The plan must cover all expected sources of revenue and expenditure and the full range of responsibilities under the management of the NHS body.

From 2016/17, a single planning document has been issued to all NHS bodies. *Delivering the Forward View: NHS Planning Guidance 2016/17 – 2020/21* is a joint publication by NHS England, NHS Improvement, the Care Quality Commission, Health Education England, the National Institute for Health and Care Excellence (NICE) and Public Health England.

---

[11]PDC is a form of long-term government finance. See chapter 15.
[12]Published by Monitor in August 2015.

All NHS bodies must produce:

- a one year operational plan for 2016/17 for their organisation
- a five year sustainability and transformation plan (STP) which is 'place based' and produced by all NHS bodies in a geographical area.

These plans cover both financial and non-financial performance.

CCGs have a statutory duty to prepare an annual commissioning plan[13]. The plan should set out how a CCG proposes to 'exercise its functions' – this includes how it plans to spend the funding received on buying healthcare for its constituent practices' patients. These plans must be published and submitted to NHS England and all relevant health and wellbeing boards before the start of the financial year to which they relate. A CCG must also have detailed financial plans that are consistent with its commissioning plan.

Reporting financial performance

NHS bodies must report regularly on their financial performance against the plan submitted at the start of the financial year to ensure that there is effective financial management of NHS resources. This information is collated by NHS England (for CCGs) and NHS Improvement (for provider bodies).

Since 2015/16, FTs and non-foundation NHS trusts have been required to keep the amount that they pay for agency staff within a limit set by NHS Improvement. The amount spent on agency staff has to be reported on a weekly basis to NHS Improvement.

During 2016/17, NHS Improvement will work to merge the reporting systems in place for FTs and non-foundation trusts. Until then, the reporting systems developed by Monitor and the NHS TDA will continue to be used.

Chief finance officers are expected to inform the appropriate regulator if there are any significant variances against plans and to ensure that appropriate recovery plans are put into place.

Non-financial performance standards and targets

As well as financial duties, there are a number of other targets that NHS bodies are required to meet. The *Health and Social Care (Community Health and Standards) Act 2003* established the power for the Secretary of State for Health to set standards which are published by the Department of Health. Guidance issued by the NICE is also an important element of the standards system.

Since 2015/16, the non-financial performance standards are included in *Delivering the Forward View: NHS Planning Guidance 2016/17 – 2020/21* and performance against these standards will be measured through the CCG *Improvement and Assessment Framework* (see chapter 12 for more details).

Performance Assessment

External audit

The public is entitled to expect that money raised by local or national taxation is properly accounted for. To provide an assurance that this is the case, there is a need (among other things) for a wide-ranging and independent external audit covering both the financial statements and the NHS body's arrangements for securing value for money from its use of resources.

For the financial year 2017/18 onwards, all NHS bodies will be responsible for appointing their own auditors using an auditor panel set up for the purpose. Until then, the auditors for non-foundation NHS trusts and CCGs are those that were appointed by the Audit Commission prior to its abolition on 31 March 2015. FTs have always appointed their own auditors – this is the responsibility of the FT's Council of Governors.

---

[13] Section 14Z11 of the *NHS Act 2006* as inserted by s26 of the *Health and Social Care Act 2012*.

All external auditors must follow the National Audit Office's *Code of Audit Practice* which requires them to review and report on:

- the annual accounts
- arrangements for securing economy, efficiency and effectiveness in the use of resources.

By exception, auditors must also report when the governance statement does not comply with appropriate reporting requirements.

Auditors of NHS bodies have powers to report where they have specific concerns arising from their audits.

Internal audit

Internal audit is defined in the *UK Public Sector Internal Audit Standards* as 'an independent, objective assurance and consulting activity designed to add value and improve an organisation's operations. It helps an organisation accomplish its objectives by bringing a systematic, disciplined approach to evaluate and improve the effectiveness of risk management, control and governance processes'. These standards have applied to all NHS bodies since April 2013.

All NHS bodies are required to have an internal audit function and the head of internal audit's opinion is used by the Accountable Officer to inform the governance statement.

As the definition above indicates, the internal audit service fulfils two functions – assurance and consultancy. The first involves providing an independent and objective opinion to the Accountable Officer, governing body/board and audit committee on the extent to which risk management, control and governance arrangements support the aims of the NHS body. In this context, risk management, control and governance means the policies, procedures and operations established to ensure:

- the achievement of objectives
- the appropriate assessment of risk
- the reliability of internal and external reporting and accountability processes
- compliance with applicable laws and regulations
- compliance with the behavioural and ethical standards set for the NHS body.

The second role involves providing an independent and objective consultancy service specifically to help line management improve the NHS body's risk management, control and governance. When performing consultancy services, the internal auditor must maintain objectivity and not take on management responsibility.

Internal Reporting

For NHS bodies to run effectively, the governing body/board and managers at all levels need to receive up to date financial and non-financial performance information on a timely basis. This information needs to be derived from the same financial system that is used for external reporting purposes – this ensures consistency in reports and that decisions throughout the NHS body are made on the same basis.

Reporting to NHS governing bodies

NHS governing bodies or boards are responsible for ensuring that there are high standards of financial stewardship through effective financial planning, financial control and ensuring value for money. To achieve this, NHS governing bodies require an effective system of financial and performance reporting that is accurate and timely so that it can take early and corrective action where necessary. It is for the governing body/board to decide the form and content of the reports required and it should review its information needs regularly. The governing body/board should also make use of assessments carried out by external bodies.

> **Examples of Financial Information that is Reported on a Monthly Basis**
>
> Performance against the achievement of statutory and departmental duties and targets
>
> In-year revenue and expenditure position and year-end forecasts, including an analysis of performance against budgets
>
> Financial risks, the likelihood of them arising and how they will be managed
>
> Activity levels linked to financial data
>
> Progress on the achievement of any cost improvement programmes and financial recovery plans
>
> Statement of financial position
>
> Cash forecast
>
> Aged receivable and payable balances including actions taken and progress made
>
> Losses
>
> Performance of outsourced services
>
> Progress against internal and external audit recommendations
>
> Progress on major capital schemes
>
> Staffing and establishment reports

As well as considering monthly reports, there is some financial information that the governing body/board needs to consider every year, including:

- the annual accounts
- financial plans
- (for CCGs and non-foundation NHS trusts) the annual audit letter which summarises the key issues identified during the external audit.

The governing body/board should also be updated and advised regularly on the nature and development of new systems and initiatives in the NHS so that it is better able to understand the implications and prepared to manage the impact when implementation takes place.

Reporting to budget holders

The reporting of performance against the plan and any corrective action taken as a result is an essential element of financial management in the NHS. Reporting to budget holders must therefore be sufficiently detailed to ensure that all significant movements are identified and issues that need to be corrected are highlighted.

Budget monitoring information is produced at a range of levels, allowing managers to see not only summary performance, but also the performance of individual departments and teams. The exact nature of this reporting depends on the NHS body's management structure but in each case it is essential that the information is timely, accurate and fit for purpose. To ensure accuracy, financial commitments should be recognised as soon as possible and reflected in the monthly financial reports. Without accurate budget reporting at budget holder level, costs cannot be controlled properly. These reports are often referred to as the 'management accounts'. Chapter 14 looks in more detail at revenue planning and budgeting.

Key Learning Points

- All NHS bodies have a statutory duty to prepare an annual report and accounts that is audited
- The annual report is a review of the past year and performance against targets
- The annual accounts must be prepared in accordance with international financial reporting standards and additional guidance is provided by the Department of Health/NHS England/NHS Improvement
- The governance statement forms part of the annual report and accounts and reflects on the arrangements that the NHS body has in place to manage and control risk
- Quality accounts (for FTs, quality reports) must be prepared by bodies providing healthcare and focus on the quality of care provided and areas for improvement in the future
- All regulatory bodies undertake financial monitoring throughout the year and require financial information on a regular basis
- All NHS bodies have financial targets which they must meet. Some are statutory and others are administrative
- Additional assurance over the financial reporting of NHS bodies is provided by external auditors
- All NHS bodies must have an internal audit service that fulfils two key functions – assurance and consultancy
- NHS bodies are responsible for monitoring their own financial performance from the overall corporate level through to budget holders
- Governing bodies/boards should think carefully about their information needs to ensure that they can properly direct the NHS body.

References and Further Reading

Health and Social Care Act 2012: www.legislation.gov.uk/ukpga/2012/7/contents/enacted

NHS Act 2006: www.legislation.gov.uk/ukpga/2006/41/contents

International Accounting Standards Board: www.ifrs.org (you will need to register on this site even for free access to the standards)

Financial Reporting Manual, HM Treasury, 2016:
www.gov.uk/government/collections/government-financial-reporting-manual-frem

NHS Finance Manual, Department of Health: www.info.doh.gov.uk/doh/finman.nsf

Manual for Accounts 2015/16, Department of Health:
www.info.doh.gov.uk/doh/finman.nsf/4db79df91d978b6c00256728004f9d6b/
aeda7648c62c72c680257e99004acdd6?OpenDocument
(Note: this will be replaced by the Department's Group Accounting Manual from 2016/17)

NHS Foundation Trust Annual Reporting Manual 2015/16, Monitor:
www.gov.uk/government/publications/nhs-foundation-trusts-annual-reporting-manual-201516
(Note: this will be replaced by the Department's Group Accounting Manual from 2016/17)

Managing Public Money, HM Treasury:
www.gov.uk/government/publications/managing-public-money

National Health Service (Quality Accounts) Regulations 2010; National Health Service (Quality Accounts) Amendment Regulations 2011; National Health Service (Quality Accounts) Amendment Regulations 2012 www.legislation.gov.uk/all?title=quality%20account

NHS foundation trust quality reports: 2015/16 requirements, Monitor, 2016: www.gov.uk/government/publications/nhs-foundation-trust-quality-reports-201516-requirements

Quality Accounts reporting arrangements: www.nhs.uk/aboutNHSChoices/professionals/healthandcareprofessionals/quality-accounts/Pages/about-quality-accounts.aspx

Delivering the Forward View: NHS Shared Planning Guidance 2016/17 – 2020/21, NHS England, 2015: www.england.nhs.uk/ourwork/futurenhs/deliver-forward-view/

Risk Assessment Framework, Monitor, 2015:
www.gov.uk/government/publications/risk-assessment-framework-raf

Code of Audit Practice, NAO, 2015: www.nao.org.uk/code-audit-practice/

UK Public Sector Internal Auditing Standards, 2013:
www.gov.uk/government/publications/public-sector-internal-audit-standards

Chapter 12

How the NHS is Regulated

> NHS organisations are subject to regulation and inspection from a wide range of bodies that are independent of Government and the NHS. These include national agencies and organisations linked to the many different professions involved in the delivery of healthcare – ranging from the Royal Colleges[1] and the General Medical Council to HM Revenue and Customs.
>
> In an environment where demonstrating high quality performance and the effective use of public funds is essential, the role of these bodies and their impact on an organisation's reputation and morale cannot be underestimated. It is therefore essential that NHS organisations are aware of the approach and requirements of each organisation and that appropriate mechanisms are in place to facilitate the assessment process and respond to any recommendations or advice that is issued.
>
> This chapter focuses on the approach of those bodies that have a direct impact on NHS organisations in terms of their finance and governance arrangements – namely, the Care Quality Commission (CQC), NHS Improvement, the National Audit Office and local authorities.

Care Quality Commission

As we saw in chapter 9, the Care Quality Commission (CQC) is the independent regulator of health and adult social care in England. Its purpose is to 'make sure health and social care services provide people with safe, effective, compassionate, high-quality care' and to encourage care services to improve. Its remit covers:

- NHS providers
- adult social care providers
- independent healthcare providers
- dentists
- private ambulances
- NHS out-of-hours services (that are not GP practices)
- GPs and NHS walk-in centres (that do not provide out of hours services).

The CQC has four core functions:

- to **register** those who apply to them to provide health and adult social care services
- to use information and data to **monitor** services and then carry out expert **inspections**, making a judgement of each service and giving an overall **rating**
- to ask providers to improve where poor care is found (inadequate or requires improvement) and to **enforce** this if necessary
- to provide an **independent voice** on the state of health and adult social care in England, helping to share learning and encourage continuous improvement across the sector.

---

[1] 'Royal Colleges' refers to a range of representative organisations for different medical specialists such as GPs, surgeons, anaesthetists, radiologists etc. Details can be found on the Academy of Medical Royal Colleges website: www.aomrc.org.uk/

When the CQC registers and inspects services, it asks the same five questions of every service, namely is it:

- **safe** – are people protected from abuse and avoidable harm?
- **effective** – does the care provided achieve good outcomes and promote a good quality of life?
- **caring** – do staff involve and treat people with compassion, kindness, dignity and respect?
- **responsive** – are services organised so that they meet people's needs?
- **well-led** – does the leadership, management and governance of the organisation assure the delivery of high-quality person-centred care, support learning and innovation, and promote an open and fair culture?

Registration

Before care providers can operate, they must register with the CQC and demonstrate that they meet a number of requirements, including the fundamental standards (see below). Registration effectively represents a licence to operate.

Issues that the CQC considers when assessing services include:

- whether the care provider is suitable
- whether the care provider has enough staff with the right skills, qualifications and experience
- the size, layout and design of the places where care will be provided
- the care provider's policies, systems and procedures and their effectiveness
- how the care provider is run and how it plans to make decisions.

Once registered a provider must show on an ongoing basis that it is meeting the fundamental standards of quality and safety.

Fundamental Standards of Quality and Safety

Person-centred care – you must have care or treatment that is tailored to you and meets your needs and preferences.

Dignity and respect – you must be treated with dignity and respect at all times while you're receiving care and treatment. This includes making sure:

- you have privacy when you need and want it
- everybody is treated as equals
- you're given any support you need to help you remain independent and involved in your local community.

Consent – you (or anybody legally acting on your behalf) must give your consent before any care or treatment is given to you.

Safety – you must not be given unsafe care or treatment or be put at risk of harm that could be avoided. Providers must assess the risks to your health and safety during any care or treatment and make sure their staff have the qualifications, competence, skills and experience to keep you safe.

Safeguarding from abuse – you must not suffer any form of abuse or improper treatment while receiving care. This includes:

- neglect
- degrading treatment
- unnecessary or disproportionate restraint
- inappropriate limits on your freedom.

Food and drink – you must have enough to eat and drink to keep you in good health while you receive care and treatment.

Premises and equipment – the places where you receive care and treatment and the equipment used in it must be clean, suitable and looked after properly. The equipment used in your care and treatment must also be secure and used properly.

Complaints – you must be able to complain about your care and treatment. The provider of your care must have a system in place so they can handle and respond to your complaint. They must investigate it thoroughly and take action if problems are identified.

Good governance – the provider of your care must have plans that ensure they can meet these standards. They must have effective governance and systems to check on the quality and safety of care. These must help the service improve and reduce any risks to your health, safety and welfare.

Staffing – the provider of your care must have enough suitably qualified, competent and experienced staff to make sure they can meet these standards. Their staff must be given the support, training and supervision they need to help them do their job.

Fit and proper staff – the provider of your care must only employ people who can provide care and treatment appropriate to their role. They must have strong recruitment procedures in place and carry out relevant checks such as on applicants' criminal records and work history.

Duty of candour – the provider of your care must be open and transparent with you about your care and treatment. Should something go wrong, they must tell you what has happened, provide support and apologise.

Display of ratings – the provider of your care must display their CQC rating in a place where you can see it. They must also include this information on their website and make our latest report on their service available to you.

Monitoring and inspection regime

The CQC uses a detailed set of supporting questions, known as key lines of enquiry, to ensure consistency on inspections and in judgements.

Protecting the rights of those who use services is also an important part of the inspection process and equality and human rights are embedded in the questions asked. To support inspections, they use information and data gathered from a range of sources including from people using care, providers and partners.

The CQC uses teams of sector experts which include inspectors, specialist advisors (experts such as senior NHS doctors), and 'Experts-by-Experience' (people who have personal experience of using a service or caring for someone who has).

Rating services

The CQC rates services on a four-point scale:

- outstanding
- good
- requires improvement
- inadequate.

The CQC then publishes an inspection report so that the rating can be used to help people decide which care service to use. The ratings system also helps to encourage providers to improve. The CQC takes action where necessary to protect people from poor care.

The CQC is also working with NHS Improvement during 2016/17 to develop a methodology for assessing a sixth key area – how providers use their resources. This will reflect the recommendations set out in Lord Carter's review[2].

Concerns, complaints and whistleblowing

The CQC also gathers information about concerns raised by people using services and staff in three main ways:

- encouraging people and staff to make contact through its website and phone line, and providing opportunities to share concerns with inspectors during visits
- asking national and local partners to share concerns, complaints and whistleblowing information
- requesting information about concerns, complaints and whistleblowing from providers.

NHS Improvement

As we saw in chapter 9, NHS Improvement (NHSI) came into being on 1 April 2016 and brings together two separate arm's length bodies – Monitor and the NHS Trust Development Authority (NHS TDA) – along with teams from four other patient safety and improvement functions[3] from across the NHS.

During 2016/17, NHSI is developing a 'single oversight framework' that will apply to all NHS trusts. This framework will 'identify where providers may benefit from, or require, improvement support' across five themes – quality of care; finance and use of resources (including a series of 'financial rating metrics' that will focus on financial sustainability, efficiency and controls); operational performance; strategic change and leadership and improvement capability. The new approach will aim to identify problems (and risks of problems) as they emerge and pinpoint the underlying causes so that support can be tailored to meet each provider's specific needs. Providers will be segmented according to the scale of issues they face.

The proposed new framework combines and builds on the approaches used by Monitor and the NHS TDA, with changes 'intended to be as much as possible incremental in nature'. Details are set out in a consultation document issued at the end of June 2016[4].

Until the new framework is introduced, the existing regulatory approaches used by Monitor (the risk assessment framework) and the NHS TDA (the accountability framework) remain in place and are outlined briefly below.

---

[2] *Productivity in NHS Hospitals*, 2015.
[3] The Patient Safety Domain and Advancing Change Team from NHS England and the National Reporting and Learning System and Intensive Support teams from NHS Interim Management and Support.
[4] *The Single Oversight Framework*, NHS Improvement, June 2016.

Monitor

The risk assessment framework (RAF)[5]

Monitor's approach to regulation assesses an FT's compliance with two aspects of its licence – continuity of services[6] and governance.

The RAF comprises four stages:

- monitoring licence holders
- assessing risks
- investigating breaches of licence conditions
- prioritisation and regulatory action.

Monitoring

Monitoring information is required so that an FT's compliance with its licence (and specifically its financial sustainability and governance) can be assessed. The information requested falls into four categories:

- annual submissions – for example, a 3 to 5 year strategic plan and operational plans
- in year – for example, monthly financial and service performance information
- exception – for example a Royal College report that raises concerns about quality
- 'other' – for example, an independent report commissioned by the FT to review its governance arrangements.

Assessing risks

Monitor applies two risk ratings – financial sustainability and governance.

The **financial sustainability risk rating** represents Monitor's view of the level of financial risk an FT is facing in relation to the ongoing delivery of services and its own financial efficiency. It is calculated using four metrics:

- capital service
- liquidity
- income and expenditure margin
- variance from plan.

The rating ranges from 1 (the most serious level of risk) to 4 and an FT's 'score' dictates the regulatory activity it can expect with 4 resulting in no action and 1 leading to 'likely investigation'.

The **governance risk rating** is designed to assess an FT's governance standards and is based on information from a range of sources including national metrics such as A&E and cancer waiting times; outcomes of CQC inspections and independently commissioned governance reviews.

An FT's governance rating falls into 1 of 3 categories:

- green – no evident grounds for concern
- under review – potential material concerns have been identified but action has not yet been taken
- red – enforcement action is being taken.

---

[5] We are concerned with FTs only – Monitor has a separate risk assessment framework for independent sector providers of NHS services.
[6] Monitor has a statutory duty to 'prevent providers from taking actions that could undermine their continued ability to deliver services'.

Again, the rating awarded dictates the regulatory activity that an FT can expect with green resulting in no action and red leading to formal regulatory action under s105; s 106 or s111 (see below).

Investigating breaches of licence conditions and prioritisation

When the RAF has identified that an FT is (or is at risk of) failing to comply with its continuity of services or governance licence conditions, Monitor looks to see if there are grounds to investigate if a breach has occurred or may occur. To make this assessment, Monitor uses four 'prioritisation criteria':

- 'Likely benefit (direct and indirect) to healthcare users
- impact on patients and the provision of healthcare
- ultimate scale and scope of breach
- resources required to investigate and address the breach in full.'

If an investigation is launched and finds a breach those findings inform Monitor's regulatory response.

Regulatory powers

Under the *Health and Social Care Act 2012*, Monitor has extensive powers to intervene in the event that a licensed provider is failing to comply with its licence conditions. It can also take informal action – for example, helping providers who are having problems by requiring them to appoint turnaround experts to help avoid failure or (in exceptional circumstances) appointing a 'trust special administrator' to take control of the provider's business and work with commissioners to make sure that patients can still access services.

Monitor's Formal Intervention Powers under the Health and Social Care Act 2012

Section 89 enables Monitor to revoke a provider's licence.

Section 105 of the Act gives Monitor power to require a provider to take specific or a 'discretionary requirement'. This may take the form of:

- a compliance requirement: an instruction from Monitor to take specific steps
- a restoration requirement: requiring the provider to restore the situation to the position before the breach
- a variable monetary penalty, likely if there is significant potential for the breach to reoccur.

Section 106 of the Act enables Monitor to accept a commitment from a provider to take steps to ensure that a breach of the licence condition does not continue or reoccur – an 'enforcement undertaking'. Acceptance is at Monitor's discretion and will depend on individual circumstances.

Section 111 gives Monitor power to impose additional licence conditions and remove, suspend or disqualify director(s) and/ or governor(s).

Using 'specific enforcement powers' granted under sections 105 and 106 of the Act, Monitor can also take action against those healthcare bodies failing to provide information as required in its role as sector regulator including NHS England and clinical commissioning groups (CCGs). As sector regulator, Monitor also has power concurrent with the Competition and Markets Authority to apply competition law in the healthcare sector.

Where a provider is in financial difficulty, Monitor has a duty under section 135 of the 2012 Act to make available a source of finance to cover the costs of administration, via a risk pool arrangement – a fund that is built up via levies on providers and commissioners.

NHS Trust Development Authority (NHS TDA)

The NHS TDA's approach to monitoring and regulating non-foundation NHS trusts is set out in its 'accountability framework'. This framework extends beyond regulation to cover details of the approval process for trusts wanting to achieve FT status and the NHS TDA's 'development offer' – how it helps trusts develop capacity and capability. Our focus is on the 'oversight model' which is designed to generate a risk rating for each NHS trust.

The oversight model

The oversight model is designed to track and score NHS trust performance against a set of indicators in two domains, with the scores then contributing to an overall 'escalation rating'. This rating is updated each month and determines whether intervention is required.

The two domains are:

- **quality** – with indicators in each of five areas that are the same as those used by the CQC in its assessments – namely, caring; effective; responsive; safe; well-led. A score of 1 to 5 is attributed to each aspect and aggregated to give an overall quality domain score, again of 1 to 5

- **finance** – here two aspects are measured: in-year financial delivery and continuity of services (as per Monitor's RAF). Delivery against each category is rated red, amber or green but only the rating for in-year financial delivery is included in the overall escalation score.

In setting the overall escalation rating, the NHS TDA allows for 'softer intelligence' from third parties such as the CQC. It also takes account of a third domain – clinical and financial sustainability – with all NHS trusts allocated to one of six 'segmentation groups'. Although this score does not feed directly into the escalation rating it is a 'factor in its determination'.

The overall escalation scores are also subject to a moderation process led by the NHS TDA's directors of delivery and development.

Escalation and intervention

The end result of applying the oversight model is that each trust is placed in one of five 'oversight categories' which determines the level of intervention and support – these categories range from 'special measures' to 'standard oversight'

NHS England

Improvement and assessment framework

NHS England is responsible for authorising CCGs and holding them to account both for improving outcomes to patients and for getting the best possible value from the money they are allocated. It also has a statutory duty under the *Health and Social Care Act 2012* to carry out an annual performance assessment of each CCG that focuses on CCGs' own statutory duties to:

- improve the quality of services
- reduce inequalities
- obtain appropriate professional advice
- ensure public involvement
- meet financial duties
- take account of the local Joint Health and Wellbeing Strategy.

From 2016/17 this assessment is based on NHS England's 'improvement and assessment framework[7]' that 'draws together in one place *NHS Constitution* and other core performance and financial indicators, outcome goals and transformational challenges'. The Framework sets out six clinical priorities and a series of indicators in four domains that are reported quarterly.

The **clinical priorities** relate to 'national ambitions' as set out in NHS England's Forward View[8] and cover mental health; dementia; learning disabilities; cancer; maternity and diabetes. In relation to each of these areas, NHS England is creating ratings using a four point 'Ofsted-style' scale so that patients will be able to see how their CCG is performing.

The **four domains** cover better health; better care; sustainability and leadership – a flavour of the indicators used for each is shown below:

Domain	Focus	Example Indicators
Better health	How CCGs contribute to improving their population's health and wellbeing.	• Injuries from falls in over 65s • Inequality in avoidable emergency admissions • Carers' quality of life
Better care	How CCGs are performing against constitutional standards and outcomes. Also care redesign.	• Neonatal mortality and stillbirths • Cancers diagnosed at an early stage • Estimated diagnosis rate for people with dementia • Patients waiting 18 weeks or less from referral to hospital treatment
Sustainability	How CCGs are remaining in financial balance and securing good value.	• In-year financial performance • Outcomes and expenditure in areas with identified scope for improvement • Adoption of new models of care
Leadership	Quality of a CCG's leadership, plans, partnership working and governance arrangements.	• Sustainability and transformation plan (STP) • Staff engagement index • Effectiveness of working relationships

NHS England's assessment is 'a judgement, reached by taking into account the CCG's performance in each of the indicator areas over the full year and balanced against the qualitative assessment of the leadership of the CCG.' To ensure consistency of approach there will be regional and national moderation with NHS England's Commissioning Committee overseeing the process and signing off the ratings.

---

[7] CCG *Improvement and Assessment Framework*, 2016/17, NHS England, 2016.
[8] *Delivering the Forward View: NHS Shared Planning Guidance*, NHS England, 2015.

Intervention

If a CCG is unable to fulfill its duties effectively or there is a significant risk of failure, NHS England has powers to intervene. These powers range from telling a CCG how it should discharge its functions through to dissolving a CCG completely if it is failing. Since 2015/16, CCGs can also be subject to 'special measures'.

See chapters 4 and 5 for more about NHS England and CCGs.

National Audit Office (NAO)

The National Audit Office (NAO) plays an important role in NHS governance as it scrutinises public spending for Parliament. It does this in two main ways:

- conducting financial audits of all Government departments and agencies and many other public bodies – this includes the Department of Health and its arm's length bodies
- reporting to Parliament on whether Government departments and other bodies have used public money efficiently, effectively and with economy.

When auditing the Department of Health and its arm's length bodies (ALBs) accounts, the NAO places reliance on and takes assurance from the work carried out by auditors on the underlying accounts of individual NHS bodies. In addition, the results of NAO reports affect the Department and these can in turn have an impact at local level.

Under the *Local Audit and Accountability Act 2014* the NAO sets out, in its *Code of Audit Practice*, both the scope of external auditors' responsibilities and the standards that external auditors must meet. The Act also gives the Comptroller and Auditor General (C&AG) power to issue statutory guidance, to which local external auditors are required to 'have regard', when carrying out their work.

Since 1 April 2015, the NAO's *Code of Audit Practice* has applied to all local NHS bodies.

Local Authorities

Since January 2003, local authorities with social services responsibilities have been able to establish committees of councillors to provide overview and scrutiny of local NHS bodies by virtue of powers set out in section 38 of the *Local Government Act 2000*. The ultimate aim is to secure health improvement for local communities by encouraging authorities to look beyond their own service responsibilities to issues of wider concern to local people. This is achieved by giving democratically elected representatives the right to scrutinise how local health services are provided and developed for their constituents. This scrutiny role was extended by the 2012 Act to cover any provider of NHS funded services. Local authorities also now play a key role in public health and health improvement – see chapter 8 for details.

Other External Bodies

There is a wide range of other organisations with an interest in health which can affect governance arrangements. These include:

- professional bodies on both the clinical and managerial side. These organisations often have their own codes of conduct and disciplinary regimes that apply to their members. For example, the Royal Colleges and other independent audit and assurance bodies that provide an assurance to NHS organisations
- other government departments and agencies – for example, the Department for Communities and Local Government
- non-departmental public bodies, independent and local organisations (for example, local HealthWatch)

- representative bodies – for example, the British Medical Association (BMA), the NHS Confederation and UNISON
- think tanks and research organisations – such as the King's Fund
- the public – NHS organisations are required to engage with the public and conduct meaningful consultations.

Key Learning Points

- NHS organisations must be aware of the approach and requirements of all relevant regulatory and inspection agencies
- The CQC regulates providers of healthcare services via a system of registration and inspection
- All registered providers must comply with the CQC's fundamental standards of qaulity and safety
- Until NHS Improvement introduces its single oversight framework, FTs will be regulated and assessed by Monitor's *Risk Assessment Framework*
- Monitor has extensive powers to intervene if a licensed providers is not complying with its licence conditions
- Until NHS Improvement introduces its single oversight framework, non-foundation NHS trusts will be regulated and assessed by the NHS TDA's *Accountability Framework*
- NHS England uses its *Improvement and Assessment Framework* to monitor and assess CCGs
- The NAO conducts financial audits of all government departments including the Department of Health and its ALBs
- Local authorities have a scrutiny role that extends to all providers of NHS funded services.

References and Further Reading

Academy of Medical Royal Colleges website: www.aomrc.org.uk/

CQC: www.cqc.org.uk

The Carter Review: Productivity in Hospitals, 2015:
https://www.gov.uk/government/publications/productivity-in-nhs-hospitals

NHS Improvement – including Monitor and the NHS TDA:
https://improvement.nhs.uk/about-us/who-we-are/

The Single Oversight Framework, NHS Improvement, June 2016 (consultation):
https://improvement.nhs.uk/uploads/documents/Single_Oversight_Framework_consultation_-_final_draft_28_06_update_CC.pdf

Risk Assessment Framework, Monitor, 2015:
https://improvement.nhs.uk/resources/risk-assessment-framework/

Accountability Framework, NHS TDA, 2015:
https://improvement.nhs.uk/resources/accountability-framework/

NHS England: www.england.nhs.uk/

CCG Improvement and Assessment Framework, NHS England, 2016: https://www.england.nhs.uk/commissioning/wp-content/uploads/sites/12/2016/03/ccg-iaf-mar16.pdf

Delivering the Forward View: Shared Planning Guidance, NHS England, 2015:
https://www.england.nhs.uk/ourwork/futurenhs/deliver-forward-view/

NAO: www.nao.org.uk

Chapter 13
Governance – How NHS Organisations are Structured and Run

> This chapter's focus is governance – a subject that has received considerable attention over the years following spectacular failings across all sectors of the economy – recent examples include the 2008 banking crisis and Mid Staffordshire NHS Foundation Trust. These (and many other) crises have demonstrated just how important good governance is to the wellbeing of an organisation and made clear that it encompasses everything that an organisation does, not just its administrative and support functions. In the NHS this means that effective governance is as much of a concern to a nurse or consultant as it is to an accountant or manager.
>
> Governance is a huge subject in its own right so this chapter focuses on key aspects relating to NHS finance. The HFMA produces a separate Introductory Guide to Governance if you want to find out more.

What is Governance?

The terms 'governance' and 'corporate governance' are now interchangeable but it was the use of corporate governance as a phrase in the 1992 Cadbury Committee Report[1] that initiated widespread debate in this area. Corporate governance was defined in that report as 'the system by which companies are directed and controlled' and its focus was on how companies were run, structured, led and held to account. This report also identified the three fundamental principles of good governance as being openness, integrity and accountability.

Governance in the NHS

The NHS has been well aware of the importance of governance for many years with a wide range of separate regulatory frameworks and ethical codes in operation for the different professions working in NHS organisations. The challenge has been to bring together the practices and information systems of these different disciplines in such a way that they form an integrated and effective organisation-wide governance structure.

The importance of having an integrated approach to governance (i.e. covering all aspects of governance including financial, clinical and organisational) along with high standards and an open culture has been heightened by failures which have dented public confidence in the NHS and raised questions over how NHS organisations are run. These have included:

- the Shipman crimes in 2003/04
- the Healthcare Commission's[2] reports into Stoke Mandeville hospital (2006), Maidstone and Tunbridge Wells NHS Trust (2007) and Mid-Staffordshire NHS Foundation Trust (2009)
- the Francis Reports into Mid-Staffordshire NHS Foundation Trust (2010 and 2013)
- the Care Quality Commission's (CQC) 2015 Quality Report into Addenbrooke's and the Rosie hospitals (part of Cambridge University Hospitals NHS FT).

In each case, clear linkages were drawn between the clinical failings and the governance failings that allowed them to continue uncorrected. For example, one of the findings in the 2015 CQC report into Addenbrooke's was that 'disconnected governance arrangements meant that important messages from the clinical divisions were not highlighted at trust board level.'

---

[1] *The Financial Aspects of Corporate Governance*, 1992.
[2] The Healthcare Commission has since become the Care Quality Commission.

Investigations into governance lapses have also underlined the need for an open and questioning culture and governance policies, procedures and structures that are comprehensive and work in practice, not just on paper.

Lessons from Governance Failings at Mid-Staffordshire NHS Foundation Trust

The Healthcare Commission's 2009 investigation into Mid-Staffordshire NHS Foundation Trust (where multiple management failures led to high mortality rates), found that the Trust, which was seeking to make financial savings in order to apply for foundation trust status, appeared to 'have lost sight of its real priorities'.

The 2010 report by Robert Francis QC revealed that deficiencies in staffing and governance extended over a period of more than 5 years and yet remained un-remedied by those responsible. This report identified a number of basic areas where poor practice had exacerbated the problems and prevented their resolution:

- staffing – shortages of nursing staff went back ten years but staff concerns went unheeded. As a result, many staff became disengaged and poor standards prevailed
- outcomes – management relied too much on data and not enough on what patients were saying, too much on systems and not enough on the actual outcomes
- lack of urgency – some problems were identified and actions under way but these did not receive the constant follow-up, review and modification required for them to be effective
- the board – although recognising that the board's role is strategic, Francis says that its members should 'roll their sleeves up' and find out what is happening on the ground, when a bad situation is not getting better.

In relation to the involvement of directors, the 2010 report commented as follows:

The Inquiry has had the benefit of hearing the views and thinking of many former and current directors of the Trust. It is clear that many of the problems suffered in this Trust had been in existence for a long time and were known about by those in charge. Many thought – and still think – that they had done their best to address them. While there is no doubt that steps were taken to address many, if not all, of the problems, sadly the action taken was insufficient. I suggest that the board of any trust could benefit from reflecting on their own work in the light of what is described in my report.

Many of the complaints made to the Inquiry had already been made in precisely the same terms to the Trust. Many of them, even if taken on their own as one person's observation, should have been enough to alert a listener to the existence of a serious systemic problem. Often the responses were formulaic. Even where they were not, the action taken as a result was inadequate. Perhaps most importantly, representative stories hardly ever reached directors.

The 2013 report went further and found that the trust had failed to listen to patients' concerns, correct deficiencies and tackle an 'insidious negative culture' that tolerated poor standards and clinical disengagement from managerial and leadership responsibilities. The report concluded that 'this failure was in part the consequence of allowing a focus on reaching national access targets, achieving financial balance and seeking foundation trust status at the cost of delivering acceptable standards of care.'

These (and other) incidents have driven home to governing bodies/boards just how wide ranging their responsibilities are and emphasised how important it is to see governance arrangements relating to clinical and quality spheres as an integral part of an organisation's overall approach, rather than the preserve of clinicians. The National Quality Board's report[3] made this clear when it stated that 'final and definitive responsibility for improvements, successful delivery, and equally failures, in the quality of care' lie with the provider organisation's board and leaders.

An Audit Commission report in 2009[4] also emphasised the importance of an organisation wide approach to governance when it suggested that future failures were likely unless a systematic approach is taken to identifying and managing key risks, and to evaluating assurances.

By now it should be clear why an effective and integrated approach to governance is so important and equally obvious that if an NHS organisation gets it wrong it can have a disastrous impact on patients and undermine public confidence in the service as a whole. But what does this mean NHS organisations need to do in practice?

In broad terms every organisation needs to focus on how they:

- are led and structured
- demonstrate that they are operating in line with the three fundamental governance principles – openness, integrity and accountability
- are meeting their statutory duties and strategic objectives
- ensure that they provide (or commission) high quality healthcare
- ensure that they operate economically, efficiently and effectively.

NHS bodies must also recognise that governance is as much about behaviour, values and attitudes as about structures, systems, processes and controls. There is no point having a comprehensive governance framework if no-one is committed to it or understands why it exists and what it is designed to achieve.

Elements of Governance

Effective governance arrangements should underpin all that an organisation does but it is helpful to break it down across three key elements – we will look at each in turn with a focus on financial aspects:

- culture and values (the people issues) – for example, an organisation's leadership style and tone, openness and adherence to relevant legislation and codes of practice
- structures and processes – for example, statutory and regulatory requirements, governing body/board and committee structures and internal policies and procedures
- control frameworks – for example, assurance, risk management, internal, external and clinical audit.

Organisational Culture and Values

Every organisation develops its own unique culture and values but to be effective, it is essential that there is 'a system of shared values and beliefs about what is important, what behaviours are appropriate and about feelings and relationships internally and externally'[5]. If everyone within an organisation is to 'buy in' to these shared values they must be meaningful, make sense and be realistic. There is no point having a carefully crafted statement of values if it bears no relation to how things actually feel on the front line. For example, it would be a mistake for an organisation to claim that it has a 'no blame culture' if this is not borne out in practice.

---

[3] *Quality Governance in the NHS – a Guide for Provider Boards*, 2011.
[4] *Taking it on Trust – a review of how NHS trusts and foundation trusts get their assurance*, Audit Commission, 2009.
[5] *Vision and Values: organisational culture and values as a source of competitive advantage*, CIPD, 2004.

Principles of public life

Everyone involved in the public sector brings their own personality, experience and attitudes with them. However, the public provides the resources for which they are responsible and, as a result, certain ethical standards and values are expected of them – these standards are known as the *Seven Principles of Public Life* and were set out by the Nolan Committee in 1995.

The Nolan Principles of Public Life

Selflessness – holders of public office should take decisions solely in terms of the public interest. They should not do so in order to gain financial or other material benefits for themselves, their family, or their friends

Integrity – holders of public office should not place themselves under any financial or other obligation to outside individuals or organisations that might influence them in the performance of their official duties

Objectivity – in carrying out public business, including making public appointments, awarding contracts, or recommending individuals for rewards and benefits, holders of public office should make choices on merit

Accountability – holders of public office are accountable for their decisions and actions to the public and must submit to whatever scrutiny is appropriate to their office

Openness – holders of public office should be as open as possible about all the decisions and actions that they take. They should give reasons for their decisions and restrict information only when the wider public interest clearly demands it

Honesty – holders of public office have a duty to declare any private interests relating to their public duties and to take steps to resolve any conflicts arising in a way that protects the public interest

Leadership – holders of public office should promote and support these principles by leadership and example.

The Treasury's guidance document, *Managing Public Money* sets out the standards which it expects all public services to deliver which overlap with the Nolan principles:

Managing Public Money Standards

Honesty	Transparency
Fairness	Accountability
Impartiality	Objectivity
Integrity	Accuracy
Openness	Reliability

The Treasury adds that organisations should carry these standards out 'In the spirit of, as well as to the letter of, the law in the public interest, to high ethical standards, achieving value for money.'

The 2013 Francis Inquiry report also stressed the importance of openness and transparency and added a further key duty – candour.

> **Openness, Transparency and Candour – Francis Inquiry Report**
>
> **Openness** – enabling concerns and complaints to be raised freely without fear and questions asked to be answered.
>
> **Transparency** – allowing information about the truth about performance and outcomes to be shared with staff, patients, the public and regulators.
>
> **Candour** – any patient harmed by the provision of a healthcare service is informed of the fact and an appropriate remedy agreed, regardless of whether a complaint has been made or a question asked about it.

Together, the Nolan principles, the Treasury standards and the recommendations set out in the Francis Inquiry Report provide a blueprint for the underlying culture and values of any public sector organisation.

Leadership

Effective leadership is also important – the *Good Governance Standard for Public Services* recognises this when it states that 'Good governance flows from a shared ethos or culture' and that it is 'the governing body that should take the lead in establishing and promoting values for the organisation and its staff'. In other words, the culture and values of an organisation are set from the top. In the context of the NHS this means that the behaviour, approach and leadership style of the governing body/board and senior management are critical in establishing an organisation's tone, 'feel' and direction.

NHS Constitution

The *NHS Constitution* further emphasises the importance of having clear (and consistently applied) principles underpinning all that the NHS does. Since January 2010 all providers and commissioners of NHS care in England have a statutory duty to have regard to the *NHS Constitution* in all their decisions and actions.

Of particular note in governance terms are the principles and values set out in the Constitution as these must underpin everything that an organisation does.

> **NHS Constitution**
>
> Principles
>
> - the NHS provides a comprehensive service, available to all
> - access to NHS services is based on clinical need, not an individual's ability to pay
> - the NHS aspires to the highest standards of excellence and professionalism
> - the patient will be at the heart of everything the NHS does
> - the NHS works across organisational boundaries and in partnership with other organisations in the interest of patients, local communities and the wider population
> - the NHS is committed to providing best value for taxpayers' money and the most effective, fair and sustainable use of finite resources
> - the NHS is accountable to the public, communities and patients that it serves.

> **Values**
> - working together for patients
> - respect and dignity
> - commitment to quality of care
> - compassion
> - improving lives
> - everyone counts.

The 2013 Francis Inquiry report recognised the importance of the Constitution when it stated that:

- it 'should be the first reference point for all NHS patients and staff and should set out the system's common values, as well as the respective rights, legitimate expectations and obligations of patients.' (recommendation 3)
- its core values 'should be given priority of place and the overriding value should be that patients are put first and everything done by the NHS and everyone associated with it should be informed by this ethos' (recommendation 4).

Legislation

There are two Acts of Parliament that are worthy of note here as they both have links to an organisation's culture:

- the *Freedom of Information Act 2000* means that NHS bodies are required to answer questions from members of the public and make information available to them. In addition, the Government has introduced requirements in relation to transparency which requires the publication of items of spend over £25,000
- the *Bribery Act 2010* applies to both organisations and individuals and means that NHS bodies must ensure that they have in place adequate procedures to prevent bribery taking place. If they fail to do this, organisations can be prosecuted for the failure to prevent a bribe being paid on the organisation's behalf (for example when placing a contract for a major service or investment).

Codes of practice

Since the early 1990s, a number of codes of practice[6] have been issued to provide practical guidance on behavioural aspects of governance. For the most part, the content of these Codes has been incorporated into legislation or tailored guidance but the key messages that were set out in the *Code of Conduct: Code of Accountability* are worth repeating – namely that governing body/board members must adhere to three crucial public sector values that are at the heart of the NHS:

- accountability – everything done by those who work in the NHS must be able to stand the test of Parliamentary scrutiny, public judgements on propriety and professional codes of conduct
- probity – there should be an absolute standard of honesty in dealing with the assets of the NHS: integrity should be the hallmark of all personal conduct in decisions affecting patients, staff and suppliers, and in the use of information acquired in the course of NHS duties
- openness – there should be sufficient transparency about NHS activities to promote confidence between the NHS organisation and its staff, patients and the public.

---

[6] For example, the *Code of Conduct: Code of Accountability in the NHS* (2004 and 2013) and the *Code of Conduct for NHS Managers* (2002).

For CCGs, NHS England's guide – *CCG governing body members: role outlines, attributes and skills* – is of particular relevance. This includes amongst the 'core attributes and competencies' that each individual governing body member is expected to:

- 'embrace effective governance, accountability and stewardship of public money and demonstrate an understanding of good scrutiny
- bring a sound understanding of, and a commitment to upholding, the NHS principles and values as set out in the *NHS Constitution*
- demonstrate a commitment to upholding the Nolan Principles of Public Life along with his/her leadership role and the culture of the CCG.'

NHS trust board and CCG governing body members are also expected to follow the *Standards for Members of NHS Boards and Governing Bodies in England* issued by the Professional Standards Authority. These standards cover personal behaviour, technical competence and business practices.

Structures and Processes

Organisational structures

The Government (via the Secretary of State, the Department of Health and its ALBs) sets the structural arrangements that must be followed for the 'top' management and leadership structures of NHS organisations.

Although these structures vary according to the type of organisation, two basic principles apply to all – each must have its own governing body (often called the board) and a designated 'Accountable' (or 'Accounting') Officer. In addition:

- **FTs have a Council of Governors** to represent local interests and which 'binds a trust to its patients, service users, staff and stakeholders'[7]. The Council's key role is to 'hold the non-executive directors, individually and collectively, to account for the performance of the board of directors and to represent the interests of the FT's members and of the public'. Governors are also expected to act in the best interests of the FT and are responsible for sharing information about key decisions with their membership community.
- **CCGs have a Council of Members** on which all the CCG's constituent GP practices are represented and it is this Council that is responsible for determining governance arrangements and setting them out in a written constitution. The CCG is required to observe at all times 'such generally accepted principles of good governance as are relevant to it[8]' in the way it conducts its business. The Council of Members (i.e. the CCG as a body) has the authority to delegate functions to a governing body or to its members, employees, committees or sub-committees. The extent of delegation depends on the CCG's scheme of reservation and delegation (as set out in its constitution) and committees' terms of reference. The Council of Members remains accountable for all of its functions, including those that it has delegated.

The governing body/board – purpose

The governing body/board is responsible for the strategies and actions of the organisation and is accountable to its members (in the case of FTs and CCGs), the public and ultimately to Parliament. The governing body/board also monitors the achievement of the organisation's objectives (and looks for potential problems and risks that might prevent them from being achieved) and receives assurances that things are working as they should.

Given its status and role, there is a range of responsibilities and decisions that the governing body/board cannot delegate. These are referred to as being 'reserved to the board'.

---

[7] *Your Statutory Duties: a Reference Guide for NHS Foundation Trust Governors*, Monitor, 2013.
[8] Section 14L of the NHS Act 2006.

Examples of Activities 'Reserved to the Board'

- financial stewardship responsibilities (for example, adopting the annual report and accounts that all NHS bodies are required to produce)
- determining the organisation's strategy and policies and setting its strategic direction
- appointing senior executives
- overseeing the delivery of services
- standards of governance and behaviour.

In addition, an NHS organisation's governing body/board is free to agree other issues that only it will deal with and must also decide which responsibilities it will delegate by drawing up a scheme of delegation.

As noted above, the situation for CCGs is different as the Council of Members sits above the CCG's governing body and delegates functions to it. At the same time the legislation (and section 6.6 of NHS England's guidance on CCG model constitutions) requires the CCG governing body (not the Council of Members) to appoint the audit and remuneration committees, and to be responsible for (inter alia):

- 'ensuring that the group has appropriate arrangements in place to exercise its functions effectively, efficiently and economically and in accordance with the group's principles of good governance (its main function)
- determining the remuneration, fees and other allowances payable to employees or other persons providing services to the group and the allowances payable under any pension scheme
- approving any functions of the group that are specified in regulations
- other functions delegated to it by the CCG. '

This means that for CCGs, the pre-eminent body is formally the Council of Members. However, in practice the council delegates functions to its governing body which then operates in much the same way and with the same objectives as other NHS organisations' governing bodies/boards.

The governing body/board – composition

The governing body/board brings together in a decision-making forum the executive directors and the non-executive directors (NEDs) or lay members of the organisation and is separate from the day-to-day management structure. Each governing body/board is led by an independent, non-executive Chairperson.

NEDs and lay members play a particularly important role on the governing body/board as they provide independent, constructive challenge and a breadth of experience. By balancing the views of executive directors, they also ensure that power is not concentrated in a few hands so preventing any individual or small group from dominating the governing body/board's decision making.

The exact structure of each governing body/board is different for each type of NHS body and is set out in legislation and associated regulations[9].

The boards of both non-foundation trusts and FTs comprise a Chairperson, executive members (who are employees of the NHS organisation) and independent NEDs. The executive directors

---

[9] For non-foundation NHS trusts: regulations 2 and 4 of the 1990 *Trust Membership and Procedure Regulations* (SI 1990/2024). For FTs: schedule 7 to the *NHS Act 2006*. For CCGs: s14L of the *NHS Act 2006* (inserted by s25 of the 2012 Act) and the associated regulations (SI 2012/1631).

must include a medical director and nursing director as well as the chief executive and chief finance officer (CFO).

CCG governing bodies must include at least two independent lay members (equivalent to NEDs), at least one registered nurse and a doctor who is a secondary care specialist. The CCG's chief executive and CFO must also be members of the governing body. The two lay members have specific responsibilities: one has a lead role in patient and public involvement, while the other oversees key elements of the governance arrangements including audit. In addition, one of the lay members undertakes the role of the governing body's Chairperson or the deputy Chairperson.

The governing body/board – appointments

In FTs the Council of Governors appoints its own NEDs in line with Monitor's *Code of Governance* – this recommends that there 'should be a formal, rigorous and transparent procedure for the appointment or election of new members to the boards of directors' and that appointments should be made 'on merit and based on objective criteria.' To ensure that this is the case in practice, the Code recommends a nominations committee to ensure that independence is enshrined in the process and appointments are made on the basis of need (in terms of the board's needs) and competency (in relation to the individual's ability). The Code also states that it is 'desirable' for there to be a majority of governor votes on nominations committees. Final decisions about the appointment of NEDs must be taken at a meeting of the Council of Governors.

The Code also recommends that the board of directors appoint a 'senior independent director' from amongst the NEDs (in consultation with the Council of Governors) so that there is someone to deal with concerns of governors and/or members that cannot be resolved through 'normal channels' (i.e. via the Chairperson, the chief executive, or finance director).

In NHS trusts, the NHS TDA (since April 2016, operating along with Monitor as part of NHS Improvement) is responsible for appointing, re-appointing (and where necessary terminating) Chairpersons and NEDs to the boards. Appointees are chosen from lay people within the community that the organisation serves and are selected with a view to ensuring a balance of skills and experience. For example, there may be NEDs with professional qualifications in law or accountancy and others who have experience as a user of NHS services.

CCGs appoint their own lay members – practical guidance is available from NHS England[10].

The governing body/ board – committees

To help a governing body/board discharge its duties effectively, a number of committees are normally established. Although, it is up to each organisation to decide what committee structure best suits its needs, there are a number of mandatory committees, discussed in turn below.

Audit committee

Every NHS organisation must have an audit committee that reports to the governing body/board. This committee's distinctive characteristic is that it comprises only independent non-executive members – there is usually at least three, to allow for a quorum of two. In addition, the Chairperson of the organisation should not be a member. The fact that only non-executives can be members allows the audit committee to operate independently of executive management and to be objective when scrutinising the arrangements put in place and operated by the organisation's executive.

For CCGs, schedule 2, paragraph 7 (3) of the *Health and Social Care Act 2012* says that 'Arrangements ... **may** include provision for the audit committee to include individuals who are not members of the governing body.' However, NHS England's model constitution for CCGs recommends that they should follow the *Audit Committee Handbook* which makes clear that

---

[10]Best Practice Resource/Practical Toolkit – for the appointment of lay members to Clinical Commissioning Groups: www.england.nhs.uk/tk-appoint-lay-mem-ccg/

audit committees should be (and be seen to be) independent and comprise 'not less than three non-executive directors, with a quorum of two'.

The chief executive and all other executive directors attend whenever they are invited by the audit committee Chairperson and, in particular, to provide assurances and explanations to the committee when it is discussing audit reports or other matters within their areas of responsibility.

Detailed guidance about the role of audit committees is set out in the HFMA's *Audit Committee Handbook*. This makes clear that one of the audit committee's key duties is to 'review the establishment and maintenance of an effective system of integrated governance, risk management and internal control, across the whole of the organisation's activities (both clinical and non-clinical), that supports the achievement of the organisation's objectives'.

Auditor panels

Non-foundation NHS trusts and CCGs must also have an auditor panel to advise on the selection, appointment and removal of external auditors and on maintaining an independent relationship with them. This applies to appointments that start on or after 1 April 2017. In most cases, existing audit committees (or members of those committees) are nominated to act as the auditor panel. The HFMA has produced two briefings that provide practical guidance on how to establish auditor panels[11].

In FTs an auditor panel is not required as it is the responsibility of the Council of Governors to appoint, re-appoint and remove the external auditor and approve their remuneration and terms of engagement. Support and guidance is provided by the audit committee.

Remuneration committee

The remuneration (and terms of service) committee is another committee that is mandatory for all NHS organisations and reports to the governing body/board. Its role is to advise the governing body/board about the pay, other benefits and terms of employment for the chief executive and other senior staff.

In FTs, the remuneration committee should be composed of NEDs including at least three who are independent.

In NHS trusts, the committee's membership comprises at least two NEDs and the trust's Chairperson.

For CCGs, the requirement for a remuneration committee is set out in section 14M(1) of the 2006 Act, as inserted by section 25 of the 2012 Act. Only members of the CCG governing body can belong to the remuneration committee.

Accountable/Accounting Officers

Every NHS organisation has an 'Accountable' (or 'Accounting') officer. This is a formal role conferred upon the organisation's 'chief officer' (usually the chief executive). In a CCG, the chief officer is either the 'lead manager' or the 'lead clinician' and is nominated by the CCG itself – he or she is then appointed formally by NHS England. CCGs also have an option to share an Accountable Officer with another CCG providing that a joint memorandum of understanding was drawn up and approved by NHS England during the authorisation process.

The role of the Accountable/Accounting Officer is a key element in governance terms with a line of accountability for the proper stewardship of public money and assets and for the organisation's performance stretching up to Parliament. The Accountable (or Accounting) Officer is also accountable to the organisation's governing body/board for meeting the objectives it sets, for day-to-day management and for ensuring that governance arrangements are effective.

For non-foundation NHS trusts, Accountable Officers are accountable to the NHS TDA's Accountable Officer who is in turn accountable to the Department of Health's Accounting

---

[11] *Auditor Panels – Guidance to help Health Bodies meet their Statutory Duties (September 2015) and Example Terms of Reference*, HFMA, 2015.

Officer (and on to the Secretary of State and Parliament). For FTs, Accounting Officers are accountable directly to Parliament[12]. For CCGs, the Accountable Officers are accountable to NHS England's Accountable Officer who is in turn accountable to the Department of Health's Accounting Officer (and on to the Secretary of State and Parliament). The chief executive of NHS Improvement (not itself a statutory body) is the chief executive and Accountable Officer for both Monitor and the NHS Trust Development Authority (the statutory bodies).

Lines of Accountability

CCGs

Parliament
↑
Secretary of State for Health
↑
Department of Health Accounting Officer
↑
NHS England Accountable Officer
↑
CCG Accountable officer

Non-foundation NHS Trusts

Parliament
↑
Secretary of State for Health
↑
Department of Health Accounting Officer
↑
NHS TDA Accountable Officer
↑
NHS trust Accountable Officer

Foundation Trusts

Parliament
↑
NHS FT Accounting Officer

More detail about the role for FTs and NHS trusts is set out in memoranda issued by the relevant organisation (Monitor for FTs and NHS TDA for NHS trusts). This memorandum is signed by the nominated individual. For CCGs, Accountable Officers' responsibilities are set out in NHS England's guidance *Clinical Commissioning Group Governing Body Members: Role Outlines, Attributes and Skills*.

Chief finance officers

CFOs (also called finance directors or directors of finance) of health organisations are automatically executive directors with a seat on the governing body/board. This is in line with the Treasury's guide, *Managing Public Money* which states that the CFO should 'have Board status equivalent to other Board members' and that he or she should be 'a member of the senior leadership team'. Where a CFO fulfils the role for more than one organisation, he or she must be on the governing body/board of each organisation.

---

[12] This is the reason for the two slightly different terms – an Accounting Officer (for example in an FT or Department of Health) is directly accountable to Parliament (via the Public Accounts Committee) but an Accountable Officer (for example, in a CCG or NHS trust) is responsible to an Accounting Officer of a Government department who is in turn accountable to Parliament.

Executive management

Each NHS organisation must have an effective management structure designed to achieve its statutory duties and implement the strategic objectives and policies agreed by the governing body/board. This structure will vary between organisations but should ensure that all areas of responsibility are clearly accountable to a manager and ultimately to an executive director.

Fit and proper persons

All NHS provider organisations have a duty[13] NOT to appoint a person to an executive level post (including associate directors) or to a non-executive position unless they are adjudged to be a 'fit and proper person'. In other words that they:

- are of good character
- have the necessary qualifications, skills and experience
- are able to perform the work that they are employed for
- can supply information as set out in the regulations as required by the CQC.

Organisational processes

Effective internal procedures and controls are an essential part of an effective framework of governance. Collectively these are sometimes referred to as 'business rules'. Key elements that NHS organisations need to think about in relation to finance are:

- standing orders
- procedures for dealing with any conflicts of interest
- standing financial instructions/prime financial policies
- policies and procedures.

Standing orders (SOs)

All NHS organisations must have standing orders (SOs) which provide a comprehensive framework for carrying out activities and are therefore a critical element in the governance framework. Effectively, SOs are the link to an organisation's statutory powers and translate these powers into a series of practical rules designed to protect the interests of both the organisation and its staff. In FTs and CCGs, SOs form part of the constitution.

What Standing Orders Contain

The majority of provisions within SOs relate to the business of running the governing body/board and structure of its committees – for example:

- the composition of the board and committees
- how meetings are run
- form, content and frequency of reports
- what constitutes a quorum
- record of attendance
- voting procedures.

---

[13] As set out in the *Health and Social Care Act 2008 (Regulated Activities) Regulations 2014.*

Governance – How NHS Organisations are Structured and Run

Other areas covered include:
- appointment of committees and sub-committees
- scheme of delegation – a detailed listing of what the governing body/board alone can decide on and who it empowers to take actions or make decisions on its behalf
- decisions reserved to the board – those decisions that the governing body/board cannot delegate
- standards of business conduct – for example, relating to how contracts should be awarded to prevent bias
- declarations of interest
- register of interests and hospitality
- duties and obligations of governing body/board members.

Conflicts of interest

One area covered by SOs that often receives particular attention relates to standards of business conduct, declarations of interest and registers of interests/hospitality.

Governing body/board members must declare any personal or business interests or relationships that may influence (or be perceived to influence) their judgement or decisions. The fundamental principle is that no one should use their public position for private gain, either for their own benefit or for the benefit of those close to them. For example, if a governing body/board member or member of staff has any interest in a contract, that interest must be disclosed and they must take no part in the evaluation process or decision.

It is important that both actual and potential conflicts of interest are declared as any outside interest, hospitality or sponsorship represents a risk of a conflict arising. The procedures followed to manage conflicts of interest also help protect individuals from any subsequent allegations of bias.

In addition, the *Bribery Act 2010* makes it an offence to accept gifts or hospitality as an inducement or reward for doing something in your public role and staff are advised to refuse to accept such gifts or hospitality rather than declare them subsequently. There is usually some leeway for minor gifts (for example, pens or diaries) but the offer of higher value items should be questioned. The key point here is that governing body/board members and staff must be open about any gifts they have received or been offered. A good test is to think about how it would look on the front page of the local newspaper: if the action or gift could not be defended then it should not be carried out or accepted.

Standing financial instructions (SFIs)/prime financial policies (PFPs)

SFIs/PFPs cover financial aspects in more depth and set out detailed procedures and responsibilities. They are designed to ensure that NHS organisations account fully and openly for all that they do. Although FTs are not required to have SFIs/PFPs, many do and others have written financial procedures that fulfil the same function.

Other policies and procedures

For NHS bodies to run smoothly and effectively, many more policies and procedures (both financial and non-financial) are required, all of which contribute to the achievement of the organisation's overarching objectives. These policies and procedures cover a wide variety of areas and are usually pulled together in manuals and made available to all staff via the organisation's intranet. They should include a whistleblowing policy, to ensure that concerns raised by staff and other stakeholders about possible improprieties in financial, clinical or safety matters are taken seriously, without adverse consequences for the person raising that concern.

Control Frameworks

Internal control

Internal control comprises the systems and processes that an organisation has in place to give the governing body/board (and other stakeholders) reasonable assurance that things are running as they should and that the organisation is achieving its objectives and meeting its legal and other obligations. It includes the governance framework, risk management, information and communications, monitoring processes and assurance activities.

The governing body/board is responsible for ensuring that there is an effective system of internal control and that it:

- identifies and prioritises the risks to the achievement of the organisation's objectives
- evaluates the likelihood of those risks being realised and the consequent impact
- manages the risk efficiently, effectively and economically.

In practice, this means that at the core of an effective internal control system there needs to be a structured approach to identifying objectives, risks and problem areas. In the NHS this structure is provided by an 'assurance framework' underpinned by a risk management system.

Assurance framework

The HFMA's *NHS Audit Committee Handbook* describes the assurance framework as 'the key source of evidence that links the organisation's 'mission critical' strategic objectives to risks, controls and assurances, and is the main tool that the governing body uses in discharging its overall responsibility for internal control'.

Each organisation designs its own 'assurance framework' (sometimes referred to as a 'Board Assurance Framework' or BAF) based on a sound understanding of the strategic risks that could prevent the organisation achieving its agreed objectives and the potential effect each risk could have on those objectives.

However, there are a number of essential components identified in the Department of Health's 2003 publication *Building an Assurance framework: a Practical Guide* as set out below.

How to Build an Assurance Framework

1. Establish strategic objectives
2. Identify the principal (or strategic) risks that may threaten the achievement of these objectives
3. Identify and evaluate the design of key controls intended to manage these principal risks
4. Identify the arrangements for obtaining assurance on the effectiveness of these key controls
5. Evaluate the reliability of the assurances identified
6. Identify positive assurances and areas where there are gaps in controls and/or assurances
7. Put in place plans to take corrective action where gaps in controls and/or assurances have been identified in relation to principal (strategic) risks
8. Maintain dynamic risk management arrangements including, crucially, a well-founded risk register.

Risk management

For an organisation's assurance framework to be effective it must be underpinned by a robust approach to risk management. This involves identifying and managing risks, particularly those that present the biggest challenge in management terms.

The basics of risk management are straightforward – it is about being aware of potential problems, thinking through what effect they could have and planning ahead to prevent the worst-case scenario.

Internal audit

All NHS bodies are required to have an internal audit function that plays a key role in assurance by providing an independent and objective opinion to the Accountable/Accounting Officer, governing body/board and audit committee on the extent to which risk management, control and governance arrangements support the aims of the organisation. Each year the head of internal audit must produce an opinion that is used by the Accountable/Accounting Officer to inform the governance statement. This statement forms part of each organisation's annual accounts and draws together 'position statements and evidence on governance, risk management and control, to provide a more coherent and consistent reporting mechanism'. See chapter 11 for more details about this statement and the annual accounts.

Clinical audit

Another important element of the overall risk management and assurance framework is clinical audit – a process that is carried out by healthcare professionals themselves and involves:

- setting standards
- measuring current practice
- comparing results with standards
- changing the way things are done
- re-auditing to make sure practice has improved.

In its guide – *Best Practice in Clinical Audit* – the National Institute for Health and Care Excellence (NICE) states that it sees clinical audit as being 'the component of clinical governance that offers the greatest potential to assess the quality of care routinely provided for NHS users' and that it (clinical audit) 'should therefore be at the very heart of clinical governance systems'.

For NHS governing bodies/boards, managing clinical risk is just as important as managing financial and business risk. Good clinical audit is, therefore, an enormous asset and source of assurance. In addition, organisations are required to declare their participation in clinical audit in the annual quality accounts (see chapter 11).

Counter fraud and corruption

The emphasis on dealing with fraud and corruption in the NHS has increased significantly over recent years. Both are overseen by NHS Protect which is part of the NHS Business Services Authority. Its role is to lead on identifying and tackling crime across the NHS – for more details, see its website.

Key Learning Points

- The three fundamental principles of governance are openness, integrity and accountability
- An effective approach to governance should underpin everything that an organisation does
- Clinical scandals have shown clear links to governance failings – if an NHS organisation gets its approach to governance wrong it can have a catastrophic impact
- There are three key elements to governance – culture and values; structures and processes; control frameworks
- Good leadership and management are crucial to sound governance as is a shared ethos or culture and a 'tone' that is set from the top
- Everyone who works in the public sector should adhere to the seven principles of public life
- The principles and values set out in the NHS Constitution should underpin all that an organisation does
- Every NHS organisation must have a governing body/board, audit and remuneration committees, an Accountable/Accounting Officer and a chief finance officer
- CCGs and non-foundation NHS trusts must have an auditor panel
- The governing body/board (which includes both executive and non-executive members) is responsible for the strategies and actions of the organisation and is ultimately accountable to the public and Parliament
- One of the audit committee's key roles is to review the system of integrated governance, risk management and internal control across the whole of the organisation's activities
- The remuneration committee advises the governing body/board about pay, benefits and terms of employment of senior staff
- The Accountable/Accounting Officer is accountable to the organisation and (ultimately) to Parliament
- CFOs are automatically executive directors with a seat on the governing body/board
- Standing orders provide a framework for carrying out activities and translate statutory powers and duties into practical rules that all must abide by
- Organisations need an effective and comprehensive system of internal control that provides an assurance that things are running as they should
- All NHS organisations must have clear objectives and an understanding of the risks that could prevent their achievement, the possible impact and how they can be avoided
- An assurance framework links key objectives and risks with the main sources of assurance used by the governing body/board to ensure effective internal control
- Managing clinical risk is just as important as financial and business risk – clinical audit is therefore a key source of assurance in this area
- Counter fraud and security management are overseen by NHS Protect.

References and Further Reading

The Financial Aspects of Corporate Governance (the Cadbury Committee Report, 1992) available via: www.icaew.com/en/library/subject-gateways/corporate-governance/codes-and-reports/cadbury-report

The Mid Staffordshire NHS Foundation Trust Inquiry (the Francis Report): www.nhsemployers.org/your-workforce/need-to-know/the-francis-inquiry

Quality Governance in the NHS – A guide for provider boards, National Quality Board (Department of Health), 2011: www.gov.uk/government/publications/quality-governance-in-the-nhs-a-guide-for-provider-boards

Taking it on Trust – a review of how NHS trusts and foundation trusts get their assurance, Audit Commission, 2009

The Nolan Principles: www.gov.uk/government/publications/the-7-principles-of-public-life

Managing Public Money, HM Treasury: www.hm-treasury.gov.uk/psr_mpm_index.htm

Good Governance Standard for Public Services, The Independent Commission on Good Governance in Public Services, 2005: www.jrf.org.uk/publications/good-governance-standard-public-services

The NHS Constitution: www.gov.uk/government/publications/the-nhs-constitution-for-england

Freedom of Information Act, Bribery Act, Health and Social Care Act and other legislation referred to is available via: www.legislation.gov.uk/

The Code of Conduct: Code of Accountability in the NHS, Department of Health, 2004 (archived web pages): webarchive.nationalarchives.gov.uk/+/www.dh.gov.uk/en/Publicationsandstatistics/Publications/PublicationsPolicyAndGuidance/DH_4093864

Code of Conduct for NHS Managers, Department of Health (first published in 2002): www.nhsemployers.org/your-workforce/need-to-know/the-francis-inquiry/regulation-and-standards/core-standards-for-managers

Clinical Commissioning Group Governing Body Members: Role Outlines, Attributes and Skills, NHS England, 2012: www.england.nhs.uk/wp-content/uploads/2012/09/ccg-members-roles.pdf

Standards for Members of NHS Boards and Clinical Commissioning Group Governing Bodies in England, Professional Standards Authority, 2012 – available via: www.nhsemployers.org/your-workforce/need-to-know/the-francis-inquiry/regulation-and-standards/core-standards-for-managers

NHS Foundation Trust Code of Governance, Monitor, 2014: www.gov.uk/government/publications/nhs-foundation-trusts-code-of-governance

NHS Audit Committee Handbook, HFMA, 2014: available via the publications section of the HFMA website (enter 'audit committee handbook' in the search function): www.hfma.org.uk/publications

Auditor Panel Briefings, HFMA, 2015: available via the briefings section of the HFMA website (enter 'auditor panels' in the search function): www.hfma.org.uk/publications

Fit and Proper Persons Briefing, NHS Confederation, NHS Employers and NHS Providers, 2014: www.nhsconfed.org/resources/2014/12/fit-and-proper-person-test-briefing

Building an Assurance Framework: A Practical Guide, Department of Health, 2003 (archived web pages): webarchive.nationalarchives.gov.uk/+/www.dh.gov.uk/en/Publicationsandstatistics/Publications/PublicationsPolicyAndGuidance/DH_4093992

Principles for Best Practice in Clinical Audit – NICE, 2002.

Clinical audit: a Simple Guide for NHS Boards and Partners, HQIP, 2010:
http://www.good-governance.org.uk/wp-content/uploads/2014/02/clinical-audit-a-simple-guide-for-nhs-boards-and-partners.pdf

NHS Protect: www.nhsbsa.nhs.uk/Protect.aspx

Chapter 14
Revenue Planning and Budgeting

> NHS organisations are responsible for spending taxpayers' money to ensure that patients have access to high quality care, free at the point of delivery. As this is taxpayers' money there is an absolute requirement to demonstrate that the money is used well and for its intended purpose. Every NHS organisation also has a specific statutory duty to make 'proper arrangements for securing economy, efficiency and effectiveness in its use of resources'[1]. To be able to meet this requirement, each organisation needs to plan the activities it will deliver or commission and establish the associated resource implications – not just in terms of money but also in relation to staffing, equipment, supplies and so on.
>
> Planning and budgeting takes place in two areas – revenue and capital – that are then brought together in an overall plan. This chapter focuses on the revenue side – in other words, how NHS organisations plan and budget for their day-to-day activities. Capital planning is covered in chapter 15.

Why are Revenue Planning and Budgeting Important?

Revenue planning and budgeting are an integral part of an organisation's business planning process and helps it by establishing:

- an agreed way ahead
- key aims and objectives
- how those aims will be achieved and by when
- a framework for day-to-day operations and decisions
- a performance management and accountability framework.

What the Planning Process Involves – Key Documents

The planning process is designed to facilitate the efficient and effective delivery of high quality services, demonstrate accountability and ensure consistency with national policy and local plans, targets and outcomes frameworks. There are five key documents:

- a long term (5 year) **strategic plan** for the local health economy. This is known as the sustainability and transformation plan (STP)
- a long term (usually 3 to 5 years) strategic **business plan** for the organisation. This is sometimes referred to as the integrated business plan or IBP
- a **long term financial plan** that looks at best case and 'downside' scenarios
- an **annual operational plan** that outlines expected activities for the year ahead and shows how the organisation intends to meet its strategic aims. This forms the first year of the STP
- an **annual financial plan** that sets out the overall budget for the year. Alongside the financial plan, an annual activity plan is developed.

The annual financial plan is sometimes incorporated within the annual operational plan so that an organisation is able to refer to one integrated plan.

---

[1] Section 26 of the *NHS Act 2006*.

Sustainability and transformation plan (STP)

Introduced to the NHS for the first time for the year beginning 1 April 2016, the purpose of the STP is for 'every health and social care system to come together, to create its own ambitious local blueprint for accelerating its implementation of the Forward View'[2]. The emphasis is on developing a plan that meets the needs of local populations within a specific geographical area rather than focussing on individual organisations. The scope includes health, local government and voluntary organisations (where appropriate) within the locality or 'footprint'.

The STP is expected to address national and local priorities with an emphasis on creating a clear vision and plan for the local area in terms of reducing:

- the 'health and wellbeing gap' – this is concerned with reducing health inequalities and improving outcomes for patients
- the 'care and quality gap' – plans for new care model development, improving against clinical priorities and rollout of digital healthcare
- the 'finance and efficiency gap' – the local health economy must be financially sustainable; a balanced financial plan for the local health economy is a vital part of the STP.

Strategic business plan

Each individual NHS organisation also has its own long term strategic business plan. The business plan is the written end product of a process that identifies the aims, objectives and resource requirements of the organisation over a three to five year period. It is a detailed document that sets out the assumptions that underlie service plans and budgets for the period covered.

What a Business Plan Includes

An activity and income and expenditure plan

Details of planned service developments

Savings or cost improvement plans (CIPs)

Performance measures

Workforce implications

A strategy for the organisation's support services (for example, the estate and information technology)

An analysis of the needs and priorities of the wider health community and how and where the organisation fits in; it is particularly important that this is in line with the requirements set out in the STP.

The business plan is considered and approved by the organisation's governing body/board and then used as a benchmark against which to measure progress towards achieving the organisation's aims and objectives. In practice, this means that the business plan is kept under constant review and updated to reflect the impact of external changes (for example, Government announcements) and internal developments (for example, new clinical techniques).

Long term financial plan

Accompanying the business plan, a long term financial plan is used by NHS organisations to look at the financial impact of achieving their goals over the medium to long term (again over a

---

[2] *Five Year Forward View*, NHS England, October 2015.

three to five year period). This plan focuses on the assumptions made in the business plan and enables the organisation to see how potential changes (for example, in local demographics) could affect financial viability. The long term financial plan also includes an analysis of best case and 'downside' scenarios – enabling the organisation to anticipate what might happen if things don't go as planned and have in place strategies to mitigate the impact if they do.

Operational plan

Operational plans show how national targets (for example as set out in the *NHS Constitution*) and local priorities (for example, as set out in Joint Health and Wellbeing Strategies and Joint Strategic Needs Assessments developed by Health and Wellbeing Boards – see chapter 8) will be delivered within available resources. They are used by commissioners to outline how they intend to address health inequalities, improve health outcomes and better focus healthcare provision in line with commissioning intentions and strategies, national and local priorities. For providers, the focus of an operational plan is how they will deliver the contracts agreed with commissioners and meet their own objectives and priorities (for example, the need to achieve required cost improvements or carry out service re-design/integration).

Operational plans are reviewed regularly throughout the year and if significant issues arise that affect progress, adjustments are made – for example, if serious financial problems develop in the health economy.

Financial plan

Alongside the operational plan, all NHS organisations must produce an annual financial plan (usually referred to as the budget) that shows the expected income and expenditure of its planned activities for the coming year (both revenue and capital) and demonstrates that the organisation will achieve its financial duties. Chapter 11 looks in detail at these duties but in relation to the budget, the key statutory requirement for NHS providers and commissioners is that they must not spend more money than they have coming in – in other words, they must at least break even (achieve a 'balanced budget') or deliver a surplus. Although NHS foundation trusts do not have a specific statutory duty to break-even they must remain solvent if they are to continue as going concerns. In 2016/17, in addition to achieving their statutory duties, NHS provider organisations must meet a nationally established control total to ensure that the NHS as a whole achieves meets its departmental expenditure limit or DEL (see chapter 10 for more about DELs).

To assess the financial position accurately, the budget must cover all expected sources of income and expenditure across the full range of activities for which the organisation is responsible and take account of other non-financial information such as activity levels, savings schemes and staffing requirements. The budget is approved by the governing body/board in March and is then used to monitor progress and performance throughout the year so that an organisation knows how much income it is receiving, what it is spending and how much it is overspending or saving at any point in time.

For commissioners, the expenditure side of the budget is based on the activity levels that they have commissioned from providers to meet their commissioning intentions. For providers, the expenditure budget is based on the capacity and workforce they need to have available to meet these levels of activity – this will include the costs of running a service, department or organisation on a day-to-day basis (for example, to meet the costs of staff pay, travel expenses, overheads, drugs and other consumables). Providers will also have a budget for income – for example, split between income for patient care activity, teaching and education, and other areas such as research and development activity and commercial activities such as catering and the treatment of private patients.

The capital budget is based on plans for major spending on land, buildings, equipment and other durable items that are expected to be used for more than one year and have a value of £5,000 or more. This expenditure is subject to separate funding and regulations – see chapter 15 for details.

Budgeting in Practice

Approaches

Although organisations refer to their 'budget' (singular), it is actually made up of a series of separate budgets for each activity, service, department or practice. Each part of the organisation develops its own financial, workforce and activity plans to indicate how it will use its share of the money to meet needs and priorities within the overall strategy. There are three basic budgeting approaches – historic, zero-based and activity-based. The NHS tends to use a combination of all three.

Approaches to Budgeting

Historic or incremental budgeting – this uses the previous year's budget, adjusted for known savings (for example, as required in cost improvement programmes); cost rises (for example, pay awards and other inflationary factors) and developments (for example, if a new service is introduced or another discontinued or if National Institute for Health and Care Excellence (NICE) guidance changes). Allowance is also made for the financial consequences of any new policy developments.

Zero-based budgeting – this involves starting with a blank sheet of paper each year and results in a completely fresh financial plan. It tends to be used for the introduction of new services or when activities are under review.

Activity-based budgeting – this approach looks at what drives costs and is linked to activity levels. It requires those involved in setting the budget to know and understand the costs of delivering particular activities and services – for example, being clear about what costs are fixed and those that are variable (i.e. costs that will increase or decrease as activity increases or decreases – see chapter 17 for more on costing). The aim is to ensure that no matter what the actual level of activity, the correct resources are available to fund it.

Budget management

Another important feature of any budget in the NHS is that it is not the sole responsibility of the finance experts. Instead, it is essential to have a single named individual responsible for developing and managing each budget (the 'budget holder' or 'budget manager'). That person uses their knowledge and experience to help develop the budget and has the authority to take decisions relating to it. This means that responsibility for a budget must be aligned with the ability to control income and expenditure (i.e. the ability to take decisions that will incur a cost or result in a flow of income). To be effective a budget holder must understand what needs to be delivered and which organisational, local and national objectives they contribute to.

In practice, this means that each budget is managed at the lowest practicable level in the organisation by the person who understands the activity or service covered and who is responsible for committing the expenditure. This is what is known as 'devolved budget management'.

Budget monitoring

Once a budget is agreed, it is used by the budget holder to monitor how the budget is performing via regular (usually monthly) monitoring. In other words, actual performance is compared with what was planned so that when necessary, corrective action can be taken. For example, there may be an unexpected increase in the cost of equipment or a new initiative may fail to deliver the level of savings expected.

The Planning Process – Key External Constraints

Given that all NHS organisations are statutory bodies, they do not have a free hand when it comes to developing their plans. Instead they must follow national planning guidance, reflect national policy imperatives, meet targets and financial duties set by Government and reflect local priorities. The main factors that directly affect revenue planning are:

- the *NHS Constitution*
- the *NHS Outcomes Framework* ('the *Outcomes Framework*')
- annual planning guidance
- efficiency requirements
- quality, innovation, productivity and prevention (QIPP) plans
- allocations – the money received from the Treasury via the Department of Health or NHS England
- the *National Tariff Document*
- National Institute for Health and Care Excellence (NICE) guidelines.

The NHS Constitution and the Outcomes Framework

The *NHS Constitution* and the *Outcomes Framework* are key documents for all NHS organisations as they set out overall objectives and responsibilities that apply across the board. Whilst the Constitution's focus is on overarching rights, values and principles (see chapter 12), it also sets out a series of specific pledges – for example, in relation to referral to treatment times, A & E waits, cancelled operations and ambulance response times. The *Outcomes Framework* has a more direct impact on day-to-day planning as it sets out what NHS organisations are expected to achieve in terms of healthcare outcomes for patients across five broad domains. For each domain a number of areas for improvement are identified but there are no set targets associated with them.

Outcomes Framework – the Five Domains

1. Preventing people from dying prematurely
2. Enhancing quality of life for people with long term conditions
3. Helping people to recover from episodes of ill-health or following injury
4. Ensuring people have a positive experience of care
5. Treating and caring for people in a safe environment and protecting them from avoidable harm.

Annual planning guidance

As well as the overarching *Outcomes Framework*, annual planning guidance is issued. The guidance for 2016/17 (including a timetable for the development of NHS organisations' plans) was issued jointly by NHS England, NHS Improvement, the Care Quality Commission, Health Education England, the National Institute of Health and Care Excellence and Public Health England. The guidance sets out the national priorities for 2016/17 and longer-term challenges for local systems, together with key financial assumptions and the business rules underpinning reimbursement.

As noted earlier, all organisations are required to construct two separate but linked plans:

1. A sustainability and transformation plan (STP) – a five-year plan from October 2016 to March 2021 for the local health and care system. This is a placed-based plan for the local population and must reflect local health and wellbeing strategies
2. An operational plan for 2016/17 – this is organisation specific and forms the first year of the STP.

These two plans must be submitted to NHS England (for clinical commissioning groups or CCGs) or NHS Improvement (for providers).

Efficiency requirements

The NHS budget is now growing at a much slower rate than over recent years but demand for its services continues to rise. This means that all NHS organisations must deliver year on year real cost savings (or 'on-going 'efficiencies' every year) and reflect this in their annual plans. In recent years the NHS has been set an efficiency target of 4% however, for 2016/17 it is 2% in recognition that the NHS cannot continue to deliver this level of efficiency and sustain a comprehensive level of high quality services.

At a more detailed level, if the cost of an organisation's plans to purchase and/or deliver services exceeds its anticipated levels of income, further savings must be included within the budget to bring it back in line with the available resources.

QIPP plans

To help achieve efficiency targets whilst maintaining and improving quality, the Department of Health introduced the 'quality, innovation, productivity and prevention (QIPP) challenge'. In practice, this means organisations follow the 'lean management principles' of avoiding duplication, preventing errors that need to be corrected, and stopping ineffective practices. International evidence has shown that it is possible to improve the quality of care and patient experience while reducing costs. CCGs are responsible for leading the QIPP agenda but all NHS organisations have a role to play in its delivery.

Allocations

As mentioned earlier in this chapter, all non-foundation NHS organisations must achieve a balanced budget each year (and FTs must remain solvent) and so the income level they receive is of critical importance. For commissioners the key factor is the funding allocation they receive from NHS England and for providers, the income secured through contracts with commissioners. For more about the allocation process and how services are funded, see chapter 10.

The national tariff

Another set of guidelines that both commissioners and providers must take account of when preparing their plans relate to the national tariff – the NHS payment mechanism. Under the national tariff, commissioners pay providers for each patient seen or treated. Some healthcare activities have a nationally set price (or tariff) that takes account of the relative complexity of the patient's healthcare needs.

The volume of activity with a nationally set price amounts to around a third of CCG budgets overall. However, for some acute hospitals, it can drive a significant proportion of income. This activity is difficult to plan for as prices can vary between years as a result of three key factors:

- the different levels of efficiency savings included within the national tariff (each year the guidance specifies the percentage savings that are built in)
- an adjustment for cost increases
- the use of a more recent set of costs – in the summer of each year, all providers of services to NHS patients funded with NHS money must submit details of activity levels, unit cost data and average lengths of stay for a range of specified activities; this is known as the reference cost submission (see chapter 17 for more details).

A change in nationally set prices between years can also reflect changes in casemix, activity levels, improvements in costing practice and clinical practice. In addition, changes in the underlying business rules and the introduction of specific measures to influence the behaviour of NHS organisations can mean that providers are paid significantly more or less than they were for the same activity in the previous year.

As part of the planning process, organisations must also take into account the 'market forces factor' (MFF) which is paid in addition to the national tariff to reflect unavoidable cost differences between organisations (for example, staff costs are higher in London than elsewhere in the country). The MFF is set annually for each service provider and ranges from 1.00 to nearly 1.30, meaning that the organisation with the highest MFF receives a top-up to the national prices of nearly 30% for all relevant activity to reflect its higher unavoidable costs.

See chapter 18 for more about the national tariff.

NICE guidelines

NICE provides national guidance and advice that is designed to improve the quality of health and social care. Of particular importance in planning terms are its quality standards – these are developed by NICE in collaboration with relevant professions using a variety of evidence sources.

The standards are reflected in the *Clinical Commissioning Group Outcome Indicator Set* that is designed to help CCGs by providing them with comparative information about the quality of health services commissioned and health outcomes achieved.

The quality standards are also used to inform payment mechanisms and incentive schemes such as the Quality and Outcomes Framework (QOF) – see chapter 6 for more details.

The Planning Process – Other Influences

As well as reflecting national guidelines in its annual financial and operational plans, an organisation must allow for a range of other factors including, for example:

- service developments (as outlined in its business plan)
- nationally agreed changes to pay and agreed increments for staff
- the impact of changes in clinical practice
- changes in drugs or medical devices used (NICE guidelines are relevant here)
- income streams that are no longer available or received
- changes in national and/or local priorities.

Key Learning Points

- The planning process is designed to ensure efficient and effective delivery of services, demonstrate public accountability and ensure consistency with national and local plans and targets
- The sustainability and transformation plan (STP) is designed to meet the needs of the health and social care system in a geographical area
- The business plan sets out the assumptions that underlie service plans and budgets
- The operational plan shows how national targets and local priorities will be delivered within the resources available and forms the first year of the STP

- The financial plan or budget shows organisations' expected income and spending levels for the year ahead and demonstrates how their financial duties will be met
- Although organisations refer to **the** budget, it is made up of a series of separate budgets for individual activities or services
- There are three main budgeting approaches (historic, zero-based and activity-based), all of which are used in the NHS
- Budgets are managed by budget holders who monitor actual performance during the year and take corrective action when needed
- When NHS organisations develop their plans, they must take into consideration both external and internal requirements. Of particular importance are the *NHS Constitution*, the *NHS Outcomes Framework* and the annual planning guidance.

References and Further Reading

Five Year Forward View, NHS England, 2014:
https://www.england.nhs.uk/wp-content/uploads/2014/10/5yfv-web.pdf

The NHS Constitution for England, Department of Health, 2015:
www.gov.uk/government/publications/the-nhs-constitution-for-england

The NHS Outcomes Framework, NHS England:
www.england.nhs.uk/resources/resources-for-ccgs/out-frwrk/

Delivering the Forward View: NHS Shared Planning Guidance 2016/17 – 2020/21
NHS England, 2015:
www.gov.uk/guidance/delivering-the-forward-view-nhs-planning-guidance-for-201617-to-202021#nhs-shared-planning-guidance

For more about NICE and its guidelines: www.nice.org.uk/

Clinical Commissioning Group Outcome Indicator Set, HSCIC, 2015:
www.hscic.gov.uk/catalogue/PUB19278

Chapter 15
Capital Funding, Planning and Accounting

> This chapter looks at what capital is and how it is controlled and funded in the NHS. It also runs through the various sources of capital funding and explains how to account for non-current assets and changes in their values.

What is Capital in the NHS?

Expenditure is classified as either revenue (spending on day-to-day operations) or capital (also referred to as 'non-current assets'). Capital spending is incurred when an asset intended for use on a long term basis is acquired – this is also described as capital investment. Specifically, non-current assets are defined as:

- being held for delivering services or for administrative purposes
- having a useful life greater than one year
- having a cost which can be measured reliably
- generating future economic benefits or service potential for the organisation.

Non-current assets can be both tangible (things that physically exist) and intangible (assets that do not exist as physical entities) – examples are shown below:

Asset Examples

Tangible assets	Intangible assets
Land	Software licences
Buildings	Development costs for software and systems
Dwellings	Licences and trademarks
Assets in the course of construction	Patents
Plant and machinery	Other development costs which may result in an asset
Transport equipment	
Information technology (including integral software)	
Fixtures and fittings	

Asset Registers

Every NHS organisation maintains a register of its non-current assets (tangible and intangible) so that they can be managed effectively and to demonstrate accountability. The register records a range of information about each asset and is used to help in the preparation of the organisation's financial accounts.

Asset Registers – what is Recorded for each Asset

Identification, description and location

Date, method of acquisition and initial capital outlay

How the asset has been financed (for example, is it owned, leased or covered by a PFI agreement?)

Opening balance on the 1st April

Any additions to the asset

The value if reclassified for sale

Gains from revaluation (so that there is a clear link to the revaluation reserve – see later in this chapter)

Impairments (i.e. a loss in value – see later in this chapter) including any reversals

Cumulative depreciation charges and estimated life

Closing balance at 31st March

Theoretically, each non-current asset should be recorded in the asset register. However, to include all very low value items would be a costly administrative burden. As a result, NHS organisations use a minimum level of expenditure or 'threshold' below which property, plant or equipment is not considered to be a non-current asset. Items that fall below this threshold are charged as a revenue cost in the year of purchase and are not recorded in the asset register. The threshold (or 'de minimis level') generally used is £5,000[1] (this is the figure set in the Department of Health's Manual for Accounts) although some NHS foundation trusts (FTs) use a higher figure which they have agreed with their external auditors.

Where assets are interdependent (they only work together) then the de minimis level applies to the cost of the group of assets[2]. An example of grouped assets is IT hardware attached to a network. Groups of similar assets (for example, hospital beds) cannot be grouped together or classed as interdependent as each can be used independently.

The Capital Regime – Allocations, Limits and Controls

Allocations

As part of the Spending Review in November 2015, the NHS in England has been allocated £4.8bn per annum for capital spending for the next four years. This allocation covers capital spending by all NHS providers and commissioners.

As statutory bodies, all NHS organisations must work within a statutory and regulatory framework to ensure that this allocation is spent appropriately. Overall responsibility for ensuring that this is the case and that the allocation is not overspent rests with the Department of Health.

The vast majority of capital expenditure is incurred by the provider sector. Providers' spending is controlled by the use of restrictions on the amount of finance that they can access. These controls are explained below.

Some clinical commissioning groups (CCGs) are given a capital allocation each year which is based on their 'capital resource limit' (CRL) as set by NHS England. These allocations also

---

[1] The £5,000 'threshold' includes VAT where this is not recoverable, installation costs and external fees such as architect, surveyor or installation fees.
[2] This may be different for the devolved nations. For example, in Scotland, in addition to the individual asset value of £5,000, the group value must be more than £20,000.

come out of the overall NHS capital allocation (i.e. from the annual £4.8bn total over the next four years).

CCG CRLs are used to control their spending (see below for details). However, very few CCGs incur significant levels of capital spending as the assets that they use are generally owned and managed by NHS Property Services Ltd. Similarly, leases of properties developed under NHS LIFT arrangements are held and managed by Community Health Partnerships Ltd (see later in this chapter). CCGs can generate their own funds internally to spend on capital investments but, in practice, this is rare.

Capital resource limit

Non-foundation trusts and CCGs are given a 'capital resource limit' (CRL) each year. For CCGs, remaining within this limit is a statutory duty – they should not exceed it and it is monitored throughout the year. The Department of Health (rather than statute) requires non-foundation trusts to remain within their CRL.

Performance against the CRL must be reported in the annual report and accounts. The organisation should not spend more than its CRL after adjusting for asset disposals and grants and/or donations towards the purchase of non-current assets. Underspends against the CRL cannot be carried forward to the following financial year unless they are known in advance and built into submitted plans.

For CCGs, the CRL represents the amount of finance given to them for capital expenditure. For non-foundation trusts, the CRL does not represent the amount of finance given to the trust which is why trusts have other controls to meet.

FTs do not have a CRL.

External financing limit

Non-foundation trusts are also required to remain within their 'external financing limit' (EFL). This was established to control the amount of cash that could be spent on capital in a year. However, since 2008/09, it has been set to include all sources of capital finance, including from:

- the Department of Health (i.e. public dividend capital (PDC)[3] and loans)
- internal generation
- external sources (including finance leases).

This means that the EFL is a 'financing limit' – i.e. the maximum amount of cash that can be accessed through external borrowing. Achievement of the EFL is an absolute financial duty. There is no tolerance above the EFL target as it is designed to control the cash expenditure of the NHS as a whole to the level agreed by Parliament. By controlling net cash flows, the EFL sets a limit on the level of cash that an NHS trust may:

- draw from either external sources or its own cash reserves (a positive EFL) or
- repay to external sources for capital borrowing (a negative EFL).

Commissioners and FTs do not have an EFL.

Capital to revenue transfers

The Department of Health is responsible for ensuring that the NHS does not spend more than the amount allocated to it on capital. The Department also manages the revenue allocation – see chapter 10 for more details.

If the Department expects that the NHS will underspend on its capital allocation but is in danger of overspending against the revenue allocation it can apply to HM Treasury to transfer

---

[3] PDC is a type of government finance – it is discussed later in the chapter.

some of the allocation from capital to revenue. This means that the NHS can spend more on day to day expenditure but less than planned on longer term investment in assets.

FTs and non-foundation trusts can apply for capital to revenue transfers from the Department. In summary, the transfer means that the provider body repays some of their PDC in cash to the Department and then receives additional income for the healthcare services they have provided. The repayment of public dividend means that the provider bodies cannot access as much finance as they would otherwise be able to access and therefore can incur less capital expenditure.

Risk Assessment Framework – capital service capacity metric

FTs do not have either an EFL or CRL but their capital expenditure counts towards the overall NHS capital allocation. Control over FTs' capital expenditure is via Monitor's *Risk Assessment Framework* (see chapter 12). This framework includes a capital service capacity metric as part of the financial sustainability risk rating. This looks at the amount that the FT has to pay in relation to its borrowing (both in terms of interest and principal repayments) relative to its revenue to assess the financial risk to the FT.

Planning the Capital Programme

There is an absolute requirement when spending public money to demonstrate that it has been used wisely and for its intended purpose. As a result, NHS organisations need to plan, monitor and manage their capital investments.

Affordability

The overriding constraint when planning for capital is that organisations must not spend more than they have available and can afford, both in relation to the initial cost of the non-current assets and the associated on-going revenue costs. This means thinking through a number of factors including:

- the need for new infrastructure and strategic developments
- the need to replace medical, IT and other equipment
- maintenance costs
- depreciation costs – non-current assets wear out and over their 'useful life' an annual (non-cash) charge is made to the revenue account to reflect this (see later for more about depreciation)
- impact on PDC dividend – this is a cash charge paid to the Department of Health which is based on the average net assets of the organisation. An increase in non-current assets results in an increase in the dividend charged (see later in this chapter for more about PDC).

Business cases

Most NHS organisations will have a rolling programme of capital investment to ensure that its asset base is fit for purpose. When additional capital investment is needed, the first stage is usually to develop a business case to consider the options available, their impact and affordability. In the context of capital spending, a business case is usually a written statement of the need for investment in capital. The business case process is designed to lead to a consideration of changing circumstances, future requirements and opportunities and an agreed corporate view of the best way forward backed up by sound and reasoned assumptions and projections. It is helpful to use a standard format so that key issues are covered.

Capital Funding, Planning and Accounting

What a Business Case Includes

The strategic 'fit' of the proposed investment within the local health economy, including a clear and concise statement of need.

Effective project management arrangements, clear lines of communication and details of those key individuals who will be personally accountable.

An indication that the proposal has the support and approval of key stakeholders including commissioners, staff and patients.

Quantified analyses of the investment and its lifetime costs, benefits and cash flows.

Quantified analyses of the costs/benefits of any alternative methods of financing the investment.

Evidence-based information to support the proposal in terms of priority, cost-effectiveness, clinical service management and the best use of scarce resources.

If a major investment is being considered, the business case should also bring together the arguments for the preferred option (including current and future service requirements), affordability, the organisation's competitive service position and the ability to complete the project within the specified budget and in line with agreed timescales.

Delegated limits

Business cases for non-foundation trusts are currently subject to a system of 'delegated limits'. This means that the capital value of a project determines what approvals are required. Non-foundation trusts have a delegated limit for all business cases that is currently £5m or 3% of turnover, whichever is lower (turnover is measured using the trust's previous year's financial accounts turnover figure). This means that projects with a capital value of less than £5m (or 3% of turnover) require only the approval of the trust's own board. Above this level, external approval is required as shown below.

Delegated Limits for Non-foundation NHS trusts

Financial value of the capital investment	Approving person or group
Between £5m or 3% of turnover whichever is lower, and £15m	NHS Trust Development Authority (NHS TDA)[4] Director of Finance
£15m to £35m	NHS TDA Investment Committee
£35m to £50m	NHS TDA Investment Committee AND NHS TDA Board
Over £50m	NHS TDA Investment Committee AND NHS TDA Board AND the Department of Health AND the Treasury

Source: *Capital Regime and Investment Business Case Approvals, Guidance for NHS Trusts*, NHS TDA, 2015.

---

[4] The NHS TDA and Monitor now operate as part of NHS Improvement. However, they both remain separate statutory bodies (or 'legal entities') and so continue to have their own boards. Since 1st April 2016, the NHS TDA and Monitor boards have had identical membership and meet as one board. See chapter 9 for more details.

CCGs are unable to approve their own business cases.

FTs are not subject to strict limits. However, significant transactions are reported to Monitor[4] and some will require its approval. Whether a project or transaction is significant depends on the associated risks.

Any provider body that is in receipt of 'distressed funding' (cash support) may have additional restrictions placed on them over their capital spend approvals. This may, for example, require approval by NHS Improvement for any 'discretionary' capital spend above £250k, and trusts would be required to commit only to essential capital projects.

Sources of Capital

The potential sources of funding for capital investments vary by type of NHS organisation.

As mentioned earlier, it is unlikely that CCGs will have significant levels of non-current assets as the only source of funding available to them is internally generated funds or any capital allocation given to them by NHS England.

The situation is much clearer for non-foundation trusts and FTs – they have access to a number of well-established funding sources:

- internally generated resources (via retained surpluses, depreciation and proceeds from the sale of non-current assets)
- borrowing (including PDC)
- public private partnerships
- leases
- donations and grants.

Internally generated resources

The main source of capital funding is from internally generated resources. In other words, retained surpluses, depreciation and proceeds from the sale of non-current assets.

As we mentioned earlier, all NHS bodies must make a charge to the expenditure side of their revenue account to reflect the cost of using an asset over its useful life – this is known as depreciation. This charge does not involve actual cash being paid out (it is 'non-cash') and so an organisation that breaks even or achieves a surplus on its revenue account will generate a cash surplus equivalent to the value of the depreciation charge (all other things being equal). The cash 'generated' and/or any surplus is available to invest in capital projects, such as replacing equipment, enhancing existing assets or building new ones subject to the organisation meeting the capital controls set out earlier in the chapter. It can also be used for revenue purposes – maintenance or sustaining the 'working capital[5]' position.

Another source of finance is the sale of existing assets. While an FT is able to retain the total proceeds from the sale of an asset, the amount of money that a non-foundation trust can retain is capped and is also reflected in its CRL.

Borrowing

The way in which money can be borrowed depends on the type of organisation considering the loan.

Under the *National Health Service Act 2006*[6], the Department of Health is required to produce guidance in relation to the powers that it has to provide financial assistance to FTs. The

---

[5] Working capital is the money and assets that an organisation can call upon to finance its day-to-day operations (it is the difference between current assets and liabilities and is reported in the statement of financial position as net current assets/liabilities). If working capital dips too low, organisations risk running out of cash and may need a loan to smooth out cash flows.

[6] Section 42A of the *NHS Act 2006* which was inserted by section 163 of the *Health and Social Care Act 2012*.

guidance that the Department of Health issued, in October 2014[7], is also applicable to non-foundation trusts. In this context, financial assistance includes the provision of loans, issue of PDC, giving of grants and other payments.

To support an investment, non-foundation trusts may borrow from the Department of Health in the form of a capital investment loan (normally interest bearing) which must be linked to specific capital expenditure and local priorities. The loan and its repayments must be affordable and within both the trust's EFL and CRL as noted above. However, it is not generally possible to access the funds until the need arises for the cash – i.e. when the supplier has to be paid for the equipment or the contractor for building works. If the loan is not received in a timely manner, the trust's EFL may be breached – this is a particular risk at year end.

Exceptionally, loans may be approved even if they are not supported by a trust's EFL – for example, where the capital investment itself will lead to future income streams that will enable repayment of the loan.

FTs have greater borrowing freedoms available to them. They can borrow from the Department of Health as set out in the guidance referred to above. They are also able to borrow from the open market, including commercial loans from banks and other private lending organisations as long as they can demonstrate the affordability of the loan.

In reality most NHS bodies now borrow from the Department of Health. Access to these loans is through the Independent Trust Financing Facility (ITFF) which was set up to provide independent professional advice to the Secretary of State in respect of decisions to provide financial assistance to NHS bodies.

The key underlying principle for all organisations is that total borrowing must be affordable.

Borrowing, in the context of borrowing limits monitored by the Department of Health, has a wide definition and includes all loans (whatever their source) as well as finance leases including private finance initiative (PFI) schemes (see later in this chapter).

Public dividend capital (PDC)

Before the introduction of loan funding for capital investment, NHS trusts received capital funding allocations. These took the form of public dividend capital (PDC) – a type of long-term government finance. Although new PDC has in effect been replaced with loan funding it is possible that it can be issued to non-foundation trusts and FTs on either an interest or non-interest bearing basis. In some cases, new PDC is issued to assist an NHS body in financial difficulties and in others it is used to allow access to Department of Health capital budgets for specific initiatives (for example, in relation to carbon efficiency).

Where PDC funding has been agreed with the Department of Health for a capital project, then a 'PDC limit' is set (by the Department). This is similar to a cash based capital resource limit. Non-foundation trusts and FTs can only access PDC once all internally generated funds have been used and once the cash is required to pay for the capital project. In other words, cash backed PDC cannot be accessed ('drawn down') in advance of need.

It is worth noting that if an asset is transferred between two NHS trusts, a 'circular flow of funds' is required whereby the asset is paid for with PDC; PDC equivalent to the value of the asset is then removed from the 'seller'. This flow of funds does not involve the transfer of cash between any of the bodies involved.

Public private partnerships

Although there has been a fall in the use of public private partnerships since 2009/10, they remain an option for delivering capital investment schemes. Appropriate business case approvals are required in the same way as for any other investment. The main routes are discussed below.

---

[7] Secretary of State's Guidance under section 42A of the NHS Act 2006.

Private finance initiative (PFI)

Traditional (PFI) schemes were used for a number of years and involved the creation of partnerships between the public and private sectors, allowing the NHS to raise funds for capital projects from commercial organisations. The financing of the construction of the asset was the responsibility of the PFI provider and the idea was that capital investment was funded without recourse to public money. Private companies were contracted to design and build the assets which were then 'leased back' to the public sector, usually over a period of around 30 years. The contract set out in detail the obligations of each party over the agreed period. The contract usually contained a service element relating to the building – for example, cleaning, catering, security and maintenance.

Private finance 2

Following a review of public private partnerships by the Treasury in 2012, a new approach to private sector involvement in public sector infrastructure projects has been developed and has replaced traditional PFI schemes. Under this approach, the Government acts as a minority equity co-investor with investments managed by a commercially focused central unit located within HM Treasury. Recognising the importance of greater transparency, information is published in relation to the progress of individual projects.

Local improvement finance trusts (LIFTs)

Local improvement finance trusts (LIFTs) have been used to develop and improve primary care and community-based facilities. Delivered by Community Health Partnerships (CHP – a limited company wholly owned by the Department of Health) on behalf of the Department, a partnership is established with the local health economy through a LIFT company. This is a limited company with the NHS, CHP and the private sector partner as shareholders. The company owns and maintains the building and leases the premises back to the NHS.

There are a small number of LIFT schemes where a non-foundation trust or FT is the lead lessor and their interests are not held by CHP.

Leases

A lease is often considered a suitable alternative to the outright purchase of a non-current asset.

A lease is defined as an arrangement between two parties (the 'lessor' and the 'lessee') 'whereby the lessor conveys to the lessee in return for a payment or series of payments the right to use an asset for an agreed period of time'.

Currently, there are two types of lease:

- the lessor transfers to the lessee substantially all the economic benefits and risks of asset ownership. This is referred to as a finance lease
- any lease which is not a finance lease is an operating lease. These are likely to relate to smaller assets and equipment such as cars and photocopiers or parts of larger assets such as a floor of an office block or arrangements which are for significantly less than the expected life of the asset.

The type of lease depends on who bears the risks or benefits from the rewards of using the asset and is assessed using a series of tests set out in international accounting standard 17 (IAS 17). Land is not normally treated as a finance lease unless it is expected that the title will pass to the lessee at the end of the lease or the lease is very long term (999 years).

A new accounting standard, IFRS 16, was issued in January 2016. It is expected to be effective from 1 January 2019[8]. Under this new standard, lessees will account for all leases on the same

---

[8] The effective date of the new standard is dependent on EU adoption of the standard and the Treasury incorporating it into the Financial Reporting Manual (FReM). See chapter 11 for more information on financial reporting.

basis[9] removing the distinction between operating and finance leases. Lessors will continue to distinguish between operating and finance leases.

Donations and grants

Charitable donations can be an important source of funds to support capital investment but the trustees (usually the NHS corporate body) must ensure that the expenditure is in line with the charitable fund's purpose as set out in its governing documents.

Some NHS bodies also receive grants from bodies such as the Lottery Fund to finance the purchase of non-current assets.

Charitable donations and grants are recognised as income by the NHS body in the year that any conditions attached to the donation are met. When a donation or grant is used to buy a non-current asset this means that the income is recognised in the year that the asset is purchased. However, the cost of the asset is spread over the life of that asset in the form of depreciation charges which results in a timing difference between the recognition of the income and expenditure. This timing difference is adjusted for when determining whether or not the NHS body has met its financial duties.

For more about NHS charitable funds, see chapter 19.

The Cost of Capital

In terms of the cost of capital, there are three elements – PDC; depreciation and interest. Each is discussed in turn below.

PDC dividend

The PDC dividend is derived by applying a percentage 'rate of return' to an organisation's 'average relevant net assets', calculated as follows:

Average Relevant Net Assets Calculation

The average of the organisation's relevant net assets (i.e. the opening balance at 1st April added to the closing balance at 31st March divided by 2):

Total public dividend capital and reserves

Less   the net book value of donated assets and lottery-funded assets held

Plus   the value of any deferred income balance that funds a donated asset or lottery-funded asset

Less   charitable funds

Less   net cash held in Government Banking Service accounts[10]

Less/plus PDC dividend receivable/payable.

The percentage used is 3.5% for non-foundation trusts and FTs and is payable in two instalments during the year.

Depreciation

Depreciation is calculated annually to reflect the cost of 'using up' the asset during its useful life – a number of assumptions are used:

---

[9] Leases with a term of less than 12 months and leases for low value assets can be accounted for differently.
[10] The Government Banking Service is the banking shared service provider to Government and the wider public sector. It is responsible for holding the working balances of Government departments and other public bodies in high-level accounts at the Bank of England. The balance included in this calculation is the average daily cleared balance rather than the average between the opening and closing balance for the financial year.

> **Depreciation – Assumptions Used**
>
> Land is considered to have an infinite life and is not depreciated
>
> Buildings, installations and fittings are depreciated over their assessed useful lives, with both the value and life expectancy determined periodically by a qualified valuer
>
> Assets in the course of construction are not depreciated until they are brought into use
>
> Equipment is depreciated over its useful economic life
>
> Leased assets classified as capital are depreciated over the shorter of the lease term remaining or the asset's remaining economic life.

Depreciation is usually calculated on a 'straight line basis' which means it is assumed that the asset will be 'used up' evenly over its life. As depreciation is calculated on asset values which are subject to revaluation, the depreciation charge and total value of the assets held will vary each year.

Interest

All NHS organisations must pay interest on capital investment loans taken out from the Department of Health in addition to the repayment of the loan amount itself. Linked to the National Loans Fund rate, interest payments are largely fixed over the duration of the loan unless the loan is re-financed during that period.

FTs must also pay interest charges on any borrowing including commercial loans which attract a market rate.

For all NHS organisations, interest is also payable on the balance of outstanding finance leases.

Accounting for Capital

Accounting for capital can be complicated and is often an area of the accounts subject to audit scrutiny. This is because, by its very nature, the amounts involved are usually 'material'[11] but also because there is a level of judgement and estimation required to reach a true and fair view.

Accounting standards

The Treasury has developed a *Financial Reporting Manual* that sets out how accounting standards should be implemented in the public sector. The Department of Health, NHS England and NHS Improvement also produce manuals and guidance for NHS bodies. The following accounting standards are of particular relevance when accounting for capital:

- IAS 16 *Property, Plant and Equipment*
- IAS 17 *Leases* (to be replaced by IFRS 16 from 2019/20)
- IAS 20 *Accounting for Government Grants and Disclosure of Government Assistance*
- IFRS 5 *Non-current Assets Held for Sale*
- IAS 36 *Impairment of Assets*
- IAS 38 *Intangible Assets*

---

[11] Materiality is an accounting concept that allows the preparers and auditors of accounts to make a judgement about whether an item or transaction will influence the reader/user of the accounts. If it is decided that it would influence the reader/user of the accounts then the item is material and should be included and explained in the accounts. Immaterial items do not need to be explained.

- IAS 40 *Investment Property*
- IFRIC 4 *Determining whether an arrangement contains a lease* (to be replaced by IFRS 16 from 2019/20)
- IFRIC 12 *Service Concession Arrangements*
- IFRS 16 *Leases* (this standard will replace IAS 17 and IFRIC 4 from 2019/20).

Valuation

One of the reasons that accounting for capital can be complicated is that, in the public sector, non-current assets are not recorded in the accounts at the amount that they cost to buy. Instead, they are held at 'fair value'. In accounting terms, fair value has a specific meaning but it is essentially the amount that the asset could be bought for on the open market.

On acquisition, non-current assets are recorded at the cost but they are subsequently revalued to their fair value. The timing of that revaluation is dependent on a number of factors which are discussed below.

For NHS organisations, identifying the fair value for non-current assets is difficult as they are held to provide services and there is a limited open market for NHS assets. Specialised property such as hospitals for which a market value cannot be determined easily, is valued at the cost of replacing it with an equivalent, modern one, not an exact replica of what currently exists. This is the 'depreciated replacement cost' approach, also known as the 'modern equivalent asset basis'. Determining the modern equivalent asset valuation for a hospital can only be done by a professional valuer[12] and will be carried out in conjunction with the NHS body's finance and estates teams.

Assets which are not specialised, such as offices and some clinics, are valued based on what they could be sold for.

The timing of the valuation is a matter of judgment. Under IAS 16, organisations must consider whether the recorded value of their assets continues to reflect fair value taking into account market volatility. For example, if the local property market is particularly volatile or the organisation embarks upon a significant capital expenditure project, annual revaluations may be needed to keep the recorded value up to date. When an individual asset (for example, a piece of medical equipment) is revalued, all assets of its type must also be revalued. In the absence of a significant change, revaluation may be needed less frequently.

Each year, an assessment must be made of whether the valuations are materially correct or not. This will involve consideration of the volatility of the property market and usually requires discussion with a professional valuer. In years where a professional valuation has not been undertaken, the value given to land and buildings will need to be reviewed and any changes appropriately evidenced to support the preparation of the accounts. Valuation is also required when:

- organisations merge
- there is a major change in use
- an asset formerly under construction is brought into use.

Most intangible assets (i.e. assets that have a financial value even though they are not visible – for example, goodwill) are recorded at cost less 'amortisation' (equivalent to depreciation but for intangible assets) as a proxy for fair value. However, where a market value is readily available then this should be used.

---

[12] This is someone with a qualification from the Royal Institution of Chartered Surveyors (RICS).

Gains

Gains (or increases) in asset value may occur following a revaluation by an external reviewer or, for equipment assets, by a review undertaken by the finance and/or estates departments to provide a new fair value.

The gain is not treated in the same way as revenue or income. Instead, it is reflected in the revaluation reserve.

Losses (including impairments)

Impairments occur where there is a loss (or reduction) in the value of a non-current asset compared to its recorded value. This can be due to:

- a loss of economic benefit to an asset itself – for example, it is physically damaged
- the asset becoming surplus to requirements
- a change in the asset or its environment which has permanently reduced its capacity to provide services.

IAS 36 is relevant here. However, HM Treasury guidance diverges from IAS 36 and requires organisations to identify the cause of impairment as the result of either:

- the consumption of economic benefits or service potential or
- a loss following revaluation.

In the first scenario, the resulting loss is charged to operating expenses in the year that the impairment occurs.

However, where there has been a previous upward revaluation for the asset and a revaluation reserve balance exists, a transfer is made from the revaluation reserve to the general fund/retained earnings.

In the second scenario, a revaluation loss, the reduction should initially be charged to the revaluation reserve to the extent that a balance exists for the asset. Any remaining amount is charged to operating expenses.

If impaired assets then have an upward valuation, the charge made to expenditure can be reversed to the extent that the upward revaluation reverses the original impairment. It is therefore important to record all impairment charges by individual asset to enable entries to be reversed if needed.

Asset sale or disposal

When assets are sold or scrapped, the difference between the value at which they are held and the amount of income received is the profit or loss on disposal. In the case of assets which are scrapped the income will be nil so there is likely to be a loss on disposal.

Profits on sale are reflected in other operating income. Losses are an operating expense in the year of disposal.

Leases

As mentioned earlier, currently there are two types of lease and they are accounted for differently by the lessee (this is the entity which is using the asset).

When a finance lease is entered into, the asset is recorded in the asset register with a corresponding, matching lease liability. The asset is treated as if it had been bought outright as soon as it becomes operational. It forms part of average relevant net assets for PDC dividend calculations, is subject to depreciation and is revalued in the same way as any owned asset. The lease liability is written down as the capital element is repaid. The interest payments on the lease are treated as an expense each year.

For operating leases, the rental payments are treated as operating expenditure.

When the new lease accounting standard is introduced all leases will be reflected in the accounts as an asset and a liability.

Leases are a complex area in accounting terms.

PFI and LIFT schemes

PFI and LIFT schemes are also complicated arrangements to account for. Relevant accounting standards that need to be considered are IFRIC 12 (*Service Concession Arrangements*) and SIC 29 (*Service Concession Arrangements: Disclosures*).

Key Components in Accounting for PFI and LIFT schemes

Organisations must consider whether the scheme represents a service concession under IFRIC 12 for which a number of specific 'tests' exist, and if not, whether the scheme is a finance lease or an operating lease.

The asset is recognised in the organisation's accounts at 'fair value' – the capital cost of the asset at the inception of the scheme which is determined using the contractor's financial model.

A finance lease liability is shown equal to the fair value of the asset.

The unitary payment (i.e. the payment made by the public sector organisation to its private sector partner) is allocated between:

- payment for services
- payment for the property:
    - repayment of the liability
    - interest charge relating to the lease
    - contingent rent (this is a rent which is not fixed throughout the contract – it usually varies in relation to RPI or a percentage of RPI over the life of the contract)
- life cycle costs relating to future capital expenditure.

Depreciation and other changes in value must be accounted for as with any other asset owned by the organisation.

Donated assets

Assets funded by donation require specific identification in the asset register. The most common method of receiving a donated asset is for it to be purchased by the NHS organisation and for an invoice to be raised to the charitable body funding the asset; this can help with identification. It is worth noting that donated assets do not form part of the PDC dividend calculation.

Income will fluctuate in line with the receipt of new donated assets, either improving or worsening the revenue position of the NHS body according to whether more or less donated income is received as compared to the depreciation charge on the overall value of donated assets.

Key Learning Points

- Non-current assets deliver a benefit to an organisation over a period of time
- Non-current assets can be tangible or intangible
- In order to account appropriately for non-current assets, a detailed asset register must be maintained and kept up to date
- Commissioners do not hold many non-current assets
- Most of the capital expenditure incurred in the NHS is incurred by provider bodies
- NHS Property Services Ltd holds most of the assets used by CCGs
- Organisations work within a system of controls and financial limits to ensure that taxpayers' money used to finance capital expenditure is safeguarded
- It is important to consider capital needs and plan to meet them; organisations must consider the affordability of financing capital investment as well as the on-going revenue costs within the context of the capital controls
- A well-structured, logical and concise business case can help explain the case for capital investment. It may be subject to external approval depending on its value
- The potential sources of funding for capital investments vary by type of NHS organisation – not every option is available to every type of organisation
- Commissioners have limited access to sources of capital funding
- Non-foundation trusts and FTs have access to a number of sources of capital funding: internally generated resources; borrowing; public/private partnerships; leases, grants and donations. NHS organisations may also have access to public dividend capital (PDC) in certain circumstances
- Accounting for capital can be complicated – detailed guidance is available from the Treasury, Department of Health, NHS England and NHS Improvement.

References and Further Reading

Capital Regime and Investment Business Case Approvals, Guidance for NHS Trusts, NHS TDA, 2015: http://www.ntda.nhs.uk/blog/2014/07/11/capital-regime-and-investment-business-case-approvals-guidance-for-nhs-trusts/

Secretary of State's Guidance under section 42A of the NHS Act 2006:
www.gov.uk/government/uploads/system/uploads/attachment_data/file/365134/SofS_Finance_Guidance_under_Section_42A.pdf

Independent Trust Financing Facility:
www.gov.uk/government/groups/independent-trust-financing-facility

Public Private Partnerships guidance, HM Treasury:
www.gov.uk/government/uploads/system/uploads/attachment_data/file/221555/infrastructure_new_approach_to_public_private_parnerships_051212.pdf

Private Finance 2 (PF2), HM Treasury:
www.gov.uk/government/organisations/infrastructure-and-projects-authority

Accounting for PFI under IFRS and Accounting for NHS LIFT under IFRS, Department of Health, 2009:
www.info.doh.gov.uk/doh/finman.nsf/4db79df91d978b6c0025672800 4f9d6b/
5c86c759beddaecf80257654003623c5? OpenDocument

NHS Property Services Ltd: www.property.nhs.uk/

Community Health Partnerships (including LIFT): www.communityhealthpartnerships.co.uk/

Manual for Accounts, Department of Health (FINMAN website):
www.info.doh.gov.uk/doh/finman.nsf/

Government Financial Reporting Manual, HM Treasury: www.gov.uk/government/collections/government-financial-reporting-manual-frem

UK Accounting Standards: http://www.icaew.com/en/library/subject-gateways/accounting-standards/knowledge-guide-to-uk-accounting-standards

International Accounting Standards: http://www.ifrs.org/Pages/default.aspx

Guidance on asset valuation, HM Treasury:
www.gov.uk/government/uploads/system/uploads/attachment_data/file/328549/guidance_on_asset_valuation.pdf

Chapter 16
Commissioning

> This chapter explains what commissioning is, what it aims to achieve and what it involves in practice. In particular it works through the 'commissioning cycle' and explains what each step involves.

What is Commissioning?

The Department of Health has described commissioning as 'the process of ensuring that the health and care services provided effectively meet the needs of the population. It is a complex process with responsibilities ranging from assessing population needs, prioritising health outcomes, procuring products and services, and managing service providers'. However, what it boils down to in practice is commissioners negotiating agreements with service providers (in the NHS, private and voluntary sectors) to meet the health needs of a particular population.

The Aim of Commissioning

Service quality is the focus for NHS commissioners and the 'organising principle' that underlies all that they do. This means that the overarching goals for commissioning are to achieve the following within available funds:

- improved health outcomes
- reduced health inequalities
- improved provider quality
- increased productivity.

Commissioners are constrained by the fact that demand for healthcare always exceeds the level of funds available and so there is a need for them to make choices and to prioritise availability of services. This involves a focus on local needs, targets and desired outcomes together with reviewing services in the search for greater effectiveness, economy and efficiency. As a result, not all NHS services are available everywhere in the same way.

NHS commissioners are also expected to achieve improvements in relation to the five domains set out in the *NHS Outcomes Framework* and follow national planning guidance issued each year.

> **NHS Outcomes Framework Domains**
>
> Domain 1 Preventing people from dying prematurely.
>
> Domain 2 Enhancing quality of life for people with long-term conditions.
>
> Domain 3 Helping people to recover from episodes of ill health or following injury.
>
> Domain 4 Ensuring that people have a positive experience of care.
>
> Domain 5 Treating and caring for people in a safe environment; and protecting them from avoidable harm.

The Commissioning Cycle

Commissioning does not follow a pre-set template and cannot be done once and forgotten about – rather it is a continuous process with many different elements. It is only by going through the entire process – often referred to as 'the commissioning cycle' – that a realistic commissioning plan can be drawn up and an associated budget developed. This cycle is shown below in diagrammatic form[1]:

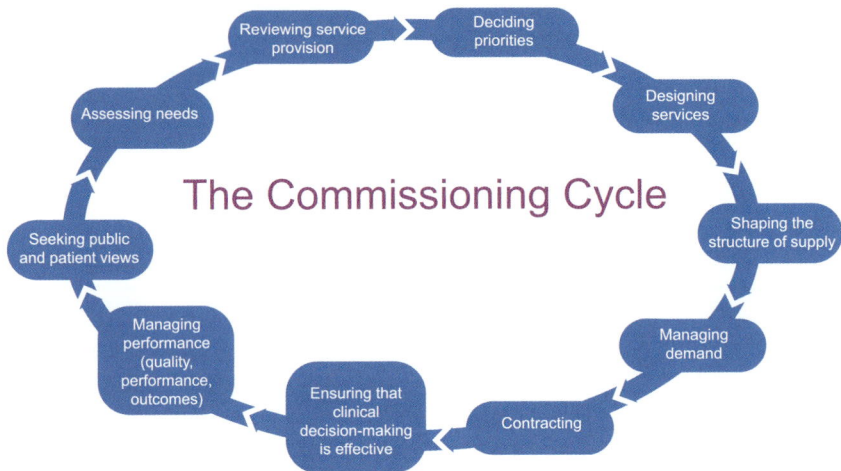

These activities are usually grouped into three key phases – planning, procurement and managing/monitoring.

Planning

Assessing health needs

Assessing health needs involves planning ahead so that an organisation knows what services are needed to meet the requirements of the population served. This cannot be done in isolation – commissioners must work with others (for example, local authority and public health professionals, local authority Health and Wellbeing Boards (HWBs), patients and the local community) to gather the information they need.

In looking at needs, it is important that the focus is on commissioning services that will result in good patient outcomes. For example, the test of effective commissioning for knee operations could be whether or not patients can return to work or drive again rather than the number of operations that are carried out over a set period of time. As we will see later, this outcomes focus involves thinking about developing new and innovative ways of contracting which incentivises providers to deliver the desired outcomes.

There are a number of tools that can help commissioners decide where to focus attention including:

- benchmarking data – for example, from NHS England's Commissioning for Value packs that contain a range of data and on-line tools
- outcomes indicator set – produced and maintained by the Health and Social Care Information Centre (HSCIC), this provides comparative information about the quality of health services commissioned and health outcomes achieved. It contains indicators from

[1] Adapted from a version that appeared in the Department of Health's 2006 guidance *Health Reform in England: Update and Commissioning Framework.*

the *NHS Outcomes Framework* that can be broken down to CCG level and other additional indicators – for example, linked to the National Institute for Health and Care Excellence's (NICE) quality standards

- better care, better value indicators – developed by NHS Improving Quality[2] to identify potential areas for improvements in efficiency
- atlas of variation – maps that place health economies into quintiles of performance for individual outcome and efficiency measures.

Reviewing service provision and identifying gaps or areas where change is needed

This stage involves:

- looking at outcomes from services – in other words, are services delivering what they should?
- reviewing the latest guidance and assessing its impact – for example, from NICE
- analysing feedback from service users
- being aware of any guidance or recommendations that inspectors or regulators have issued – for example, the CQC and NHS Improvement
- using the local Joint Strategic Needs Assessment (JSNA) and the Joint Health and Wellbeing Strategy (JHWS) – both led by the HWB established by the local authority (see chapter 8).

Deciding priorities

This involves commissioners taking tough decisions about exactly how to spend the limited pot of money that they have available. Inevitably, not all needs can be met and so relative priorities must be established in a logical and objective way. Commissioners need to link these decisions to national priorities, performance targets (national and local), business rules (how providers of NHS services are reimbursed) as well as their overall objectives, plans and budgets. They must also take account of patient choice and the views of the local community and other partners. Another consideration is the need for openness and transparency in the approach to deciding priorities so that everyone can understand why decisions are made and see that the approach is objective and impartial.

Procurement

Once planning has been carried out, the next stage is for commissioners to contract for the services that are required whilst bearing in mind the need to provide for both competition and patient choice. This may involve a procurement exercise that will take into consideration those services already provided and the underlying relationship with service providers themselves.

Designing services

The first step in this process is to ensure that the way services are designed is in line with the agreed priorities. This may involve reshaping the way things are delivered in consultation with GP practices and other providers. This is where NHS England's commissioning guidelines and model care pathways fit in.

Shaping the structure of supply

Once commissioners are clear about what it is they want to buy they need to make sure this is specified clearly so that service providers know exactly what they are expected to deliver. In some instances, commissioners may also need to encourage changes in provision to

---

[2] In November 2015, NHS Improving Quality moved to NHS England to become its Sustainable Improvement Team.

meet their requirements – for example, so that services are provided closer to home or in different ways or to fill gaps in the range of services available. This involves working with local authorities and potential service providers to:

- develop service specifications
- understand any barriers that might prevent potential providers from coming forward and (in some cases and where it is appropriate) addressing them
- identify incentives that could stimulate supply – for example, using multi-year contracts that recognise that the level of work will increase gradually, or that service changes will be incremental or staged.

Managing demand whilst ensuring appropriate access to care

Managing demand is one of the trickiest aspects of commissioning as the care and services that patients need during the year must be matched with contracts that are agreed in advance, available capacity and financial resources. Effective demand management is therefore inextricably linked to shaping the supply of services and ensuring that the services that are available are clinically appropriate. It also involves reducing clinical variation in referrals made by GPs and in consultants' clinical practice.

Patient activity tends to be classified in two main ways – non-elective and elective:

- non-elective activity is the consequence of individuals feeling unwell, becoming unwell or having accidents and may occur as patient attendance at GP practices, urgent care centres or accident and emergency departments, either self-presenting or conveyed via the ambulance service. Patients may subsequently require admission to secondary or tertiary care for further investigation or treatment. Generally speaking, non-elective activity has to be dealt with at the time of presentation and is inherently unpredictable
- as the name suggests, elective (or planned) care consists of interventions or interactions that are known about and planned in advance. At primary care level this may be through regular appointments, follow ups or health checks. In relation to community and outpatient services it consists of booked appointments, while at secondary and acute care it will be planned admissions for procedures or investigations. NHS providers plan elective care in conjunction with assessments of their capacity but this can be affected by increases in non-elective patient activity which reduces overall system capacity.

In practical terms, managing demand means that commissioners must:

- have access to reliable, timely activity monitoring information – for example, in relation to referral patterns
- anticipate in-year changes – for example in screening programmes, care pathways, new providers, NICE guidance
- have in place activity management plans
- identify and follow best practice
- ensure that enough resources are devoted to health promotion and education, preventative measures and communication
- have in place effective communication plans – for example, the use of social media to encourage patients to access the appropriate part of the healthcare system
- be prepared to review services for effectiveness and value for money, and restrict access to or decommission services that give less benefit.

Increasingly, commissioners also look beyond the costs of individual treatments that may be needed during a year to consider the likely total cost of patient care across several years (this may include social care costs). There are a number of tools and techniques that commissioners can use to 'join up' information so that they can assess future demand in this way – for example:

- risk stratification – to identify patients with long term conditions who may need closer management or those who use hospital services regularly and are more likely to have re-admissions
- predictive modelling – by identifying the probability of future events affecting groups of patients, interventions can be planned and executed.

The role of GPs

With their detailed knowledge of patients' needs, GPs are at the forefront of demand management, specifying services and developing new care pathways. They can also influence how their patients behave – for example, by encouraging self-care and preventative measures and by educating them about which services should be accessed when (for example, when to use pharmacy services rather than minor injuries units). This can help reduce the number of referrals and improve the overall quality of patient care.

However, GPs also need to be mindful of actual and potential conflicts of interest. There are two central issues here: individual commissioning decisions taken by GPs and commissioning decisions taken by the CCG.

It is important to promote the choices open to patients, particularly if the GP is also a service provider. For example, the GP may be part of a consortium that operates a private clinic to which patients could be referred. It would therefore be appropriate for a patient to be made aware of these facts so that they can take this into consideration when making a decision about their treatment or care.

On a larger scale, there is the potential for conflicts of interest to arise in commissioning decisions taken by CCGs – for example, in relation to service reconfiguration. This can be particularly challenging when redesigning local services. In March 2012, NHS Peterborough CCG was found to have inappropriately managed a potential conflict of interest when redesigning primary and urgent care services. The ruling by the Co-operation and Competition Panel (CCP) found that '...NHS Peterborough had failed to manage a potential conflict of interest resulting from the involvement in its consultation process of two lead clinicians who were partners in GP practices that would be directly affected'[3] by the proposed changes.

Contracting

Contracting is a key stage in any procurement process but, unlike other sectors of the economy, the NHS uses a standard contract for the commissioning of all NHS clinical services (except primary care[4]). This contract can be adapted to suit a broad range of services and delivery models – in other words the standard contract provides a framework that can then be added to locally.

The healthcare services that are covered by the contract may be provided by NHS or other public or private sector providers (i.e. by 'any qualified provider'). Contracts should be signed before the start of the financial year with any disputes resolved swiftly and will take a variety of forms, from 'block'[5] to 'cost per case'. In the longer term, block arrangements are generally constrained by capacity, whilst cost per case arrangements can flex to meet demand. In the short term, both will be constrained by capacity.

---

[3] *CCP warns commissioners to avoid conflicts*, March 2012, Co-operation and Competition Panel: www.ccpanel.org.uk/cases/Peterborough_PCT_Conduct_Complaint.html
[4] The standard contract is not used for primary care services provided by GPs, dentists, opticians and community pharmacists – these are governed by separate contracts and form part of NHS England's direct commissioning activities – see chapters 4 and 6 for more details.
[5] Largely based on historical patterns of care, a block contract allows a healthcare provider to receive a 'lump sum' payment to provide a service irrespective of the number of patients treated or the type of treatment provided.

Commissioners must enforce the standard terms of the contract. These include penalties for under-performance and requirements such as a duty of openness and the need for a 'friends and family test' to be offered to patients across most NHS services.

NHS England is responsible for reviewing and updating the standard contract documentation. Details are available on its website.

See chapter 18 for more about how NHS services are paid for.

In letting contracts, commissioners must also consider how and when to introduce competition to improve services. To help commissioners in this area NHS England and NHS Improvement have developed choice and competition guidance[6].

Managing and monitoring

Ensuring effective clinical decision-making

Although contracts are agreed by NHS England or CCGs, each referral that a primary care clinician (usually a GP) makes is effectively a mini commissioning decision that commits money. Ideally, those making these decisions need to:

- recognise the broader context
- be aware of service options
- be able to justify their decisions
- accept peer review of performance
- understand the implications of their decisions.

In reality, most clinicians will make a decision based on their clinical judgement and the needs of the patient. The CCG therefore plays an important role in providing clear thresholds and pathways to enable the GP to refer patients to the right service, once the level of need is established.

Managing performance

Commissioners need to ensure that the services they have bought are delivered in line with the specifications they set out in their contracts in terms of quality, quantity and price. They must also review performance in relation to:

- achieving national standards – for example, the NHS Constitution 18 week waiting time and patients not having an urgent operation cancelled twice. NHS England expects commissioners to 'use their contracting muscle' to penalise such failings
- quality – the NHS standard contract between commissioners and providers allows for a proportion of providers' income to be conditional on quality, innovation and the achievement of local quality improvement goals through Commissioning for Quality and Innovation (CQUIN) schemes
- never events – there is a national set of 'never events' that must be included as part of contract agreements with providers. Any such events must be reported to the CQC via the National Reporting and Learning System[7] as well as to the relevant commissioner. NHS England guidance requires commissioners to withhold payment for an episode of care in which a never event occurs and for the treatment of the consequences of a never event. The full list is included within the standard contract documentation – examples include wrong site surgery; retained instrument post operation; wrong route of administration of medication and a patient falling from a poorly restricted window

---

[6] Procurement, choice and competition guidance: https://www.gov.uk/government/collections/procurement-choice-and-competition-in-the-nhs-documents-and-guidance
[7] Now operating as part of NHS Improvement: https://report.nrls.nhs.uk/nrlsreporting/Default.aspx

- key performance indicators – regular review of performance against national and local key performance indicators (for example, the time taken from referral to the commencement of treatment) helps to keep service delivery on track and identify potential issues for greater focus
- outcomes – the achievement of defined outcomes for patients are closely monitored. For example, review time against minimum cluster review periods for mental health patients
- activity management – for example, analysing referrals to providers or agreeing an extension to a provider's waiting list to keep activity within the agreed contract.

Undertaking patient and public feedback

Every CCG has a duty to prepare an operational plan before the start of each year that shows how it intends to use its budget and improve outcomes for patients. As mentioned earlier, these plans are discussed with the relevant HWB to ensure that they reflect the JSNA and JHWS. CCGs (and NHS England) are also under a duty to ensure that people who receive services 'are involved in its planning and development, and to promote and extend public and patient involvement and choice.' This means making use of patient satisfaction surveys and using these to inform the next commissioning round. To ensure that this information is available, the requirement for patient feedback is often built into service specifications.

Effective Commissioning

To be effective commissioners need to:

- have the necessary skills and experience (either themselves or via commissioning support units/services – see chapter 4)
- engage with a broad range of clinicians
- improve community engagement
- ensure choice for patients.

They must also have access to information and skills that will support their decisions. To help them in this area, a national information system known as the 'secondary uses service' (SUS) collects patient level activity information from providers and makes anonymised data available to commissioners. This system then applies the relevant price to providers' activity information, calculates the payment due and notifies each commissioner.

Other important sources of information include:

- population risk assessments
- referral patterns – CCGs monitor variations in referrals and query referral practice where appropriate
- details of past spending patterns and how this compares (for example, with other GP practices)
- information to monitor actual activity against plans and expenditure against budgets
- additional data made available by service providers.

These other sources of information are particularly important as CCGs do not have access to identifiable patient data: whilst ensuring patient confidentiality this means that understanding pathways and individuals' use of different services can be challenging. This situation is exacerbated when working with other public services such as local authorities.

Who are the Commissioners in the NHS and how do they approach their Responsibilities?

The *Health and Social Care Act 2012* led to the creation of NHS England and CCGs both with a role in commissioning services for patients. The creation of CCGs placed primary care clinicians at the heart of the commissioning process – they are fully accountable for managing the funding they receive from NHS England and negotiating contracts with providers of services. NHS England also directly commissions some services itself and others jointly with CCGs.

Local authorities are also involved as they are responsible for health improvement and public health spending and are parties to pooled budgets[8] with CCGs. These organisations' structures, accountabilities and roles are described in chapters 4, 5 and 8 but it is worth noting here that they can use a number of different approaches – for example:

- NHS England commissions some services – see chapter 4
- CCGs commission services themselves – see chapter 5
- where it makes sense for the health economy as whole (for example, to achieve economies of scale), CCGs may work together collaboratively. This may mean using a lead commissioner approach where a single contract is negotiated by the lead commissioner with the local service provider and is managed across all member CCGs. NHS England has produced a model collaborative commissioning agreement for CCGs to use when working together in this way
- partnership working with local authorities. Since April 2013, local authorities have been responsible for public health activities and lead on health improvement and reducing health inequalities. They also jointly commission some services with CCGs through pooled budgets (see chapter 8).

Key Learning Points

- Commissioners negotiate agreements with service providers to meet the health needs of their population
- The aim is to improve health outcomes, reduce health inequalities, improve provider quality and increase productivity
- Commissioners have to make tough choices as demand for healthcare services always exceeds the level of funds available
- Commissioning is a continuous process with many different elements grouped under three phases – planning, procurement and managing/monitoring
- A standard NHS contract is used by commissioners for all providers of secondary and community services
- Commissioners must ensure national standards (for example, as set out in the NHS Constitution) are met by providers and penalise any failings
- Contracts allow for a proportion of providers' income to depend on quality
- 'Never events' must be included as part of the contract agreements. When they occur they must be reported to the Care Quality Commission
- The key players in the commissioning field are NHS England, CCGs and local authorities.

---

[8] A type of partnership arrangement where NHS organisations and local authorities contribute an agreed level of resource into a single pot that is then used to commission or deliver health and social care services.

References and Further Reading

The NHS Outcomes Framework, NHS England:
www.england.nhs.uk/resources/resources-for-ccgs/out-frwrk/

Better Care, Better Value Indicators, NHS Improving Quality:
http://www.productivity.nhs.uk/Content/About

Atlas of Variation: http://www.rightcare.nhs.uk/index.php/nhs-atlas/

Clinical Commissioning Group Outcome Indicator Set, HSCIC, 2015:
www.hscic.gov.uk/catalogue/PUB19278

Commissioning for Value packs, NHS England: www.england.nhs.uk/resources/resources-for-ccgs/comm-for-value/

NHS Standard Contract 2016/17, NHS England: www.england.nhs.uk/nhs-standard-contract/

NHS Friends and Family Test Guidance, Department of Health, 2013:
www.gov.uk/government/publications/nhs-friends-and-family-test-guidance-on-scoring-and-presenting-results-published

Regulations on healthcare procurement, patient choice and competition, 2013:
https://www.gov.uk/government/publications/regulations-on-healthcare-procurement-patient-choice-and-competition-laid

The Never Events Policy Framework, NHS England, 2015: www.england.nhs.uk/patientsafety/wp-content/uploads/sites/32/2015/04/never-evnts-pol-framwrk-apr2.pdf

Secondary Uses Service (SUS): http://www.hscic.gov.uk/sus

Model Collaborative Commissioning Agreement for CCGs, NHS England, 2013 – under CCG development on the CCG resources page: www.england.nhs.uk/resources/resources-for-ccgs/

Chapter 17

Costing

> Understanding the cost of NHS patient care is vitally important, both locally and nationally, in making decisions about how to manage and deliver sustainable high quality services.
>
> There is a recognition that the NHS needs to develop new ways of working to meet the challenges posed by a growing and ageing population and the prevalence of long-term conditions. This cannot be done without an understanding of the existing costs of meeting healthcare needs and how they might change if services are provided differently.
>
> Good cost data can also help NHS organisations to understand variations in the way that patients are treated and the impact on available resources. When this information is linked to health outcome measures, the NHS can make value-based rather than volume-based decisions.
>
> Robust cost data is also vital for informing the payment system – the system of financial flows that moves money around the health service; see chapter 18 for more details.

What is Costing?

Costing is the quantification, in financial terms, of the value of resources consumed in carrying out a particular activity or producing a certain unit of output. Costing therefore involves:

- being clear about the activity whose costs you are seeking to identify – it must be defined clearly and unambiguously
- making sure that the correct costs of everything and everyone involved in carrying out that activity are included in the costing calculation.

It is also important to analyse the costs themselves, how they are related to what is being costed and how they behave. We will look in more detail at these cost classifications later on in this chapter.

What is Costing Information used for?

In the NHS, costing involves looking closely at healthcare services and identifying how much they cost. This can be at a variety of levels – for example, the total annual cost of the orthopaedic department in a hospital, the cost of a particular activity or group of procedures within that department (for instance, hip replacements) or the cost of treating an individual patient undergoing a hip replacement.

It is important to recognise that costing is not an end in itself – it is only worth doing if the information generated is used in a meaningful way to deliver improvements in healthcare services. In the NHS, costing information is used both within organisations and at a national level.

NHS organisations need costing information for a variety of reasons, for example to:

- support value-based decision making. Robust cost data, alongside quality and outcomes, is fundamental to understanding and measuring value[1]
- help run their organisations effectively and efficiently

---

[1] Value is concerned with the delivery of the best quality of care possible within the resources available.

- help decision makers, managers and budget holders decide how services should develop in the future
- manage 'services lines' – this involves looking in detail at the income and costs of an organisation's services in much the same way as a private sector company analyses its business units. In practice, this means that the focus is on profitability information (or the contribution made) by specialty. The information gleaned from service line reporting (SLR) is used to 'manage' each service line (hence 'service line management' or SLM) and develop business plans with the organisation overall effectively managed as 'a portfolio of autonomous and accountable business units'
- identify the costs of different activities at different levels (for example, for a particular specialty/department or for an individual patient)
- support the development of commissioning strategies, including new and emerging ways of working – for example, collaborative partnerships
- compare potential investment opportunities
- build up realistic budgets and plans
- monitor performance and benchmark services
- support negotiations for funding and the agreement of local prices.

At a national level, costing information provided by NHS bodies is used in a variety of ways including to develop:

- healthcare resource groups (HRGs)
- reference cost comparisons
- the prices for healthcare activities where they are set nationally.

The Move to Patient-Level Costing

Patient-level costing represents a change in the costing methodology in the NHS from a predominantly 'top down' allocation approach, based on averages and apportionments, to a more direct and sophisticated approach based on the actual interactions and events related to individual patients and the associated costs.

While the majority of acute trusts have implemented patient level costing and information systems (PLICS), it is still early days for mental health and community services.

PLICS can play a vital role in improving the efficiency and effectiveness of how patient care is delivered, bringing together information about the resources consumed by individual patients on a daily basis and combining this with the cost of the resource. This type of blended financial information is new for many organisations and is incredibly powerful. When PLICS is analysed alongside other performance and quality information it becomes even more powerful in understanding the delivery and performance of services. It also facilitates much more meaningful and constructive discussions within multi-disciplinary teams.

Approved Costing Guidance

Unless the underlying costing data supplied by health organisations is accurate and collected on a consistent basis, the resulting information will not itself reflect reality or be meaningful. For this reason, NHS Improvement issues annual *Approved Costing Guidance* setting out the recommended approach for all NHS providers covering:

- costing principles
- clinical costing standards for acute and mental health services
- guidance for reference cost collection

- guidance for the voluntary collection of patient-level information and costing systems (PLICS) data.

The guidance explains the approach to costing and cost collection that should be followed and sets out what service providers will need to do in this area to meet the conditions of their provider licence.

Costing principles

The overriding principle for costing in the NHS is that all costs must be 'fully absorbed'. In other words, every cost (whatever its nature) must be attributed to an activity. NHS Improvement's guidance sets out six principles that should be used for all costing exercises.

Six Principles

1. Stakeholder engagement – including frontline clinical staff and departments providing clinical support services such as pathology
2. Consistency – across and within organisations
3. Data accuracy – given that multiple data sources are used
4. Materiality – costing effort should focus on material costs and activities
5. Causality and objectivity – costing should be based on an understanding of how resources are used during the patient pathway to minimise subjectivity
6. Transparency – costing processes and outputs should be transparent and auditable.

Based on the concept of patient-level costing, the guidance lists six steps to support the implementation of the costing principles.

Steps to Implementing the Costing Principles

1. Define the element of patient care to be costed
2. Identify the activities involved in delivering the patient care
3. Identify the costs incurred in delivering the patient care
4. Classify costs by understanding the nature of the costs
5. Assign costs to the activities in the correct proportion
6. Validate the outputs by clinical and other stakeholder review.

Cost classifications

NHS Improvement's guidance gives details for each step but because it is such an important area we are going to look more closely at step 4. This recommends that costs should be categorised using two types of classification namely whether a cost is:

- direct, indirect or an overhead – to examine how costs relate to an element of patient care
- fixed, semi-fixed or variable – to examine how costs behave and inform the way that they can be controlled.

Direct costs

Direct costs relate directly to the delivery of patient care and arise as a result of individual patient episodes of care. For example, within a hospital ward the cost of drugs supplied and consumed can be directly attributed to that ward by the pharmacy system. Hence, drugs would be a direct cost of the ward.

Indirect costs

Indirect costs are indirectly related to the delivery of patient care but cannot always be specifically identified to individual patients. Examples include catering and linen services.

Overheads

Overhead costs are the costs of support services that contribute to the effective running of an NHS provider. These costs cannot be traced or easily attributed to patients and need to be allocated via an appropriate cost driver – something that causes a change in the level of costs. For example, the total heating costs of a hospital may be apportioned to individual departments using floor area or cubic capacity on the basis that the larger the floor area occupied by a department the greater the amount of heating used. The key here is that overheads are apportioned on a logical and consistent basis.

Fixed costs

Fixed costs are costs that do not change as activity changes over a 12-month period – for example, depreciation.

Semi-fixed costs

Semi-fixed costs are fixed for a given level of activity but change in steps as activity levels exceed or fall below these given levels. In other words, semi-fixed costs do not move with activity changes on a small scale, but 'jump' or 'step up' when a certain threshold is reached – for example, nursing staff.

Variable costs

Variable costs vary proportionately with changes in activity. In other words, they are directly affected by the number of patients treated or seen – for example, drugs and consumables costs.

Clinical Costing Standards

Developed by the HFMA since 2011/12, the clinical costing standards are designed to support a bottom-up approach to costing, setting out recommended best practice for the production of patient level costs. The acute and mental health standards form the second chapter of NHS Improvement's *Approved Costing Guidance*.

Organisations are able to assess and improve the quality of their costing process and data using the materiality and quality score (MAQS) templates included within the costing standards.

Reference Costs

Reference costs provide the richest source of financial data available about the NHS, enabling detailed comparisons relating to the cost of treating patients. There are three publications:

- the national schedule of reference costs showing the national average unit costs derived from the unit costs of NHS providers

- the reference cost index (RCI) that measures the relative efficiency of NHS organisations from an index centred around 100. For example, a RCI of 110 suggests a provider's costs are 10% above average; a score of 90 suggests they are 10% below average

- the database of source data that this allows a more detailed analysis of organisation-level costs.

NHS Improvement's latest reference cost audit report[2] indicated that 49% of the acute trusts audited had made materially inaccurate reference cost submissions. The findings show that many trusts are not undertaking the detailed work necessary to produce accurate costing

[2] *Reference Cost Assurance Programme: Findings from the 2014/15 Audit*, Monitor, September 2015.

information. The majority of trusts found to be inaccurate had costing systems and processes in place, but had problems with their design and operation.

The Future of Costing in the NHS

NHS Improvement and NHS England recognise that improvements to the payment system and to the underpinning information are critical to developing and delivering the new ways of working outlined in the *Five Year Forward View* (see chapter 2 for more details). As a result, NHS Improvement has embarked on a programme to transform NHS costing over the next few years, with the intention of mandating patient-level costing for all licensed providers. Known as the costing transformation programme, the changes include:

- an improved costing method including standard definitions and rules
- a single cost collection across:
  - acute trusts by financial year 2018/19
  - mental health and ambulance trusts by 2019/20
  - community service providers by 2020/21.

During the transition period and until the first mandated cost collection under the costing transformation programme, the HFMA clinical costing standards will remain part of the *Approved Costing Guidance*. Acute trusts are likely to be asked to adopt (on a voluntary basis) the new standards developed under the costing transformation programme from January 2017.

Key Learning Points

- Costing involves quantifying the value of resources used to carry out an activity
- Costing is not an end in itself – it is used to help deliver improvements in healthcare services
- Costing information has many uses at both organisational and national level
- NHS Improvement's *Approved Costing Guidance* sets out the principles and standards that NHS organisations should follow. It also contains guidance on reference cost collection and patient-level information and costing systems
- All costs in the NHS must be attributed to activities in a structured and logical way
- Costs are classified as direct, indirect or an overhead – here the focus is on how costs relate to an element of patient care
- Costs can also be viewed in relation to how they behave – as fixed, semi-fixed or variable
- The HFMA's clinical costing standards set out best practice for producing patient level costs
- Reference costs are collected each year and record activity levels, unit cost data and average length of stay for a range of specified activities. They provide useful management information and are used to develop national prices where applicable
- A national reference cost index is published each year – this allows comparisons between NHS organisations
- It is likely that over the next four years all providers will be required to implement patient-level costing, adopting NHS Improvement's new standards.

References and Further Reading

Approved Costing Guidance, Monitor, 2016:
www.gov.uk/government/publications/approved-costing-guidance

Reforming the Payment System for NHS Services: Supporting the Five Year Forward View, Monitor and NHS England, 2014:
www.gov.uk/government/uploads/system/uploads/attachment_data/file/381637/ReformingPaymentSystem_NHSEMonitor.pdf

Improving the Costing of NHS Services: Proposals for 2015–2021 and Monitor's response to feedback, Monitor, 2014 and 2015:
improving-the-costing-of-nhs-services-proposals-for-2015-to-2021

Reference Cost Assurance Programme: Findings from the 2014/15 Audit, Monitor, 2015:
https://www.gov.uk/government/publications/nhs-reference-cost-assurance-programme-findings-from-the-201415-audit

Reference costs – collection guidance and published reference costs, Department of Health:
www.gov.uk/government/collections/nhs-reference-costs

Clinical costing standards and supporting guidance, HFMA: www.hfma.org.uk/costing/standards

Healthcare Costing for Value Institute, HFMA: www.hfma.org.uk/costing

Chapter 18

How NHS Services are paid for

> We saw in chapter 10 that commissioners are allocated funding to purchase healthcare for local populations. The providers of those healthcare services are paid in line with contracts (see chapter 16). Contracted activity is paid for under the payment mechanism or national tariff. This chapter looks at what the national tariff is and how it works in practice.

What is the National Tariff?

The national tariff is the payment mechanism (a system of financial flows to move money around the health service) used to reimburse providers of NHS healthcare in England. It is a legal framework that covers prices for treatments and procedures, the methodology for setting them (where they are set nationally) and the underpinning rules. Under the national tariff, payments made to providers of care for NHS patients, be they from the NHS, private or independent sector, are linked to the activity and services actually provided. For most secondary care activity, payment is based on a national pre-set price for a defined measure of output or activity while recognising the type, mix, complexity and severity of the treatment provided. For the remaining services, payment is negotiated locally within the rules set out in the national tariff.

The First Payment Mechanism

The first payment mechanism – payment by results (PBR) was a key element in the NHS reform agenda set out in the Labour Government's 2000 *NHS Plan*. The Government at the time wanted to be sure that the large increases in resources that it planned over a five year period would be used to develop and deliver a higher volume and quality of clinical services. To achieve this aim there needed to be a financial system that contained the right balance of reward, incentive and equity – hence the introduction of PBR.

PBR was originally designed to bring about fundamental change to the way funds moved between commissioners and providers for the payment of secondary care services. PBR and now the national tariff, does not affect the way funds flow *to* commissioners: CCGs receive an allocation with which to purchase healthcare for the patients registered with their constituent practices. However, in simple terms, it affects the way that commissioners spend that allocation as they pay providers for each patient seen or treated in many cases, at the national pre-set rate. Therefore, if more patients are treated than originally planned, the commissioner will spend more money.

PBR and now the national tariff, does affect the income received by providers – they are paid for the actual work they do often at a national pre-set rate. Therefore if more or less patients are treated than planned, the provider may have more or less income than anticipated.

The National Tariff

The *Health and Social Care Act 2012* established the move from PBR (the responsibility of the Department of Health) to the national tariff (the joint responsibility of Monitor – now operating as part of NHS Improvement – and NHS England). Although they have different roles, NHS Improvement and NHS England work together to have an effective payment mechanism in place. Although this chapter refers to NHS Improvement (NHSI) in relation to the national tariff, as it is a legal framework, the documents relating to it for 2016/17 are issued by Monitor as the statutory body responsible.

Introductory Guide – NHS Finance

NHS Improvement (NHSI)

Where national prices apply, they are set by NHSI. NHSI is also responsible for designing the way that the national tariff works – setting down the underpinning rules and methodologies, including those to be applied when no nationally set price exists.

NHS England

In terms of the national tariff, NHS England has primary responsibility for determining and developing the unit of output/healthcare activity or 'currency' that commissioners buy on behalf of patients – for example, an outpatient attendance, a stay in hospital or an ambulance journey. Different parts of the NHS use different currencies to best reflect the way that patients are seen, treated and care delivered.

Tariff release process

The *Health and Social Care Act 2012* also means that the process of producing the national tariff and the associated documents is now set out in law. NHSI and NHS England work to a staged process for the development and publication of the *National Tariff*[1] *Document* as set out in the following diagram:

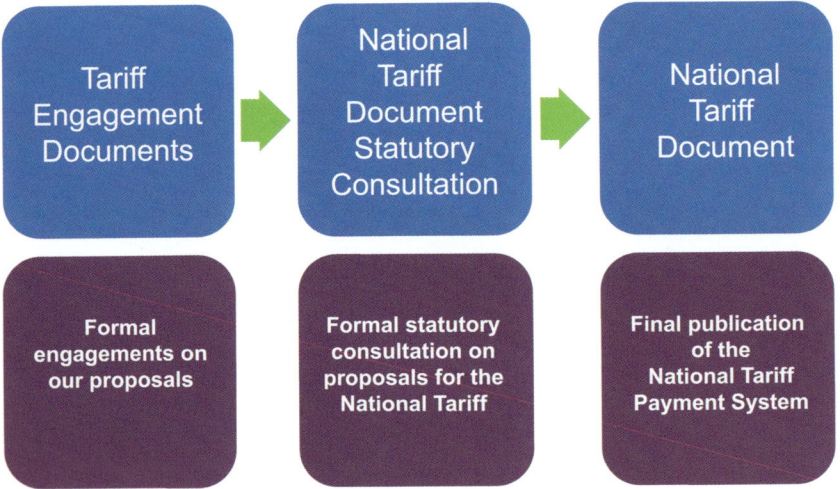

The stages, timing and documents and their statutory basis are set out in the table below:

Stage	Documents Released	Statutory Basis
National Tariff Engagement	Tariff engagement documents	Not applicable
Statutory Consultation[2]	Proposed *National Tariff Document* for the coming year including proposed final prices	Section 118 of the *Health and Social Care Act 2012*
Publication of the National Tariff	Final *National Tariff Document* for the coming financial year	Section 116 of the *Health and Social Care Act 2012*

---

[1] The *Health and Social Care Act 2012* requires the document to be called the 'national tariff'.
[2] Section 118(13) requires a statutory consultation period of 28 days beginning the day after the notice is published.

The publication the '*National Tariff Document* (NTD)' is fundamental here. It details:
- the services covered by the payment mechanism and their prices where applicable
- how the prices have been calculated
- national variations to nationally-set prices
- how and when the local agreement of a change to a national price may be appropriate
- the underpinning rules associated with payment.

Services covered by the national tariff

The national tariff contains three basic models suited to different types of healthcare service:
- national currency, national price
- national currency, local price
- local currency and price.

National currency, national price

This model is used where the unit of output or healthcare activity (the currency) is well defined and there is sufficient data collected over time to enable a price to be set for that currency. It is mainly used to reimburse providers of acute healthcare and covers the following:
- admitted patient care (covering a spell of care from admission to discharge)
- procedures undertaken in outpatients
- outpatient attendances
- accident and emergency attendances.

As both the currency and its price are predetermined, commissioners can focus on agreeing the quality of services to be provided and the number of patients who are likely to be seen or treated.

National currency, local price

Even if the currency is well defined, the data needed to calculate a price may not yet exist. For these services, the national mandatory currency provides a common basis for agreeing contracts alongside local flexibility to negotiate an appropriate price. This model of 'national currency, local price' currently covers the following:
- adult and neonatal critical care
- ambulance services
- HIV outpatient services
- specialist rehabilitation
- health assessments for looked after children placed out of area
- renal transplants
- adult mental health services
- working age and older people mental health services
- positron emission tomography and computerised tomography (PET/CT)
- cochlear implants
- transcatheter aortic valve implantation (TAVI)

- complex therapeutic endoscopy
- dialysis for acute kidney injury.

Local currency and price

To be able to contract for healthcare services where there is no nationally defined currency or price, providers and commissioners negotiate local payment arrangements in line with the rules set out in the *National Tariff Document*. Any local price needs to take account of the costs incurred by the provider so that they can afford to deliver the agreed level and quality of care. Local prices must also be agreed formally and reviewed annually.

In order for the first two models to work, two key issues must be considered:

- how is the activity measure defined?
- how is the price set?

Defining the activity measure

For the payment mechanism to work, it is important to decide what is being paid for – what is the unit of healthcare or 'currency'? Different parts of the NHS use different currencies to best reflect the way that patients are treated and care delivered. The healthcare resource group (HRG) is the currency used for admitted patient care (covering a spell of care from admission to discharge or death), procedures undertaken in outpatients and accident and emergency attendances.

HRGs group services that are clinically similar and require similar resources for treatment and care. The HRG applies to a procedure or treatment regardless of where it takes place and supports the provision of components of healthcare outside of hospitals through the use of 'unbundled tariffs' whereby the payment or tariff can be shared between different providers. It provides the ability to differentiate between procedures and treatments, recognising the different costs associated with treating patients of different ages, those with multiple co-morbidities (related chronic illnesses) or where there are additional complications.

The currency for outpatient attendances is the attendance itself, split between first and follow-up attendances, the broad medical area (defined by a treatment function code) and whether the attendance relates to a single professional or a multi-professional team.

The currency used for adult mental health and learning disability services is the 'care cluster'. It describes the common needs of a group of patients/service users over a period of time. Each of the 21 clusters includes a number of different diagnostic codes; the 'mental health clustering tool' enables service users to be matched with the appropriate cluster.

For ambulance services, four broad activities are used as the currency:

1. urgent and emergency care calls answered
2. hear and treat/refer
3. see and treat/refer
4. see, treat and convey.

Prices per call (1), per patient (2) and per incident (3 and 4) are locally agreed.

Calculating national prices

A national set of prices is published annually, and is currently based on the average reference costs for HRGs as reported by providers of NHS funded services. Chapter 17 explains what reference costs are but in this section we are looking at how they are used to build prices. There is effectively a four stage process.

> **The Four Stage Process**
>
> Stage 1 – activity is coded. Clinical coders assign diagnosis or procedure codes to activity based on the patient notes or discharge summary.
>
> Stage 2 – HRGs are assigned. Activity is automatically assigned to an HRG (via software called the grouper) based on the diagnosis or procedure codes – as logged by the clinical coder.
>
> Stage 3 – 'reference costs' for activity with a national activity currency are submitted to the Department of Health.
>
> Stage 4 – the prospective national tariff is calculated by NHSI. At present, this involves working out the national average cost for each HRG/service where a national price applies. Prices are then adjusted for factors that affect the whole of the NHS known as 'national variations'.

National variations to national prices

Adjustments to national prices are made for the following factors that affect the NHS as a whole:

- inflation
- efficiency requirements
- generic cost pressures
- changes in technology and practice (for example, the cost of recommendations made by the National Institute for Health and Care Excellence – NICE).

Given the current pressures on public spending, the level of efficiency that healthcare providers are expected to deliver is particularly important.

Efficiency

An assumption about the savings that the NHS can make is built into national prices each year as an 'efficiency requirement'. For 2016/17, this equates to 2% and reduces the price paid by this percentage. Taken together with the other national adjustments, this can sometimes mean that the required efficiency improvement is greater than any increase to reflect inflation and national cost pressures.

Other adjustments

A number of other adjustments are made that affect the amount a provider is paid for treating a patient. These include:

- the marginal rate emergency tariff – a provider is paid a percentage of the national price for each patient admitted as an emergency over and above a set threshold (see below)
- the short stay emergency adjustment – for patients admitted as emergencies that stay in for less than two days, the national price is adjusted in relation to a patient's expected length of stay
- a long stay payment – payments are only intended to cover costs up to a nationally set length of stay for the treatment or care received. For patients whose length of stay exceeds these 'trim points', providers may receive additional payments
- a 'specialised service' top-up payment – these payments recognise the additional costs of undertaking specialised activity. Top ups for children's services, neurosciences, orthopaedics and spinal surgery are restricted to specific specialist providers.

Market forces factor

There are some differences in cost that a provider cannot avoid – some costs are higher just because the provider's location means that labour, land, buildings and even equipment cost more. As these costs are unavoidable and in order to ensure that the providers concerned are not disadvantaged, a compensating adjustment is made – the market forces factor or MFF. The actual price paid for a spell of care is the national price adjusted by the MFF. Where prices are locally agreed, there is no additional MFF paid as the local price should already reflect any local cost pressures. The same MFF is used to adjust commissioners' allocations, ensuring that CCGs have broadly equal purchasing power irrespective of where they are located. The most obvious area affected is London and the South East where the MFF can add up to 30% to the amount paid per patient.

Local agreement to change a national price

The national tariff allows for commissioners and providers to negotiate a local agreement to vary what is specified in the *National Tariff Document* if certain conditions are met.

Local variations

These are adjustments to:

- a national price
- a national currency
- a payment approach – for example, moving from paying per patient per attendance to paying for a year of treatment.

Adjustments are agreed by commissioners and providers and must be published as well as notified to NHSI. Local variations facilitate innovative approaches – for example, to pay for a new patient pathway.

Local modifications

A 'modification' to a national price can be agreed in the event that local circumstances make it uneconomic to provide a particular service at the pre-set price. The modification increases the price paid so that the service continues to be available for patients. A number of conditions must be met including that the higher costs incurred cannot be avoided by the provider. To date, only one local modification has been approved: University Hospitals Morecambe Bay NHS Foundation Trust is paid higher prices for a number of elective and non-elective essential services.

The underpinning rules

The *National Tariff Document* also sets out the rules underpinning the payment mechanism. These include billing, payment and activity reporting as well as payment for NHS funded healthcare services provided by local authorities.

All licensed healthcare providers are required to comply with the national tariff and provide information to support its development. Section 5 of the provider license sets out a number of 'pricing conditions' including one that requires licensees 'to charge for NHS healthcare services in line with the national tariff' (pricing condition 4).

Influencing behaviour

The national tariff is also used to influence the behaviour of those commissioning and providing healthcare services and to support the overall strategic aims of the NHS. As policy and objectives develop and change over time, so must the national tariff.

Emergency medicine

One area where this policy has been applied in recent years is in relation to urgent and emergency care. For example, to help reduce emergency admissions to hospitals two rules have been introduced.

Emergency activity

Since 2010/11, providers of accident and emergency services have been paid at full price for the number of patients attending emergency departments up to the value of the activity recorded for an agreed baseline. However, attendances over and above this baseline are paid at a marginal or per patient rate of 70%[3] of the pre-set price. Where accident and emergency attendances consistently exceed the contracted level there is an added incentive to redesign services and manage patient demand for those services. The money that commissioners would have spent on paying for the activity at full price is reserved to fund changes in the way emergency services are provided.

Re-admissions to hospital

In a similar vein, providers do not receive any further payment for a patient admitted within 30 days of their discharge following a previous admission if the 're-admission' is deemed to be avoidable. In other words, hospitals are penalised if the patient is readmitted within a 30 day period if the readmission is related to the original reason for care and could have been avoided. The application of this 'rule' is subject to a locally agreed and evidenced threshold. Any resulting savings made by commissioners must be disclosed and reinvested to support patients following discharge from hospital. This applies to activity where a national price exists even if the patient is readmitted to a different hospital than the one where their original treatment was received. A number of patient groups are excluded including maternity, cancer, renal dialysis and paediatric patients.

Service quality and patient outcomes

Another key factor affecting the development of the national tariff has been the focus on service quality and improved outcomes for patients. This can be seen through best practice tariffs. Best practice tariffs reflect the costs of delivering treatments in line with NICE guidance – for example, by undertaking cholecystectomies as a day case procedure or admitting stroke patients directly to a dedicated stroke unit. The standard tariff (i.e. *not* best practice) is set lower than the normal tariff price. An addition to this is then applied to give the best practice price. This creates a financial incentive for providers to adopt best practice patient pathways and treatments as those providers failing to deliver best practice will attract a lower payment for the activity. This approach is designed to deliver national improvements in the quality of care delivered and the scope of best practice tariffs continues to expand. It currently (2016/17) covers 20 areas of healthcare.

The reimbursement of mental health services is moving to payment for a year of care/patient episode or payment for a defined group of patients (a capitated payment). Both of these approaches are linked to the achievement of defined patient outcomes – for example, the percentage of people with severe mental illness in paid employment.

Key Learning Points

- A system of financial flows or a payment mechanism is used to move money around the NHS in England. This is known as the national tariff
- The national tariff is a legal framework subject to a process set out in law
- The production of the national tariff is the joint responsibility of two of the Department's arm's length bodies – Monitor (operating as part of NHSI) and NHS England
- Three models operate under the national tariff: national currency, national price; national currency, local price; local currency and price

[3] 2016/17 rate.

- The unit of healthcare or the 'currency' used for admitted patient care, procedures in outpatients and A & E attendances is the HRG
- For outpatient attendances, the currency is the attendance and broad medical area
- For mental health and learning disability services, the currency is the care cluster
- National prices are subject to national variations to take account of factors affecting the whole of the NHS – for example, inflation and efficiency requirements
- National prices may be subject to local variation or modification if certain criteria are met
- The national tariff is also used to influence behaviour and support the overall aims of the NHS. This is seen in relation to payment for urgent and emergency care, reimbursement aimed at improving service quality and the linking of payment to specific outcomes for patients.

References and Further Reading

The NHS payment system, documents and guidance, Monitor and NHS England: www.gov.uk/government/collections/the-nhs-payment-system-regulating-prices-for-nhs-funded-healthcare

Information about healthcare resource groups, Health and Social Care Information Centre: www.hscic.gov.uk/hrg

NHS Standard Contract 2016/17, NHS England: www.england.nhs.uk/nhs-standard-contract/

Chapter 19
NHS Charitable Funds

> This chapter looks at the management of funds held on trust and is based on the legislative framework as it applies to England and Wales. The key Act is the *Charities Act 2011* which brings together all relevant charities legislation from previous years (other than a few minor provisions) including Acts passed in 1992, 1993 and 2006.

Background

As at March 2015, there were around 260 NHS charities, with a combined income of £327 million and asset value of £2 billion. The top 30 NHS charities accounted for over two-thirds of total NHS charity income/assets in 2012/13.

To a large degree, the accumulation of these funds is a consequence of the historical funding of early health services through charitable sources. When the NHS was created, most existing charitable assets were pooled into the Hospital Endowments Fund. The main exceptions to this were teaching and university hospitals, which retained control of their endowments through boards of governors and management committees respectively.

Over the years, the NHS has been reorganised many times and laws passed to allow the charitable funds to transfer to NHS organisations that can use them for their intended purpose. More recently, funds have been boosted through capital growth and income from investments, legacies, donations and fundraising appeals.

The Nature and Purpose of Charitable Funds

A charitable fund is created when funds are accepted by a trustee to be held and used for the benefit of a beneficiary. The arrangement is usually governed by an instrument that sets out the terms of the trust and the purpose to which funds are to be applied by the trustee. In order to be deemed charitable, funds held on trust must exist to provide public benefit, be exclusively charitable and be used to further the funds' objectives. There are thirteen acceptable charitable purposes set down in legislation[1]. The Act also provides for the continuing admission of other categories that are analogous to these principal categories. The categories are subject to the overriding requirement of demonstrable public benefit.

The Thirteen Charitable Purposes

1. The prevention or relief of poverty
2. The advancement of education
3. The advancement of religion
4. The advancement of health or saving lives
5. The advancement of citizenship or community development
6. The advancement of the arts, culture, heritage or science
7. The advancement of amateur sport
8. The advancement of human rights, conflict resolution or reconciliation or the promotion of religious or racial harmony or equality or diversity
9. The advancement of environmental protection or improvement

---

[1] These purposes were set out originally in the *Charities Act 2006*, since consolidated into the *Charities Act 2011*.

10. The relief of those in need by reason of youth, age, ill-health, disability, financial hardship or other disadvantage
11. The advancement of animal welfare
12. The promotion of the efficiency of the armed forces of the Crown, or of the efficiency of the police, fire and rescue service or ambulance services
13. Other purposes beneficial to the community not falling under any of the other headings.

There are three classes of charitable funds recognised in law:

- **unrestricted funds** – which may be spent at the discretion of the trustees in line with the charity's objectives

- **restricted funds** – which can only be spent in accordance with written restrictions imposed when the funds were donated or granted or in accordance with the specific terms of an appeal raised for the charity

- **endowment funds** – where capital funds are made available to a charity and trustees are legally required to invest or retain them. Endowment funds can be 'permanent' (i.e. trustees have no automatic power to spend the capital, only the income generated through its investment unless they apply for and are given consent by the Charity Commission or by resolution following the *Trusts (Capital and income) Act 2013*) **OR** 'expendable' (here the trustees can convert capital to income and spend it on the fund's purpose).

Funds may also be 'designated' or 'earmarked' which means that trustees can set aside unrestricted funds for a specific purpose or more typically for an area of the hospital's operations – for example, cardiology, urology or nursing staff benefits. Designating funds can be useful where it is planned to build up funds through periodic transfers from unrestricted funds over time for a significant project or where funds are needed to meet on-going costs (for example, staffing) to which formal commitments have been made. It may also be a useful way to recognise the apparent 'wishes' of donors (which do not create 'restrictions').

Major public appeals may also be treated as an unrestricted designated fund where examples of the intended use of the funds is given (i.e. rather than a specific purpose) – for example, an appeal to raise money for a cancer treatment building. Such an unrestricted fund will be a subsidiary registered charity (a special trust under Part 14 of the *Charities Act 2011*) under the group registration of the NHS charity. The reason this can be treated as unrestricted is that the monies raised may be used on any of the costs of the project including building costs, professional fees, future maintenance costs (when specified in the subsidiary charity's objects clause) and meeting fundraising and administrative costs.

If trustees want to accumulate funds generally (i.e. not for a specific project), they must request a 'power of accumulation' from the Charity Commission (unless the governing document already allows them to do so).

Charitable Funds Income

As mentioned above, the origins of NHS charitable funds date back to pre-NHS days when early health services were funded largely by charity or through endowments. Over the years, funds have been added to gradually and today there are five main sources of new money for charitable funds.

> **Charitable Funds Income – Sources**
> - Donations
> - Fundraising
> - Legacies
> - Investment income and interest
> - Grants.

In some circumstances income can also be generated through:

- trading – but only if it is in pursuance of the fund's primary purpose (for example, at a training course for NHS staff there may be an ancillary trade in refreshments)
- charging for part or all of a service provided by the fund (but only if it is for public benefit – the charges must not restrict access).

We will look at each of the five income sources in turn but first it is important to note that trustees are not obliged to receive funds on trust and should refuse where the conditions imposed by the donor are too onerous or where they are unlikely to be able to use funds as directed. To avoid criticism and safeguard their own position, trustees are advised to seek advice from the Charity Commission before refusing a donation. Acceptance of all donations should be tested against the general principle that it does not, nor appear to, place an NHS body or the Department of Health/Welsh Government under an inappropriate obligation.

Donations

Donations can be solicited (for example, through posters, leaflets or other appeals) or unsolicited (for example, where, at the end of a hospital stay, a patient asks how they can donate to the ward or hospital charity).

Donations of both types can be unrestricted or restricted. For example, an unrestricted donation would arise when a patient or relative gives money 'for the hospital charity' or 'for the ward funds' without specifying how it should be used. Even if there is a particular use suggested, it will only be a 'restriction' if the terms are strictly limited – for example, 'it must be used' or 'must only be used' – and it is formalised in writing. A donation made in response to a fundraising leaflet soliciting donations for a general fund would also be unrestricted.

It is desirable to minimise the proportion of donations received as 'restricted' funds because this limits spending flexibilities. One way to do this is to use a standard form of receipt that invites donors to record how they 'wish' their donation to be used 'without imposing any trust'. The wishes expressed can be reflected through the designation of donations, but donations on these terms are 'unrestricted'. The Charity Commission's *NHS Charities Guidance* includes a model receipt form as an appendix and it is also available on their website. Such a receipting system can also assist with accountability and the receipt can incorporate an invitation to donate under Gift Aid arrangements.

Fundraising

Fundraising income results from events (anything from coffee mornings and sponsored swims through to high profile celebrity events) and targeted appeals. If the money is sought for an explicit purpose (for example, if tickets or a poster for a charity dinner state 'all proceeds from this event will be used to buy monitors for the special care baby unit') then it must be used for that and nothing else. The power of NHS trustees to raise funds is set out in section 222 of the *NHS Act 2006* and in section 169 of the *NHS (Wales) Act 2006*. These Acts permit funds to be used more flexibly where there is an insufficient response (a failed appeal) or an excess of funds over and above the appeal target, provided certain safeguards are met.

Legacies

Legacies can be restricted or unrestricted depending on the terms on which the bequest is made. The 'wishes' or 'desires' of a donor are normally non-binding designations, however reference should be made to the terms of the gift to ensure that a binding restriction does not mean that the legacy is restricted funds.

If the legacy cannot be fulfilled (for example, if the function it was intended for no longer exists or has been transferred to another body) the NHS trustee(s) concerned should consider whether they received the legacy under section 91 of the *NHS Act 1977* (re-enacted as section 218 of the *NHS Act 2006*), which may provide a power to redirect the funds. Advice may be sought from the Charity Commission. If it appears that section 218 does not apply then an application must be made to the Charity Commission for a scheme that allows the legacy to be used in another way.

Investment income and interest

Where charitable funds have surplus monies not needed to fund immediate charitable activities, trustees may invest to generate additional income. However, they must do so in line with legislation and Charity Commission guidance. The relevant legislation is the *Trustee Act 2000* which includes a general power of investment that can be used in relation to any charity property held on trust (except property of charitable companies) subject to any 'restriction or exclusion' affecting the charity. This power allows a trustee to place funds in any kind of investment, excluding land, as though he or she was the absolute owner of those funds. The *Trustee Act 2000* also gives all charity trustees power to acquire freehold or leasehold land in the UK.

Investment income and interest (and any gains or investment losses) must be apportioned to the restricted fund that generates it. Where the trustee(s) administer(s) more than one charity, the income and investment gains and losses must also be apportioned to the respective charities. In the case of designated unrestricted funds of a charity the trustee(s) is permitted to apply investment gains for any of the objects of the charity concerned.

Grants

Grants are usually restricted income given for a specific purpose. As well as the general principles that apply to the use of (and accounting for) restricted funds, grants often have additional requirements attached. For example, how an acknowledgement is made in the accounts or other public documents.

Charitable Funds Spending

A charitable fund can only spend money in line with its charitable purpose. In other words, in the interests of the fund's beneficiaries (i.e. NHS patients) and not the NHS organisation to which it is linked. This does not mean that the charitable fund must itself purchase items of equipment etc. for use in its linked NHS organisation. Instead, NHS trusts often purchase items with the charitable fund providing grant funding. This ensures that ownership (and any related liabilities) rest with the NHS trust.

Types of Trustee

It is important to appreciate that health service bodies are not themselves charities. Only the property they hold on trust for exclusively charitable purposes constitutes a charity.

The charitable fund's governing documents set out who or what controls, manages and administers the charity – these are the trustees. At present (and until the end of 2017/18), there are three main types of trustee in the NHS – corporate, special[2] and appointed[3]. There are also

---

[2] Under section 7 of the 1946 NHS Act endowment and trust funds were vested in the board of governors of designated teaching hospitals who acted as trustees. Subsequently the 1973 NHS Reorganisation Act provided for the reorganisation of charitable funds held historically.
[3] Under a number of different Acts, the Secretary of State for Health appointed trustees to hold and administer the charitable funds associated with an NHS trust (often referred to as section 11 trustees); an NHS foundation trust (section 51 trustees); special health authorities; NHS England and clinical commissioning groups. In Wales equivalent powers to those of the Secretary of State are exercised by Welsh ministers.

a very small number of NHS charities that are governed by a charitable company limited by guarantee – here government ministers have the right to appoint non-executive directors.

From 1 April 2018, there will no longer be any special or appointed trustees in England. Instead there will be two options – corporate and independent.

Corporate trustees

Under this model, it is the NHS corporate body (i.e. an NHS organisation as an entity) that is the trustee. The governing body/board of the NHS body acts on behalf of the corporate trustee in the administration of the charitable funds but the members of the governing body/board are not themselves individual trustees.

Independent trustees

Under this approach, the NHS organisation's governing body/board appoints an independent charity to undertake the trustee role in relation to its linked charitable funds. This model was introduced following the Department of Health's 2011/12 review of the regulation and governance of NHS charities which allowed NHS charities in England to transfer charitable property to another specifically established independent charity.

Where this route is followed, the new charity is regulated solely by the Charity Commission and is 'free to set its own constitution including objects, legal form and trustees appointments appropriate to its needs'[4]. The transfer of assets to the new charity cannot be reversed but there are a number safeguards to protect the interests of patients and the linked NHS organisation. In particular, all assets retain the same designation and the objects of the 'original' charity continue (although they could be expanded to support wider health provision).

If an NHS charity decides to go down the independent route, it must obtain the necessary transfer order from the Secretary of State. The first charity to achieve independence was Barts Charity, which raises funds for the London-based Barts Health NHS Trust – its order came into effect on 31 July 2014.

Practical guidance to help NHS charities wishing to go down this route has been developed by the Association of NHS Charities and the Department of Health and is available online.

For charities that do not opt for independent status and for all charities in Wales where there is no such option, key requirements for governance and finance will continue to be set by the Department of Health/Welsh Government and the Charity Commission.

Trustees – Roles and Responsibilities

The Charity Commission booklet CC3 (*The Essential Trustee – what you need to know*) gives detailed information and advice about trustees' roles and responsibilities. In broad terms, trustees have a duty to ensure compliance, a duty of prudence and a duty of care, each of which is discussed below.

Compliance

Trustees must ensure that:

- the charity complies with charity law and with the requirements of the Charity Commission as regulator. As part of this, they must ensure that the charity prepares its annual report, returns and accounts as required by law

- the charity does not breach any of the requirements or rules in its governing document

- any fundraising activity undertaken by or on behalf of the charity is properly undertaken and that funds are properly accounted for

- the relevant provisions of the 2006, 2011 and 2013 Acts are complied with.

---

[4] *Review of the Regulation and Governance of NHS Charities*, Department of Health, March 2014.

Duty of prudence

Trustees must:

- ensure the charity is and will remain solvent
- ensure the charity's income and property is applied solely for the purposes set out in its governing document and for no other purpose
- use charitable funds and assets wisely and only in furtherance of the charity's objects
- avoid activities that might place the charity, its assets or reputation at risk
- take special care when investing the charity's funds
- ensure adequate financial management and control arrangements are in place
- ensure the charity's expenditure is applied fairly amongst those who are qualified to benefit from it
- not allow the charity's income to accumulate unless there is a specific power of accumulation and a future use for it in mind
- have an agreed reserves policy that is reviewed regularly. If reserves are too high, the charity is retaining funds without justification and this could constitute a breach of trust. If reserves are too low, the fund's ability to meet future commitments or needs may be at risk.

Duty of care

Trustees must:

- exercise such care and skill as is reasonable in the circumstances having particular regard to any special knowledge or experience that he or she has (or professes to have) or that it is reasonable to expect of a person acting in the course of that kind of business or profession
- act with integrity and avoid any personal or organisational conflicts of interest
- ensure they have appropriate risk management plans in place. Trustees of charities with gross annual income over £500,000 must make a statement about risk management in their annual report
- consider using external professional advice where there may be a material risk to the charity.

Regulation – Roles and Responsibilities

Department of Health

At present (2016/17), the Secretary of State for Health in England and Welsh ministers in Wales are responsible for bringing forward legislation on:

- the appointment and removal of trustees
- the terms of their office
- the transfer of property between trustee bodies – no transfers of charitable funds or trustee responsibilities can be made where NHS bodies are restructured without the Department's authority or agreement
- the preparation and audit of accounts for charitable funds – i.e. the overarching requirement to prepare accounts in line with the relevant charities Acts and the SORP (see later in this chapter for details).

However, in England the *NHS (Charitable Trusts etc) Act 2016* removes the Secretary of State's powers to appoint trustees to NHS bodies, and to appoint special trustees with effect from 1 April 2018. This means that charities with independent trustees (i.e. special trustees or appointed bodies of individual trustees) must decide whether to set up a new independent charity or revert to the corporate trustee arrangements. NHS charities with a corporate trustee can either do nothing or choose to move to the new model.

Charity Commission

The Charity Commission (the Commission) is the statutory organisation that regulates charities in England and Wales. Its aim is to maintain public confidence in the integrity of charity which it does by encouraging better methods of administration, giving advice to trustees and investigating and correcting abuse. The Commission has the power to change the objectives of a charity where this is necessary and where trustees do not have the power to do so themselves. It also keeps a register of charities, which is open to public inspection – all charities with an annual income of at least £5,000 are required by law in England and Wales to register with the Commission.

Trustees of charities in England and Wales with income in the relevant financial year in excess of £10,000 must make an annual return[5] and those registered charities with an income in excess of £25,000 must forward to the Commission a copy of their annual report together with the accounts and the report of the auditor or independent examiner within 10 months of the charity's financial year-end. For NHS charities, this means that the information is due by 31 January each year.

The NHS is required to register charitable funds with the Commission and to file audited accounts in a prescribed form and also to produce an annual report and annual return. The Commission provides advice and guidance to help charities make effective use of their resources and to help trustees fulfil their objectives and obligations.

The Management of Charitable Funds

Day-to-day management

Trustees can only delegate authority that is specified in their governing instrument or section 11 of the *Trustee Act 2000*. However, they cannot delegate their statutory duties and responsibilities. This means that although in practice the day-to-day management of charitable funds may be delegated to a sub-committee and staff, trustees remain accountable for all decisions relating to the charity and its performance. It follows, therefore, that they need to be well informed about the business of the charity if they are to meet their responsibilities effectively. They must therefore establish clear reporting lines and ensure that appropriate arrangements exist to enable them to oversee actions taken on their behalf.

However they manage their affairs, trustees need to have written rules and procedures covering the formal conduct of the charity's business. These will normally be set out in the form of standing orders or terms of authorisation (including a scheme of delegation), standing financial instructions (or prime financial policies) and policies, procedures or guidance notes.

The frequency of trustee meetings will vary depending upon the size of the charitable funds being administered and the volume and complexity of its transactions. Meetings need to be frequent enough to avoid any delays to the charity's administration that might lead to a failure to meet legal and regulatory requirements or to poor management of its resources.

---

[5] This is separate from, and in addition to, any requirement to submit the charity's annual accounts and trustees' report.

When acting on behalf of corporate trustees, governing bodies of NHS organisations must recognise that:

- the charitable funds they are managing are distinct from their exchequer (NHS) monies
- they have separate and distinct responsibilities for the administration of the charitable funds. Meeting these responsibilities is best achieved either by:
  - governing bodies/boards meeting separately to deal with charitable funds business OR
  - establishing a separate committee to deal with matters relating to the charitable funds – this committee then reports to the full governing body/board of the NHS organisation acting as corporate trustee.

Governance code

The Charity Commission also encourages all charities to follow the advice set out in *Good Governance: a Code for the Voluntary and Community Sector* which identifies six key principles that trustees should adhere to in order to provide good governance and leadership.

Good Governance Code – Key Principles

Understanding their role

Ensuring delivery of organisational purpose

Working effectively both as individuals and a team

Exercising effective control

Behaving with integrity

Being open and accountable

Financial management

As part of their overall responsibility for sound governance, trustees must ensure that the resources of the charity are managed securely and economically and deployed to the best advantage of users and beneficiaries. Robust and effective systems of control are key to achieving this aim as they help ensure that business is conducted in accordance with the law and minimise the risk of a breach of trust. They also play an essential role in demonstrating to potential donors and beneficiaries that the charity is well run and its property is safeguarded.

Sound controls that are clearly laid down and reviewed regularly are also important in helping people who, while acting with the best intentions, might put the charity, its reputation or property at risk through ignorance of the correct procedures.

To be able to discharge their responsibilities effectively, trustees need management information to inform their decision-making. As well as the more usual financial information relating to budget and spend to date, trustees will need:

- to be informed of significant donations
- a list of large or significant transactions
- a summary investment report
- a report on slow moving or overdrawn funds
- a report on the use of the Chairperson's discretionary powers.

The Charity Commission booklet (CC60), *The Hallmarks of an Effective Charity*, sets out the standards the Commission believes an effective charity and its trustees will try to uphold and the principles that its regulatory framework exists to support. As such, it provides some useful pointers to trustees when reviewing their governance arrangements.

Risk management

Trustees should maintain a risk register and review it on a regular basis to ensure the effectiveness of actions taken to mitigate identified risks. Detailed guidance is available on the Charity Commission's website.

Accounting Requirements

The detailed requirements for the preparation and submission of annual accounts of individual charities that are not charitable companies depend upon their level of income or expenditure and where they are based in the UK. The key document to refer to in England and Wales is the Charity Commission's booklet CC15b – *Charity Reporting and Accounting: the Essentials*.

All charities with a gross annual income of over £250,000[6] in the financial year (and all charitable companies) must prepare their accounts on an accruals basis (i.e. all income and expenditure relating to the financial year is included in the accounts regardless of whether cash has actually been received or paid) and follow the relevant Statement of Recommended Practice (SORP) issued by the Charity Commission[7]. Below this threshold, eligible charities may elect to prepare their accounts on a receipts and payments or accruals basis.

In England and Wales the accounts must be audited if either the charity's gross income exceeds £1million, or its gross assets exceed £3.26m and gross income exceeds £250,000.

Trustees are also required to ensure that the charity keeps proper books and records. As a minimum, all charities must:

- prepare and maintain accounting records which must be retained for at least 6 years
- prepare annual accounts and make these available to the public on request
- prepare a trustees' annual report and make it available to the public on request.

What Charity Accruals Accounts Comprise

- a statement of financial activities (SOFA) for the year that shows all incoming and outgoing resources and reconciles all changes in its funds
- a balance sheet, showing the recognised assets, liabilities and different categories of fund of the charity
- for larger charities[8] only, a cash flow statement
- notes explaining the accounting policies adopted.

The HFMA has issued an example trustee annual report and accounts that follows the requirements of the FRS 102 based SORP – it is available via the website.

The Annual Report

The annual report is one of the key tools available to charities to help them communicate with stakeholders including donors, beneficiaries and the wider public. It is normally presented with the accounts but is legally a separate document. The SORP sets out in detail the minimum data

---

[6] These thresholds are subject to change. The current thresholds are available via the Charity Commission's website.
[7] From 2016/17 there is only one Charities SORP based on Financial Reporting Standard 102 (FRS 102).
[8] Larger charities are those with a gross income exceeding £500,000.

requirements. These include[9]:

- details about how trustees are recruited and trained
- details about the charity's decision making processes – for example, what functions are delegated to sub-committees and staff
- an explanation of the charity's aims and the changes/difference it seeks to make through its work
- a statement that the trustees have had regard to the Charity Commission's guidance on public benefit
- details of the charity's objectives for the year and strategy for meeting these
- details of significant activities, projects and services that contribute to the achievement of the charity's objectives
- a description of the reserves policy adopted by the trustees
- a statement setting out the charity's grant making policies
- where material investments are held, details of the investment policy and objectives including the extent to which social, environmental and ethical considerations are taken into account
- details of investment performance against the investment objectives set
- where material funds have been designated, the reserves policy statement should quantify these, explain their purpose and, where they have been set aside for future expenditure, indicate when they are likely to be spent
- for charities with a gross annual income of at least £500,000 a report on their risk management plans including:
  - an acknowledgement of trustees' responsibility
  - an overview of the risk identification process
  - an indication that major risks identified have been reviewed or assessed
  - confirmation that control systems have been established to manage those risks
  - (for larger, or more complex charities) a more detailed description of how their risk management procedures work
- plans for the future.

Key Learning Points

- There are around 260 NHS charities with combined assets of £2bn and annual income of over £327m
- To be charitable, funds must exist to provide public benefit
- There are 13 acceptable charitable purposes
- There are three main types of charitable fund – restricted, unrestricted and endowment

---

[9] This is not an exhaustive list. Full details, including exemptions for smaller charities, are set out in the published SORP which is available via the Charity Commission's website.

- Charitable funds income comes from five main sources – donations; fundraising; legacies, investment income and interest and grants
- All charitable funds spending must be in line with its charitable purpose
- There are three main types of trustee in the NHS – corporate, special and appointed
- Trustees have a duty to ensure compliance, a duty of prudence and a duty of care
- At present, most charitable funds are covered by both NHS and charities legislation
- In England NHS charities can now opt to become independent and regulated solely by the Charity Commission
- The Charity Commission is the statutory organisation that regulates all charities in England and Wales (not just NHS charitable funds)
- Trustees cannot delegate their statutory duties and responsibilities
- Charitable funds have written rules and procedures governing the formal conduct of their business including standing orders, standing financial instructions/prime financial policies and schemes of delegation
- Charities with a gross annual income of more than £250,000 must prepare accruals accounts and follow the Charities SORP
- Charitable funds must produce a trustees' annual report which is normally presented with the annual accounts.

References and Further Reading

Charities Act 2011: www.legislation.gov.uk/ukpga/2011/25/contents/enacted

Other Acts of Parliament referred to in this chapter can be found via:
www.opsi.gov.uk/acts.htm

The Charity Commission guidance publications referred to in this chapter can be found via:
https://www.gov.uk/government/organisations/charity-commission/about/publication-scheme

NHS Charitable Funds: A Practical Guide, HFMA, 2014: www.hfma.org.uk

NHS Charities: Conversion to Independence – Outline Guidance, Department of Health and the Association of NHS Charities, 2015: https://www.gov.uk/government/publications/how-nhs-charities-can-convert-to-independent-status

Review of the Regulation and Governance of NHS Charities, Department of Health, 2014:
https://www.gov.uk/government/consultations/regulation-of-nhs-charities

Good Governance: a Code for the Voluntary and Community Sector:
www.charity-commission.gov.uk/Charity_requirements_guidance/Charity_governance/Good_governance/governancecode.aspx

Charities SORP microsite: http://www.charitiessorp.org/

Example Trustee Annual Report and Accounts, HFMA, 2016 (under briefings): https://www.hfma.org.uk/publications/details/nhs-charitable-funds---example-trustee-annual-reports-and-accounts

Guidance on the content of the annual report is available in the following Charity Commission publications:

Public benefit: reporting (PB3), Charity Commission, 2013:
https://www.gov.uk/government/publications/public-benefit-reporting-pb3

Charity reporting and accounting: the essentials (CC15b), Charity Commission, 2013: https://www.gov.uk/government/publications/charity-reporting-and-accounting-the-essentials-cc15b

Receipts and payments accounts pack (CC16), Charity Commission, 2012:
https://www.gov.uk/government/collections/receipts-and-payments-accounts-pack-cc16

Charity accounting templates: accruals accounts (CC17), Charity Commission, 2013: https://www.gov.uk/government/publications/charity-accounting-templates-accruals-accounts-cc17

Chapter 20
Health and Social Care in Northern Ireland

The primary difference between the NHS in England and services in Northern Ireland is that in Northern Ireland health services and social care are fully integrated. The Department of Health (DoH) is one of the 9 government departments that administers the responsibilities devolved to the Northern Ireland Assembly (NIA).

Currently the health and social care system in Northern Ireland consists of a single commissioner, the Health and Social Care Board (HSCB), a multi-professional Public Health Agency (PHA), five local commissioning groups (LCGs) to cover the same geographical area as five health and social care trusts (HSC trusts) and the DoH. The Northern Ireland Ambulance Service is the sixth trust in Northern Ireland and provides a regional emergency and non-emergency ambulance service. A regional Business Services Organisation (BSO) provides a range of business and administrative support functions for the health and social care service.

In April 2014 the Minister for Health in Northern Ireland commissioned the former Chief Medical Officer in England, Professor Sir Liam Donaldson, to advise on the improvement of governance arrangements. The Donaldson Report *The Right Time, the Right Place* was published in December 2014 and contains a number of recommendations covering:

- coming together for world-class care
- strengthening commissioning
- transforming your care – action not words
- self-management of chronic diseases
- better regulation.

In November 2015 following the publication of this review, the Minister announced:

- a fundamental change to the way services are commissioned, through the standing down of the HSCB. In future, planning for services will be carried out by the health trusts for their local areas, with the DoH taking firmer strategic control of the health and social care system
- the setting up of a panel of experts to lead the debate on the best configuration of health and social care services in Northern Ireland.

These changes are expected to take 18–24 months to come into effect.

Introductory Guide – NHS Finance

Who Does What?

The diagram that follows shows the current structure of health and social care in Northern Ireland. The role of each key player is outlined below.

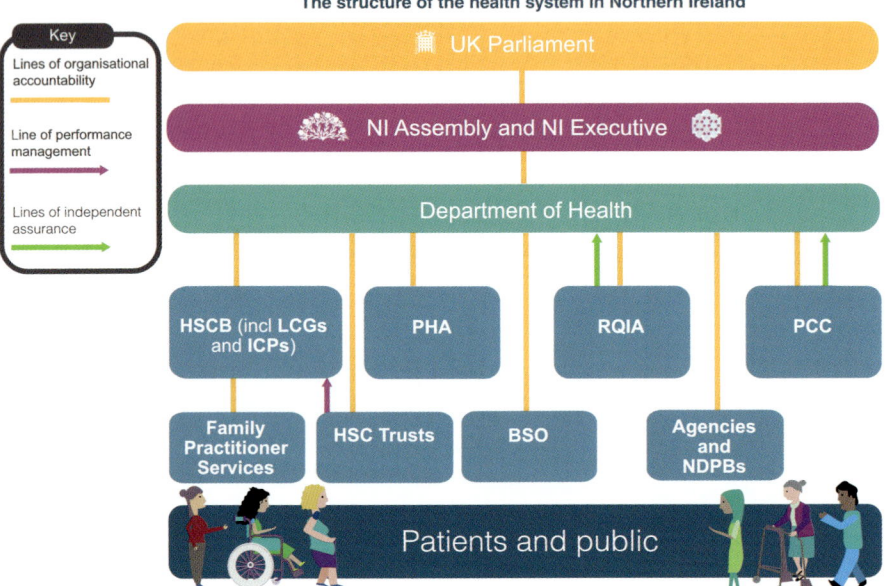

The structure of the health system in Northern Ireland

UK Parliament

The funds for running all public services in the UK ultimately come from Parliament and the public sector in Northern Ireland is expected to operate within the broad framework established by HM Treasury.

Northern Ireland Assembly

The Northern Ireland Assembly (NIA) is the devolved legislature of Northern Ireland. It has power to legislate in a wide range of areas that are not explicitly reserved to the UK Parliament, and to appoint the Northern Ireland Executive. It currently consists of 108 democratically elected members but there are moves to reduce this to 90[1].

Northern Ireland Executive

The Northern Ireland Executive is the executive arm of the NIA. It is answerable to the Assembly and consists of a First Minster, Deputy First Minister and various ministers with individual portfolios and remits. Each minister is in charge of a Department and is responsible for its policy and business.

The Department of Health

In Northern Ireland, both health and social care (HSC) are the responsibility of the Minister for Health. The Department of Health's (DoH) remit covers policy and legislation relating to:

- health and social care (this includes hospitals, family practitioner services, community health and social services)
- public health (to promote and protect the health and wellbeing of the population of Northern Ireland).

[1] *Assembly Members (Reduction of Numbers) Bill, 2016.*

The DoH's mission is to improve the health and social wellbeing of the people of Northern Ireland. It endeavours to do so by:

- leading a major programme of cross-government action to improve the health and wellbeing of the population and reduce health inequalities. This includes interventions involving health promotion and education to encourage people to adopt activities, behaviours and attitudes that lead to better health and wellbeing. The aim is a population that is much more engaged in ensuring its own health and wellbeing
- ensuring the provision of appropriate health and social care services, both in clinical settings such as hospitals and GP surgeries, and in the community through nursing, social work and other professional services.

The Permanent Secretary of the DoH is also chief executive of the health and social care system, as well as Principal Accounting Officer for all of the DoH's responsibilities. Within the DoH, the key business groups are the Resources and Performance Management Group, the Healthcare Policy Group, the Social Services Policy Group, and the Office of the Chief Medical Officer. The DoH also has a Modernisation Directorate and a Human Resources Directorate.

There are five professional groups within the department, each led by a chief professional officer:

- chief medical officer group
- office of social services
- nursing, midwifery and allied health professionals (AHP) directorate
- dental services
- pharmaceutical advice and services.

The DoH reviews any guidance issued by the National Institute for Health and Care Excellence (NICE) and decides if it is relevant for Northern Ireland. If guidance is not considered relevant, or if the DoH decides that it is only partly relevant, it advises on any changes that need to be made. The DoH is likely to approve most NICE guidance and usually decides shortly after NICE has made its decision.

Health and Social Care Board

Currently the Health and Social Care Board (HSCB), together with local commissioning groups and integrated care partnership committees (see below), is accountable to the Minister for Health for translating his vision for health and social care into a range of services that deliver modern and effective outcomes for users, good value for the taxpayer and compliance with statutory obligations.

One of the key tasks for the HSCB is to ensure effective commissioning. The HSCB is also responsible for:

- performance management and service improvement – the process of monitoring health and social care performance against agreed objectives and targets and effectively addressing poor performance
- resource management – ensuring the best possible use of the resources of the health and social care system.

A full description of the responsibilities of the HSCB can be accessed from their website at www.hscboard.hscni.net/

As mentioned earlier, the intention of the current Health Minister is to stand down the HSCB and move its commissioning functions to the five HSC trusts.

Local commissioning groups

Each local commissioning group (LCG) is a subcommittee of the HSCB and is co-terminus with its respective HSC trust area. There are five LCGs:

- Belfast
- Northern
- Southern
- South Eastern
- Western.

LCGs are responsible for commissioning health and social care to address the care needs of their local population. They also have responsibility for assessing health and social care needs; planning health and social care to meet current and emerging needs; and securing the delivery of health and social care to meet those needs.

Within LCG areas there are also integrated care partnership committees (ICPs) which were established in May 2013. There are 17 ICPs across the five LCG areas. ICPs bring together a range of providers from across the health and social care system to review how care is being provided and to consider how services could be improved and better coordinated. ICPs focus on services for frail elderly people and those with some long term conditions: respiratory conditions, diabetes and stroke.

Public Health Agency

The Public Health Agency (PHA) has four primary functions:

- improvement in health and social wellbeing – influencing wider service commissioning, securing and making best use of resources
- health protection – protecting the community from any dangers to health and wellbeing
- service development and screening – working with the HSCB to provide professional input around safety and quality standards in commissioning care
- HSC research and development – promoting research and development into initiatives designed to improve the health and wellbeing of the population of Northern Ireland.

Regulation and Quality Improvement Authority

The Regulation and Quality Improvement Authority (RQIA) is an independent health and social care regulatory body. Its functions include promoting quality through disseminating best practice; regulating a wide range of health and social care services through registration, monitoring and inspection; reviewing and reporting on clinical and social care governance in health and social care and keeping the DoH informed about the provision, availability and quality of health and social care services.

Its role is to ensure that health and social care services in Northern Ireland are accessible, well managed and meet the required standards. RQIA works to ensure that there is openness, clarity and accountability in the management and delivery of all these services.

Patient and Client Council

The Patient and Client Council (PCC) is a regional body supported by five local offices operating within the same geographical areas as the five regional HSC trusts. The overarching objective of the PCC is to provide a powerful, independent voice for patients, clients, carers and communities on health and social care issues.

Health and social care trusts

There are five HSC trusts in Northern Ireland, offering a range of acute and community services (see below). The Belfast, Northern, Southern, South Eastern and Western HSC trusts were formed from the merger of eighteen health and social services trusts. A sixth trust, the Northern Ireland Ambulance Service, manages the ambulance service for Northern Ireland.

Each HSC trust provides the full range of local acute and community services. Regional and specialist services may also be provided by individual trusts. As integrated organisations, trusts also provide social care services including nursing home and domiciliary care, mental health and learning disability and children's community services. Trusts fulfil the role of 'corporate parent' to children in care, the majority in foster care.

HSC trusts, as corporate entities, are responsible in law for the discharge of statutory social care functions delegated to them by virtue of authorisations made under the *Health and Personal Social Services (Northern Ireland) Order 1994*. Trusts are accountable to the HSCB for the discharge of such functions and are obliged to establish sound organisational and related assurance arrangements to ensure their effective discharge.

Business Services Organisation

The Business Services Organisation (BSO) provides a range of business and administrative support and specialist professional services to health and social care bodies – for example, financial services; human resources; legal services; information technology and procurement of goods and services. BSO hosts the HSC shared services department which delivers accounts payable; accounts receivable; payroll and recruitment services for all HSC bodies.

The regional procurement and logistics service (PALS) is part of BSO and is the sole provider of professional supplies services (logistics and procurement) to all public health and social care organisations in Northern Ireland. It is a recognised centre of procurement expertise established under the Northern Ireland Public Procurement Policy as approved by the Northern Ireland Assembly.

Other HSC agencies and non-departmental public bodies (NDPBs)

A variety of specialist functions are carried out by organisations on a Northern Ireland-wide basis. These include:

- Northern Ireland Blood Transfusion Service
- Northern Ireland Guardian Ad Litem Agency
- Northern Ireland Practice and Education Council
- Northern Ireland Medical and Dental Training Agency
- Northern Ireland Social Care Council.

How Health and Social Care is Financed

As mentioned earlier, overall public sector funding for Northern Ireland is provided via the Northern Ireland block vote, as part of the national spending reviews. It is based on a population driven mathematical formula known as the Barnett Formula that has been in use since 1979. Changes to the total provision for Northern Ireland are largely determined through the principle of comparability, whereby HM Treasury adjusts the Northern Ireland block vote in line with comparable programmes in England.

The NIA has the discretion to allocate devolved resources within the Northern Ireland block across all departmental spending programmes. The DoH sets its proposed allocations in the context of the Minister's overall priorities and objectives for the DoH's public expenditure programme. Spending on health and social care equates to approximately 46% of the total public expenditure within the control of the NIA.

Revenue allocation

The DoH makes direct revenue allocations to the HSCB and PHA in the form of a revenue resource limit (RRL). This is to cover hospital, community health and social care services.

The HSCB and PHA use a weighted capitation revenue allocation formula to determine target allocations for hospital, community health and personal social services on a 'programme of care' basis. The formula determines how much each of the five LCGs should receive to purchase services for its residents from trusts.

Allocations are also currently made to the HSCB to commission the four family practitioner services – general medical, pharmacy, dental and ophthalmic services.

Budgets are set for each LCG area based on a weighted capitation formula. Performance against budget for each LCG area is closely monitored particularly in those areas of high expenditure (such as prescribing).

As well as commissioning income, HSC trusts may also receive income from:

- other government bodies or charitable organisations in the form of grants
- the Northern Ireland Medical and Dental Training Agency (NIMDTA)
- the DoH to fund specific initiatives – for example, funding for professional training and development of nursing and social work staff
- contributions from clients in nursing or residential care provided through trusts where clients have been assessed as being able to pay
- charges to staff, visitors or patients – for example, catering, parking or private patient facilities
- recovering the costs incurred if a person treated after being involved in a road traffic collision subsequently makes a successful claim for personal injury compensation
- charitable donations for the benefit of and expenditure on patients and clients. These charitable funds are accounted for separately from the funds that trusts are allocated for providing healthcare to patients and running their organisations
- commercial research activities.

Capital allocation

The DoH also receives a 'capital allocation' from the NIA – in 2015/16 this amounted to just under 20% of the total budget. Capital allocations are made directly to the HSCB, PHA, trusts and smaller non-departmental bodies in the form of a capital resource limit (CRL).

Strategic capital planning is the responsibility of the DoH. Individual HSC organisations submit business cases for capital requirements that must be supported by the commissioner (HSCB) and submitted to the DoH for formal approval. Trusts are allocated funding for non-specific capital expenditure (general capital) used for replacement equipment, maintenance and minor capital works. The utilisation of this funding is also supported by business cases, samples of which are checked for compliance by the DoH.

The DoH is informed by, and contributes to, the overall 10 year *Investment Strategy for Northern Ireland* prepared by the Northern Ireland Executive. The current strategy covers the period 2011–2021.

How HSC Organisations Demonstrate Financial Accountability

HSC bodies have two statutory duties – to break even and to stay within their revenue and capital resource limits.

The HSCB and HSC trusts prepare annual accounts in formats prescribed by the DoH. Accounts are produced based on guidance in HM Treasury's *Financial Reporting Manual* (FReM) following international financial reporting standards (IFRS).

The DoH issues a detailed *Manual of Accounts* for all health and social care bodies that is updated annually as required to reflect changes in reporting requirements. Where these differ for a DoH body, the manual sets out the procedures that the body has to follow.

The accounts must be formally adopted by the DoH, in time to meet the NIA summer recess deadlines (normally June following the financial year-end on 31 March). Following this the accounts must be published on the websites of the HSC bodies and made available to members of the public.

The director of finance is responsible for preparing the accounts.

The annual accounts are audited by the Northern Ireland Audit Office (NIAO), either by its own staff or by contracting out to private sector firms of accountants and auditors. Each set of accounts is then formally laid before the NIA. The Assembly has a Public Accounts Committee (PAC) with a similar role to the committee of the House of Commons of the same name.

HSC bodies are required to have in place suitable internal audit arrangements. At present, this service is provided by BSO Internal Audit Unit. Internal audit must comply with Public Sector Internal Audit Standards (PSIAS). The adequacy of the internal audit arrangements is reviewed and reported on each year by the NIAO as part of their report to those charged with the governance of each body.

How HSC Organisations are Regulated

As mentioned earlier, the key regulatory body in Northern Ireland is the Regulation and Quality Improvement Authority (RQIA).

How HSC Organisations are Structured and Run

The governance regime for HSC bodies is similar to that in place throughout the NHS in the rest of the UK making use of codes of conduct and accountability, internal audit, external audit, board reports, annual accounts, annual reports and public board meetings.

As with the NHS in England, the board of each HSC body is the pre-eminent governing body. There are also two mandatory committees of the board – audit and remuneration.

Chief executives of HSC organisations are designated 'Accounting Officers'. They are accountable to the DoH (and ultimately to the NIA) for the appropriate stewardship of public money and assets and for the organisation's performance. Chief executives are also accountable to their board for meeting its objectives and the day-to-day running of the organisation.

Commissioning

As explained earlier, one of the current key tasks of the HSCB is commissioning. The HSCB develops an annual commissioning plan in close partnership with the Public Health Agency through a 'commissioning cycle' that covers:

- assessing needs
- strategic planning across the HSC and all programmes of care
- priority setting
- securing resources to address needs
- agreeing with providers the delivery of appropriate services (and subsequent monitoring of that delivery)
- assuring that the safety and quality of services commissioned are improving, that recommendations from the RQIA and other reviews have been implemented and that as a minimum, services meet DoH and other recognised standards

- evaluating the impact and feeding learning back into the new baseline position in terms of how needs have changed.

For the most part the HSCB/PHA commissioning plan reflects the decisions and recommendations of the LCGs as they have devolved responsibility for assessing and ultimately addressing the needs of their local populations, working within regional policy and strategy frameworks, available resources and performance targets. LCGs also have responsibility for fully integrating commissioning to deliver better health and wellbeing and improve health outcomes for their local populations as well as reducing health inequalities locally and across the population of Northern Ireland.

As mentioned earlier, these areas are co-terminus with HSC trust boundaries. This geographical orientation better reflects the needs of natural communities and the organisation of local health and social care economies, including hospitals, community networks and geographically based partners. On the other hand, commissioning around 'communities of interest' or client-groups, or 'programmes of care' can ensure that the needs of service users and carers are addressed holistically and services are planned in a coordinated way to meet particular needs.

Both approaches operate within the health and social care commissioning landscape in Northern Ireland. Whilst the establishment of LCGs gives prominence to geography, this is balanced by 'programme of care' based planning within LCGs. These teams link across LCG boundaries where necessary, to form regional strategic planning networks relevant to client or 'community of interest' groups.

Commissioning of services from independent family practitioner contractors is managed by the HSCB. These arrangements recognise regional priorities, including service framework standards.

Costing

The five HSC trusts submit annual reference cost returns that capture the cost of services across a prescribed list of health and social care activities. HRG based reference costs (similar to those calculated in England) are calculated for most hospital acute inpatients and day cases, and community and personal social services indicators are calculated for a range of community and social care services.

Organisations use these reference costs to compare their costs with those of similar organisations. This comparison establishes a benchmark that enables organisations to identify areas where they may be able to reduce costs or increase productivity by understanding and implementing best practice methodologies used in other provider organisations. The unit costs are also used to inform the revenue business case process and respond to assembly questions and external information requests.

Charitable Funds

Charitable funds accounts are held by HSC trusts in Northern Ireland and are largely comprised of donations by individuals or legacies.

As in England and Wales these funds are used for the purpose for which the original donation was intended or the bequest was made (where that is known) otherwise the uses to which the funds can be put may be unrestricted. Charitable funds are held and controlled by HSC trusts and boards as corporate trustees.

A trust prepares separate annual accounts for its charitable funds and is also required to consolidate these accounts into the overall trust annual accounts.

The Charity Commission for Northern Ireland was established on 27 March 2009 and regulates charities, including HSC charitable funds.

References and Further Reading

The Donaldson Report – The Right Time, the Right Place, 2014:
https://www.health-ni.gov.uk/files/donaldsonreport270115pdf-0

Department of Health: www.health-ni.gov.uk/

The Health and Social Care Board: www.hscboard.hscni.net/

Public Health Agency: www.publichealth.hscni.net

The Regulation and Quality Improvement Authority: www.rqia.org.uk/home/index.cfm

Patient and Client Council: www.patientclientcouncil.hscni.net

Belfast Health and Social Care Trust: www.belfasttrust.hscni.net/

Northern Health and Social Care Trust: www.northerntrust.hscni.net/

Southern Health and Social Care Trust: www.southerntrust.hscni.net/

South Eastern Health and Social Care Trust: www.setrust.hscni.net/

Western Health and Social Care Trust: www.westerntrust.hscni.net/

Northern Ireland Ambulance Service Health and Social Care Trust: www.niamb.co.uk/

Business Services Organisation: http://www.hscbusiness.hscni.net/

Health and Social Care in Northern Ireland: www.hscni.net/

Northern Ireland Audit Office: www.niauditoffice.gov.uk

The Charity Commission for Northern Ireland: http://www.charitycommissionni.org.uk/

Chapter 21

The NHS in Scotland

> Responsibility for health services in Scotland was devolved from Westminster to the Scottish Parliament in 1998.
>
> The Scottish Government is formed by the party with the majority of Members of the Scottish Parliament. The Scottish Government sets national objectives and priorities for the NHS in Scotland.

Who Does What?

The diagram that follows shows the structure of the NHS in Scotland and how accountability flows. Each element is discussed in more detail below.

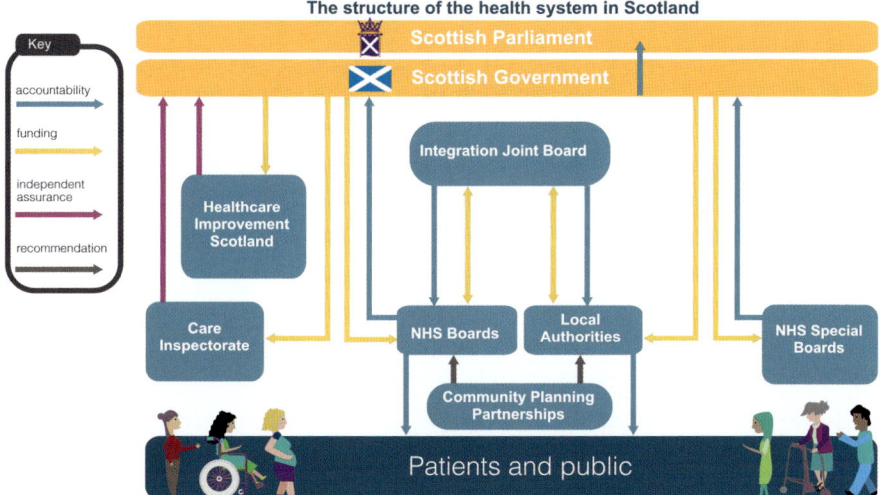

The structure of the health system in Scotland

Scottish Parliament

The Scottish Parliament is made up of 129 elected Members of the Scottish Parliament (MSPs). The last election was in May 2016.

The Scottish Parliament is responsible for passing laws relating to those matters which affect most aspects of day-to-day life in Scotland. These include health and social services.

The Scottish Parliament has recently been given more autonomy and additional areas of devolution as a result of the *Scotland Act 2016*.

Scottish Government

Immediately after each election, the Scottish Parliament nominates the First Minister who is then appointed by the Queen. The Scottish Government is led by the First Minister who is supported by a Cabinet formed of Scottish Ministers. It is the Cabinet Secretary for Health and Sport who has responsibility for the NHS as well as healthcare and social integration. The Scottish Government, led by the Cabinet, sets national objectives and priorities for the NHS.

The directorate of the Scottish Government responsible for the delivery of those objectives and priorities is the Scottish Government Health and Social Care Directorate (SGHSCD).

The SGHSCD is responsible for:

- providing strategic leadership for the NHS and social care in Scotland as well as public health
- leading the integration of health and social care into wider government policy
- supporting ministers in accounting to the public and the Scottish Parliament
- managing and allocating public money to the various parts of the NHS in Scotland
- ensuring that the highest standards of health and social care are met
- ensuring that high quality health and social care services are delivered to the Scottish population.

NHS boards

There are 14 NHS boards that cover the whole of Scotland. They are responsible for planning, commissioning and delivering NHS services to their populations. They also take overall responsibility for the health of their populations. This involves planning and commissioning community and hospital health services including services provided by GPs, dentists, community pharmacists and opticians.

From 1 April 2016, all NHS boards (except NHS Highlands) devolved responsibility for planning and resourcing the provision for integrated adult and social care to an Integration Joint Board (see the diagram above).

NHS boards are funded by and report directly to the SGHSCD. The chief executive of each NHS board is an Accountable Officer directly responsible to the Scottish Parliament

Roles of NHS Boards

- improve and protect the health of local people
- improve health services for local people
- focus clearly on health outcomes and people's experience of their local NHS system
- plan and deliver integrated health and social care services through formal integration partnership arrangements with local authorities
- provide a single focus of accountability for the performance of the local NHS system
- involve the public in the design and delivery of healthcare services.

Functions of NHS Boards

- strategic development
- resource allocation
- financial stewardship
- implementation of the local health plan
- performance management of the local NHS system
- preparation and implementation of the local health plan
- appointment, appraisal and remuneration of senior executives
- governance of the NHS board.

Special NHS boards

National or special NHS boards provide services across the whole of Scotland. They are also funded by and report directly to the SGHSCD. There are currently 7 special boards as follows:

- NHS Education for Scotland – concerned with developing and delivering quality education and training for NHS staff
- NHS Health Scotland – promotes ways to improve the health of the population and reduce health inequalities
- NHS National Waiting Times Centre – ensures prompt access to first-class treatment
- NHS 24 – provides health advice and information
- the Scottish Ambulance Service
- the State Hospitals Board for Scotland – has responsibility for secure settings for those with mental health disorders who are unable to be cared for in any other setting
- NHS National Services Scotland – supplying essential services including health protection, blood transfusion and information technology.

As with NHS boards, the chief executive of each special NHS board is an Accountable Officer directly responsible to the Scottish Parliament

Healthcare Improvement Scotland

Healthcare Improvement Scotland is the single public health body for Scotland. Its role includes:

- supporting and empowering people to have an informed voice in managing their own care and shaping how services are designed and delivered
- delivering scrutiny activity through the healthcare environment inspectorate
- providing quality improvement support to healthcare providers
- providing clinical standards, guidelines and advice.

Care Inspectorate

The Care Inspectorate regulates and inspects care services in Scotland to make sure that they meet the necessary standards. It also jointly inspects with other regulators, to ascertain how well different organisations in local areas work to support adults and children.

The Care Inspectorate is a publicly funded executive non departmental public body, which means it operates independently from Scottish ministers but is accountable to them.

Local authorities

There are 32 directly elected local authorities in Scotland funded, in the main, through a block grant from the Scottish government. They have responsibility for a wide range of public services including social work and community care. They have a mandate to tackle poverty and promote social inclusion in their local areas.

Integration

In April 2014, the *Public Bodies (Joint Working) (Scotland) Act 2014* was passed. The purpose of the legislation was to provide a framework to improve the quality and consistency of health and social care services in Scotland.

The Act requires NHS boards and local authorities to enter into an integration scheme to ensure the effective delivery of the delegated functions. The integration scheme sets out the range of functions (or services) it covers and must meet the minimum requirements set out in the legislation. At a minimum, the functions covered must include adult social care services, adult community health services and a proportion of adult acute services. The inclusion of children's services is at the discretion of the partners in each area.

An integration authority (IA) is an entity that has responsibility for ensuring that health and social care services are planned, managed and delivered in an integrated manner. The Scottish model allows the integration authority to take one of two forms:

Integration joint board

This option is illustrated in the diagram at the start of the chapter and is the model that has been adopted across Scotland with the exception of the Highlands.

The 2014 Act allows local authorities and NHS boards to create a separate legal entity known as an Integration Joint Board (IJB). IJBs are local government bodies (not NHS organisations) and are therefore subject to the same financial governance framework as local government bodies. The IJB has a chief officer who has a direct line of accountability to the chief executives of the NHS board and the local authority for the delivery of integrated services.

Voting members of the IJB comprise equal representation from the NHS boards and local authorities involved.

The IJB is responsible for the planning, resourcing and operational delivery of all integrated services delegated to it. These services are set out in the IJB's strategic plan and integrated scheme. Decisions on integrated services are now joint and integrated and made by the IJB.

NHS boards and local authorities make payments to the IJB and NHS boards can also set aside parts of their budget for the IJB. The IJB then directs and pays for the NHS board and local authority, or other providers, to deliver services in line with its strategic plan for the delivery of local integrated health and social care services. IJBs are required to produce an annual performance report on the extent to which their strategic objectives have been met.

Integration joint monitoring committee

This option has been adopted only in the Highlands and is illustrated in the diagram below.

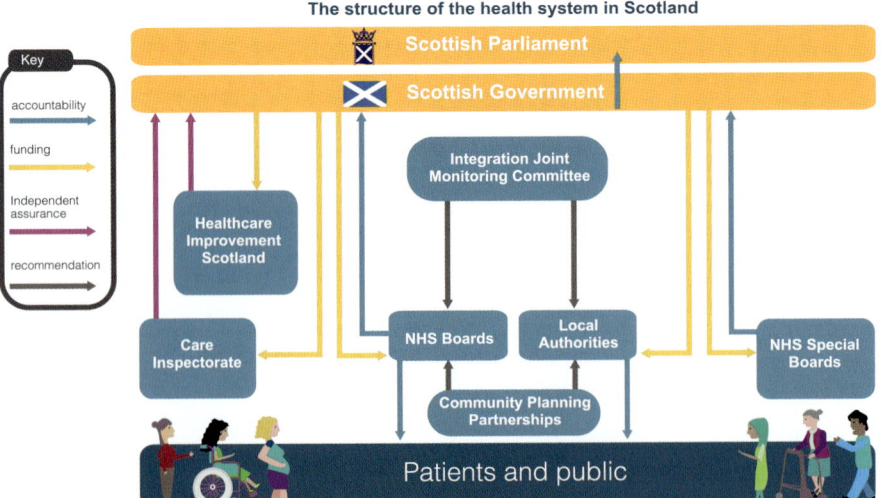

The structure of the health system in Scotland

In this case, no new entity is established. Instead, the decision is made that either the health board or the local authority will take lead responsibility for the provision of integrated health and social care services. As there is no separate entity, the chief executive of the lead body is accountable for the provision of these integrated services.

An integration joint monitoring committee is established by the health board and local authority. It not a separate legal entity but its role is to scrutinise the delivery of integrated arrangements and report on progress. It is effectively an overseeing committee whose job is to make recommendations on how the NHS board and local authorities can make best use of resources to deliver integrated health and social care services to their local population.

In order to effect integration of health and social care services in this scenario, NHS boards and local authorities can move funding between each other, with the lead body having ultimate responsibility for delivering integrated health and social care services.

Community Planning Partnerships (CPPs)

Community planning partnerships (CPPs) are the mechanism that helps public agencies to work together with the community to plan and deliver better services to make a real difference to people's lives.

The *Community Empowerment (Scotland) Act 2015*, strengthens community planning by giving CPPs a statutory footing. It also explicitly states that public bodies including NHS boards will work together with communities to improve outcomes for a local area. Whilst there are no specified lines of accountability, NHS boards and integration authorities are obligated to ensure that there is both direct contribution and leadership within their local CPP. The CPP should focus on how to improve local priority outcomes relating to health and wellbeing.

Development of NHS Scotland's Current Strategy

In 2011, the 2020 Vision was published setting out the Scottish Parliament's vision for Scotland.

> **The 2020 Vision for health and social care in Scotland is that '… by 2020 everyone is able to live longer, healthier lives at home, or in a homely setting.'**
>
> This will be delivered by the following key strategies:
>
> - integrated health and social care
> - a focus on prevention, anticipation and supported self-management
> - where hospital treatment is required and cannot be provided in a community setting, day case treatment will be the norm
> - care will be provided to the highest standards of quality and safety, with the person at the centre of all decisions, whatever the setting
> - a focus on ensuring that people get back into their home or community environment as soon as appropriate.

In 2016, the SGHSCD published *A National Clinical Strategy for Scotland* in which it provided some clarity on the Scottish Government's priorities for the reform it considers necessary to meet people's health and social care needs by 2020 and beyond.

The strategy is underpinned by the following key principles:

- quality is the primary concern
- developments should be guided by evidence where available and all changes should be evaluated before they are made
- the people using health and social care services are of central importance along with their carers and the community which supports them

- services should be built around supporting people and should be integrated and community based rather than single disease pathways
- services should be planned and delivered at a local level unless there is evidence that regional or national planning would provide better outcomes
- there should be equitable access to health and social care support to minimise the impact of health inequalities.

Statutory Provisions

The following legislation is relevant to the operation of the NHS in Scotland:

- *National Health Service (Scotland) Act 1974* and *National Health Service (Scotland) Act 1978* – these Acts establish NHS boards and their roles and responsibilities
- *Public Finance and Accountability (Scotland) Act 2000* – this sets out the rules for the Parliament's budgetary process and procedures for the approval of expenditure, use of resources, management of audit and scrutiny of the outputs obtained from that expenditure
- *Community Care and Health (Scotland) Act 2002* – this provides the legislative backing for improvements in care services
- *National Health Service Reform (Scotland) Act 2004* – this allowed for the dissolution of NHS trusts; introduced a statutory duty for NHS boards to co-operate with each other with a view to enhancing the health of the nation (for example, through regional and national planning); established powers of intervention on behalf of Scottish ministers in case of service failure; and imposed on NHS boards duties to encourage public involvement and promote health improvement
- *Patient Rights (Scotland) Act 2011* – this requires the Scottish Government to publish a charter of patient rights and responsibilities and keep it under review
- *Public Bodies (Joint Working) (Scotland) Act 2014* – this requires health bodies and local authorities to create arrangements to jointly plan and manage the delivery of a specified range of health and social care services. The legislation outlines two alternative approaches for achieving this integration of services (outlined above) and specifies the local authority and NHS board areas that must collaborate. The new arrangements introduced by this legislation went live from 1 April 2016
- *Children and Young People (Scotland) Act 2014* – this introduced requirements for local authorities, health boards and other service providers to jointly plan for children's services
- *Community Empowerment (Scotland) Act 2015* – this placed Community Planning Partnerships on a statutory footing and imposed duties on them around planning and delivery of local outcomes. It also allows CPPs to request to participate in plans being made by NHS boards and local authorities (among other bodies).

Local Delivery Plans

All NHS boards are required to publish a rolling three year local delivery plan (LDP). NHS boards that are not in recurring financial balance are also required to produce a five year plan.

The LDP covers a three year period but is updated annually. The LDP is prepared by the NHS board in conjunction with the strategic commissioning planning arrangements for joint integration boards.

> **What LDPs include**
>
> - LDP targets and plans to meet them
> - the NHS board's plans to contribute to national priorities
> - financial plans
> - a summary of workforce requirements
> - the community planning partnership's contribution.

Progress against the LDP is assessed throughout the year and a mid-year 'stock take' of progress is undertaken by each NHS board with the SGHSCD.

Shared Services

NHS Scotland operates a single shared finance system utilising a common chart of accounts and standard processes.

As part of its 2020 Vision, the Scottish government is committed to increasing shared services across all organisational 'support' services including finance and HR. This work is being progressed through NHS National Services Scotland with the close involvement of NHS board chief executives under the banner of 'Once for Scotland'.

How the NHS in Scotland is Financed

NHS Scotland funding forms part of the Scotland vote, which competes in the public expenditure survey (PES) against UK votes such as defence, social security and the environment. The First Minister for Scotland has the task of dividing up the Scottish vote among the various services for which he/she is responsible including health, prisons, education and social services. Health is one of the major areas of expenditure.

Since April 2010, the allocation of resources for hospital and community health services (HCHS) as well as GP prescribing has been based on a funding formula developed by the Technical Advisory Group on Resource Allocation (TAGRA). This formula reflects a number of factors including population share, the age and sex breakdown of that population and level of deprivation.

Cash limited/ non-cash limited

Funds allocated for HCHS are distributed via a resource allocation. These are cash limited funds – NHS boards are not allowed to overspend against their allocation (resource limit) and are highly restricted in their ability to carry forward surpluses or deficits from one year into another.

Funding for family health services (specifically dental, community pharmacy and ophthalmic services) forms part of the Scottish government health allocation. Although this is subject to a cash limit nationally much of the expenditure is not subject to cash limits at NHS board level.

Capital planning process

Capital resources are managed through the SGHSCD capital investment group ('CIG'). The following approvals apply:

For publicly funded schemes:

- less than £1m: a full business case (to be considered and approved locally)
- £1m–£5m: initial agreement and full business case (where such a project is above the NHS body's delegated limit, CIG approval is required)
- £5m+: initial agreement, outline business case, full business case (all requiring CIG approval).

For IM&T projects:

- less than £0.5m: full business case
- £0.5m–£2m: initial agreement and full business case
- £2m+: initial agreement, outline business case, full business case.

For schemes to be funded through the 'hub initiative':

- the hub initiative is managed by an independent organisation – the Scottish Future Trust. Its aim is to integrate capital projects across the whole public sector, using a mixture of private and public sector funding. All projects put forward for 'hub' funding must be approved by CIG, regardless of value.

For schemes to be funded through private financing (non-profits distribution (NPD) schemes):

- any new or re-financed NPD schemes require CIG approval, regardless of value.[1]

How Organisations Demonstrate Financial Accountability

Financial targets

NHS boards are required by statute to operate within their:

- revenue resource limit
- capital resource limit
- cash requirement.

All NHS boards have a responsibility to control their finances throughout the year. Performance is monitored by the SGHSCD. As a result, NHS boards are required to complete monthly financial performance returns (FPR) for the SGHSCD.

On an annual basis audited accounts must be produced and various statements signed by the chief executive, including an annual governance statement. The annual accounts must be published and made available publicly as part of the annual report.

NHS boards are required to prepare their accounts in accordance with the *Scottish Public Finance Manual* which is consistent with HM Treasury's *Financial Reporting Manual (FReM)*. The SGHSCD determines the format of external reporting by the production of an accounts template which is also used to produce consolidated accounts for the NHS in Scotland.

The principles of financial control and internal monitoring are set out in financial directions. It is left to local discretion to determine the exact nature of internal monitoring but it is sensible that this mirrors external requirements. Internal financial control is ensured through the adoption of standing financial instructions, standard operating procedures and formal schemes of delegation.

NHS boards meet regularly with the SGHSCD to monitor and forecast progress against the statutory targets. Where an organisation is forecast to miss a target, remedial action is expected so that the target can be achieved. In cases where a NHS board fails to operate within its revenue resource limit, it can apply for a loan known as 'brokerage'. Arrangements for the repayment of this loan must be agreed between the NHS board and the SGHSCD.

Governance and Audit

Audit Scotland and external audit

The audit of NHS Scotland is the responsibility of the Auditor General for Scotland (AGS). The AGS appoints auditors to each NHS board. The AGS is supported by Audit Scotland, which commissions audits from its own staff and commercial firms of auditors.

[1] Full details are set out in CEL 32(2010).

Auditors perform the audits of NHS boards in accordance with the *Code of Audit Practice* issued by Audit Scotland and approved by the AGS. Auditors are responsible for considering:

- financial stewardship and governance through the annual audit of NHS bodies' accounts
- achievement of value for money through a programme of national performance audit reports.

Internal audit

NHS boards maintain an internal audit function to carry out more detailed work at local level. NHS boards may provide internal audit themselves, by means of a consortium arrangement with neighbouring boards or contract out this service to private firms.

Counter fraud services

Counter Fraud Services (CFS) deters, detects and investigates frauds and other irregularities throughout NHS Scotland. CFS is hosted by NHS National Services Scotland and has links with every NHS board through partnership agreements and nominated fraud liaison officers. Concentrating initially on fraud within primary care services, the remit of CFS was expanded in 2004 to encompass all areas of fraud throughout the NHS in Scotland. CFS also undertakes pro-active exercises in areas of high risk.

Performance audits

Audit Scotland is responsible for carrying out performance audits (formerly known as value for money audits). The AGS also produces an annual overview of the performance of the NHS in Scotland that provides information on a range of performance measures – clinical outcomes, waiting times, GP prescribing, health inequalities and financial performance.

Risk assessment

The clinical negligence and other risks indemnity scheme (CNORIS) was launched in 2000 with mandatory membership for all health bodies. The scheme has two principal aims:

- financial efficiency through cost effective risk pooling and claims management
- effective risk management by encouraging a rigorous approach to the treatment of risk.

Costing and Pricing

Costing

The *Costs Book* provides cost information for NHS Scotland and a detailed analysis of where resources are spent. It is used mainly for benchmarking by healthcare providers to assess efficiency. The *Costs Book* contains NHS board information for hospital and primary care services. There are three main reports:

- hospital sector – running costs
- community health services
- family health services.

Managers at all levels can use the information as an aid to decision-making, planning and control and it also provides a set of indicators of performance for comparison purposes.

The information contained within the reports is derived from financial and statistical information prepared by the NHS boards.

Pricing

NHS Scotland has introduced a pricing or tariff system for cross boundary activity flows for acute hospital in-patients and day cases.

The price or tariff is calculated using healthcare resource groups (HRGs) to reflect the differences in casemix complexity. The Scottish tariff relates directly to the *Costs Book* and is based on national average costs distributed over Scottish activity data. However, because the Scottish costing data is not collected at detailed HRG level, the English reference costs are used to estimate costs at the HRG level. This is done by applying relative weights to Scottish costs based on the assumption that the resource differential between any two procedures or conditions in Scotland is the same as in England. For example if a hip replacement costs around 4 times as much as an arthroscopy in England, then it is assumed that this is also the case in Scotland.

Although the Scottish tariffs are based on English HRG costs, they are not directly comparable due to the different methodologies applied.

Endowment Funds

As with trust or charitable funds in England and Wales, endowment funds are derived from donations by individuals, legacies etc. and are used for the purpose for which the original donation was given where that is known. Endowment funds are held and controlled by trustees who are also members of the NHS board under the 1978 Act. The board of trustees is an unincorporated body responsible for all matters relating to the charitable funds.

References and Further Reading

On line information from NHS Scotland: www.show.scot.nhs.uk/

Legislation can be found at: http://www.legislation.gov.uk/browse/scotland

2020 Vision for Health and Social Care in Scotland, 2011:
www.scotland.gov.uk/Topics/Health/Policy/2020-Vision

A National Clinical Strategy for Scotland, 2016: www.gov.scot/Resource/0049/00494144.pdf

NHS Scotland Local Delivery Plan Guidance 2015/16: www.gov.scot/Resource/0046/00468479.pdf

National health and wellbeing outcomes framework: www.gov.scot/Resource/0047/00470219.pdf

Shared services information: http://www.gov.scot/Topics/Government/PublicServiceReform/efficientgovernment/SharedServices

Single national human resources system: www.swiss.scot.nhs.uk/index.php/eess

Resource Allocation Formula for 2016/17: https://isdscotland.scot.nhs.uk/Health-Topics/Finance/Publications/2015-09-29/2015-09-29-NRAC-Summary.pdf?62258547545

Arrangements for the management of NHS Scotland capital resources after 2010/11 – CEL 32, 2010: www.sehd.scot.nhs.uk/mels/CEL2010_32.pdf

Scottish Public Finance Manual: www.scotland.gov.uk/Topics/Government/Finance/spfm/Intro

Auditor General, Audit Scotland and the Accounts Commission: www.audit-scotland.gov.uk/about/ags/

NHS National Services Scotland: www.nhsnss.org

Counter Fraud Services: www.nhsnss.org/pages/services/counter_fraud_services.php

Scottish Health Service Costs Book, Information Services Division: www.isdscotland.org/Health-Topics/Finance/Costs/

Scottish National Tariff: www.isdscotland.org/Health-Topics/Finance/Scottish-National-Tariff/

Chapter 22
The NHS in Wales

> The National Assembly for Wales ('the Assembly') and Welsh Government were established in 1999 and have devolved responsibility for a range of areas including health, education, agriculture, transport and local government. Following a referendum in March 2011, the Assembly now has the power to create laws in 20 areas of devolved policy, including health.
>
> The Welsh Government develops and implements policy in these areas and is accountable to the Assembly.
>
> In terms of its structure, the Welsh Government comprises a cabinet of Welsh ministers led by the First Minister who is appointed by the Crown. Cabinet responsibility for the NHS in Wales rests with the Minister for Health and Social Services.
>
> Many of the principles underpinning NHS finance in Wales are similar to those in England – this chapter focuses on the key differences relating to finance and governance.

Who Does What?

The diagram that follows shows the structure of the NHS in Wales and how accountability flows. Each element is discussed in more detail below.

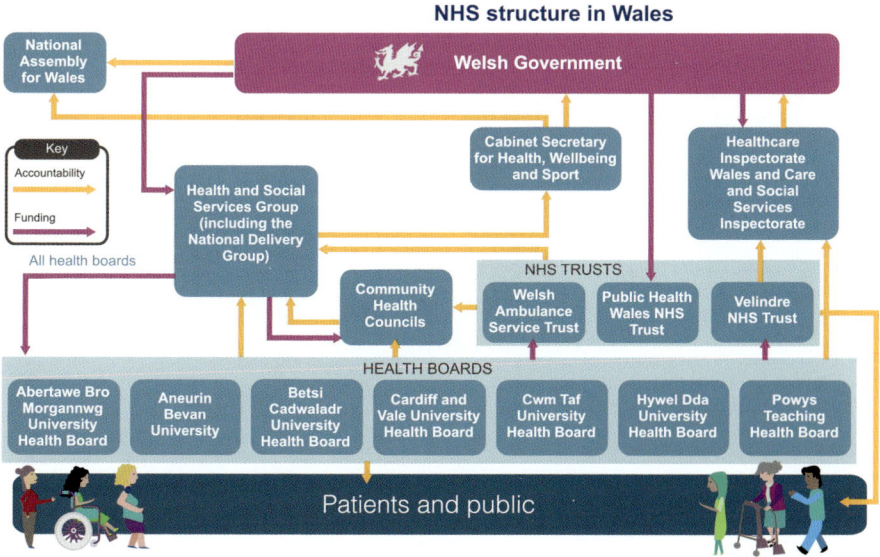

NHS structure in Wales

National Assembly for Wales ('the Assembly')

The Assembly is the democratically elected body that represents the interests of Wales and its people, makes laws for Wales, and holds the Welsh Government to account. It comprises 60 members, known as Assembly Members (AMs).

The Welsh Government

The Welsh Government is responsible for setting overall policy for the NHS in Wales and for funding the local health boards (LHBs).

The arrangements provided for in the *Government of Wales Act 2006* created a formal legal separation between the Assembly and the Welsh Government (sometimes called the executive).

The Welsh Government is usually established by the party or parties who hold the majority of seats in the Assembly. The Welsh Government consists of Welsh ministers, deputy ministers and the Counsel General and is headed by the First Minister. The role of the executive is to:

- make decisions regarding the devolved areas for the whole of Wales
- develop and implement policy
- propose Welsh laws and make statutory instruments.

The AMs scrutinise the Welsh Government's decisions and policies, hold ministers to account, approve budgets for the Welsh Government's programmes, and have the power to enact 'Assembly Measures' on certain matters.

Welsh Ministers

The Cabinet Secretary for Health, Wellbeing and Sport is the Welsh Minister responsible (and accountable to the Assembly) for the exercise of all the powers in the health and social services portfolio. The Cabinet Secretary is supported by the Minister for Social Services and Public Health.

Health and Social Services Group

The Health and Social Services Group (HSSG) is the Welsh Government department responsible for the NHS and social care in Wales. It is headed by the Director General of Health and Social Services who is also the Chief Executive of NHS Wales. The HSSG supports ministers and the Director General in discharging their responsibilities. The Chief Medical Officer for Wales is also a member of the HSSG.

The role of the HSSG is to set and implement policy in relation to:

- planning, developing and co-ordinating the delivery of NHS services, including specialist services, within the framework set down by ministers
- defining, in consultation with NHS local bodies, required outcomes and accompanying resources as part of a regular planning cycle
- facilitating the effective performance management of NHS local bodies to ensure delivery of defined outcomes.

The HSSG is also responsible for the development of social services policy for Wales.

National Delivery Group

The Chief Executive of NHS Wales is responsible for providing ministers with policy advice and exercising strategic leadership and management of the NHS. To support this role, the Chief Executive chairs a National Delivery Group, which forms part of the HSSG.

This group is responsible for overseeing the development and delivery of NHS services across Wales and for planning and performance management of the NHS on behalf of Welsh ministers. This is in accordance with the directions set by ministers.

Community Health Councils

Community Health Councils (CHCs) are statutory, independent bodies who listen to what individuals and the community have to say about the health services provided to them with regard to quality, quantity, access and appropriateness of the services. CHCs then act as the public voice in letting managers know what people want and how things can be improved.

CHCs have a statutory right to visit hospitals, clinics and primary care establishments where NHS services are delivered. This includes GP practices, dental surgeries, opticians, pharmacists and nursing homes.

There are seven CHCs which are co-terminus with the seven local health boards (LHBs).

The board of community health councils is a separate statutory body responsible for monitoring the performance of the CHCs in Wales as well as operating a complaints procedure for those who wish to make a complaint about NHS services in Wales.

Care and Social Services Inspectorate (CSSIW) and Healthcare Inspectorate Wales (HIW)

The CSSIW is responsible for the inspection and regulation of social and non-health care for adults and children in Wales. The HIW is responsible for the inspection and regulation of Welsh NHS services (including Welsh NHS funded care) and independent healthcare services in Wales.

Both organisations are managed outside HSSG within the Welsh Government, in order to maintain their independence. Special arrangements exist to ensure these organisations are able to operate in an independent manner.

A protocol exists to ensure a coordinated approach between the CHCs and the HIW in areas where there is cross-over in their work.

NHS Wales

NHS Wales comprises seven LHBs and three NHS trusts. Specialist services are planned and funded jointly by the LHBs through the Welsh Health Specialised Services Committee.

The LHBs and trusts are accountable to the Director General of Health and Social Services and Chief Executive of NHS Wales (the Director General) through their chief executives. The Director General is in turn accountable to Ministers.

Local health boards (LHBs)

The seven LHBs are responsible for planning for the health needs of their entire population With the exception of Powys LHB, all LHBs hold 'University Health Board' status. Powys LHB holds 'Teaching Health Board' status. In particular LHBs are responsible for:

- planning, designing, developing and securing delivery of primary, community and secondary care services
- specialist and tertiary services for their areas, to meet identified local needs within the national policy and standards framework set out by the Minister.

Under the provisions of the *Social Services and Well-being (Wales) Act 2014*, local authorities and LHBs are able to pool funding to jointly commission care services within their areas. The Welsh ministers have the powers to make regulations requiring local authorities and LHBs to pool budgets.

The LHBs adhere to the standards of good governance set for the NHS in Wales, which are based on the Welsh Government's *Citizen Centred Governance Principles*.

Public service boards

The *Well-being of Future Generations (Wales) Act 2015* is about improving the social, economic, environmental and cultural well-being of Wales. The Act puts in place seven wellbeing goals. Under the Act, statutory organisations called public service boards (PSBs) have been created based on local authority boundaries. The members of each PSB are the local authority, the LHB, the local fire and rescue authority and the Natural Resources Body for Wales.

PSBs must improve the economic, social, environmental and cultural wellbeing of its area by:

- assessing the state of economic, social, environmental and cultural wellbeing in its area and
- setting objectives that are designed to maximise the PSB's contribution to the wellbeing goals.

Each PSB is required to prepare a plan setting out the steps it will take to meet its objectives.

NHS trusts

There are three NHS trusts in Wales:

- the Welsh Ambulance Services NHS Trust provides emergency and non-emergency ambulance services and manages NHS Direct in Wales
- Velindre NHS Trust provides specialist cancer services for South Wales, as well as hosting several all-Wales services, including the Welsh Blood Service and the NHS Wales Informatics Service
- Public Health Wales NHS Trust provides all-Wales screening services and a National Public Health Service.

How the NHS in Wales is Funded

NHS Wales is funded by the Welsh Government which itself receives funds voted to it by the UK Parliament.

Any changes to the funding provided to the Department of Health for the NHS in England are matched by an increase in the Welsh Government's funding through the Barnett formula, but it is for the Welsh Government to determine how this funding is applied. This is done through an annual budget planning round which allocates funding to the sectors for which the Welsh Government has responsibility. The budget is formally presented to the Assembly for approval in an annual budget motion.

The Health and Social Services budget is the largest expenditure group in the Welsh Assembly's budget and accounts for approximately 48% of the total.

The allocation for health and social services comprises:

- a revenue budget for current expenditure (i.e. the day-to-day money for salaries and consumables). In 2016/17, this amounts to £6.7bn[1]
- a capital budget for expenditure on larger, long life items such as land and buildings. In 2016/17, this amounts to £273m.

The Welsh Government holds back a 'top slice' for centrally funded initiatives or services (such as the costs of training new doctors and nurses). It then decides how to share the rest of the allocations to NHS organisations. In 2016/17 the final budget for NHS delivery set in March 2016 was £6.3bn.

Revenue allocation

Each LHB has a unified allocation to fund healthcare for its population. The allocation for hospital and community health services is based on resident populations. Allocations for general medical services and prescribing are based on registered populations, and pharmacy and dental contract allocations are based on the provision of services.

The distribution of funding is largely based on historical patterns. A needs-based allocation formula was developed by the late Professor Townsend in 2001 to allocate funding based on the health needs of the local population. The formula takes as its base the population covered

---

[1] Final budget main expenditure group, components of the Welsh budget, March 2016.

by a LHB area and then adjusts that total to take account of:
- the health needs of the population
- unavoidable geographical variations in the cost of services.

LHBs contribute funding to the Welsh Health Specialised Services Committee (WHSSC) which is responsible for planning and funding specialised services on behalf of the LHBs.

Velindre NHS Trust receives its funding through 'healthcare agreements' with the LHBs and some funding via WHSSC.

The Public Health Wales NHS Trust receives the majority of its funding directly from the Welsh Government.

In 2014 the *Emergency Ambulance Services Committee (Wales) Regulations 2014* removed responsibility for the planning and securing of the provision of emergency ambulance services from the WHSSC to a separate joint committee of the LHB chief executives, called the Emergency Ambulance Services Committee (EASC).

As well as the Welsh Government revenue allocation, healthcare agreements with other LHBs and cross border income, LHBs may also receive funding from:
- the leasing of buildings
- charges to staff, visitors or patients (for example, catering or private patient facilities)
- the Welsh Government for specific initiatives, teaching and research and development
- grants from government bodies.

Capital allocation

In 2016/17 the capital budget is £273 million, which accounts for 4% of the total health budget. The Welsh Government allocates these capital resources to LHBs and NHS trusts. There are 2 types:
- discretionary capital to cover routine equipment replacement, IT developments and small-scale building works
- all-Wales infrastructure programme for specific medium to large scale schemes beyond the scope of discretionary capital.

LHBs and trusts are required to submit business cases for funding for major capital schemes using the *Five Case Model*. The HSSG has established an infrastructure investment board (IIB) to provide support to LHBs and trusts in the development of business cases, and also to scrutinise cases at all stages of their development.

All NHS infrastructure investment proposals must be prioritised at a local level and included in the integrated medium term plans of NHS organisations.

NHS trusts are allowed to retain sale proceeds from the disposal of assets up to a maximum of £500,000.

As with other parts of the public sector, the Welsh Government and NHS Wales are not able to vire funds between capital and revenue allocations.

The private finance initiative is no longer used in Wales although a small number of schemes still exist.

How the NHS in Wales Demonstrates Financial Accountability

The *National Health Services Finance (Wales) Act 2014* changed the statutory financial duties of LHBs from a single financial duty (to achieve a break-even position on an annual basis) to two financial duties:

- a duty under section 175 (1) to secure that its expenditure does not exceed the aggregate of funding allotted to it over a period of 3 financial years
- a duty under section 175 (2A) and the directions issued by the Welsh ministers under section 175(2), to prepare a plan to secure compliance with the duty under section 175(1) while improving the health of the people for whom it is responsible, and the provision of healthcare to such people, and for that plan to be submitted to and approved by the Welsh ministers.

While the Act only changed the LHB statutory financial duties, the principles behind the Act (of two financial duties) apply equally to NHS trusts.

Under the 3 year rolling duty, the first assessment of the financial duty will take place at the end of 2016/17. This three year statutory duty encompasses both revenue and capital expenditure. Full details are set out in WHC/2015/014[2].

The financial performance of NHS organisations in Wales is assessed using the following targets:

- three year break even performance for NHS trusts or resource limit for LHBs (the 3 year rolling break even duty)
- external financing limit for NHS trusts (the difference between what a trust plans to spend on capital in a year and the level of funding that it has available internally)
- preparation of a three year integrated medium term plan (IMTP) which is approved by Welsh ministers
- capital resource limits for LHBs and NHS trusts
- creditor payments (95% of non-NHS creditors, based on the number of bills, must be paid within 30 days of delivery or receipt of a valid invoice whichever is sooner).

In 2015/16 five of the seven LHBs and two of the three trusts met the requirement to produce an approved IMTP.

The format and presentation of statutory accounts for the NHS in Wales is similar to that for trusts in England. The Welsh Government produces separate *Manuals for Accounts* for LHBs and NHS trusts. The accounts must be adopted formally by the Board and presented, as part of the overall annual report of the organisation, at the annual general meeting by 30 September following the financial year end on 31 March.

The Director of Finance is responsible for preparing the accounts.

The individual accounts of LHBs and NHS trusts are summarised into two consolidated NHS accounts that are then subject to independent audit and scrutiny by the Wales Audit Office.

Each NHS organisation is also required to submit monthly monitoring statements reporting on actual financial performance and forecast outturn. This is supplemented by a detailed commentary from the Director of Finance detailing assumptions and risks behind the reported position. The overall position is monitored by the Welsh Government. Ministers will occasionally make a statement to the Assembly on the financial position of the NHS in Wales.

Health and Social Care Strategy in Wales

The regulation and performance management of the NHS in Wales is undertaken in the context of the Welsh Government's health and social care strategy. The health strategy for the period from 2011 to 2016 was titled *Together for Health*, but this is likely to be updated with a new strategy during 2016.

[2] http://gov.wales/docs/dhss/publications/150511WHC014en.pdf

In 2014, the former Minister for Health and Social Services launched the concept of 'Prudent Healthcare for Wales', based on the following main principles:

- achieve health and wellbeing with the public, patients and professionals as equal partners through co-production
- care for those with the greatest health need first, making the most effective use of all skills and resources
- do only what is needed, no more, no less; and do no harm
- reduce inappropriate variation using evidence based practices consistently and transparently.

In February 2016, the Welsh Government and NHS Wales jointly published *Prudent Healthcare: Securing Health and Well-being for Future Generations* to support national action.

Programme for Government

A Labour Minority Government was formed following the Assembly elections in May 2016. The Government will develop a Programme for Government which sets out its priorities to be delivered until the next Assembly elections in 2021.

How the NHS in Wales is Regulated

Performance management

As indicated above, under the *National Health Services Finance (Wales) Act 2014*, LHBs and trusts are directed by the Welsh Government to prepare and submit integrated medium term plans (IMTP) covering a three year period. The format and content of these plans was set out in an annual planning framework document issued by the HSSG[3].

The IMTP is a plan which sets out the organisation's strategy for complying with its financial duties while improving:

- the health of the people for whom it is responsible and
- the provision of healthcare to such people.

Whilst developing the IMTP, wider statutory duties such as the requirement to undertake a joint assessment of the local population's care and support needs under the *Social Services and Well-being (Wales) Act 2014* and to plan services jointly with other public bodies under the *Well-being of Future Generations (Wales) Act 2015*, must be taken into account.

The *NHS Outcomes Framework* was introduced in 2015/16 to try to focus the plans on outcomes rather than process and is based around measuring outcomes under seven domains:

- staying healthy
- safe care
- effective care
- dignified care
- timely care
- individual care
- our staff and resources (including financial).

---

[3] The 2016/17 requirements can be found here: gov.wales/docs/dhss/publications/151012whcnhsplanningen.pdf

The IMTPs must therefore contain details of how the organisation plans to meet the Framework's requirements.

LHBs are also required to submit delivery plans for specific services (for example, stroke and heart disease) to outline actions to achieve nationally agreed performance measures and outcomes.

A number of regular meetings are held between the HSSG and LHBs and trusts in order to monitor performance against both the IMTP and the individual service delivery plans. These include Joint Executive Team (JET) meetings and Quality and Delivery (Q&D) meetings.

As mentioned earlier, the HSSG is supported by a National Delivery Group in relation to performance management and improvement of NHS Wales organisations.

Audit

The external audit arrangements in Wales are different to England. The Wales Audit Office was created in April 2005 and the Auditor General for Wales is now responsible for auditing all public accounts and laying them before the Assembly.

Each NHS organisation is responsible for providing an effective internal audit service to meet Public Sector Internal Audit Standards (PSIAS). All NHS bodies are required to submit a governance statement as part of their annual accounts. Accountable officers (i.e. chief executives) are required to sign the statement on behalf of the board.

Standards

In 2013, the Welsh Government agreed the need for a review of the *Doing Well; Doing Better: Standards for Health Services in Wales 2010* and the *Fundamentals of Care Standards (2003)*. Jointly these two sets of standards had provided common frameworks for quality services in healthcare and social care respectively. An amended set of integrated *Health and Care Standards* was published in April 2015. They are structured as follows:

Source: figure 1, *Health and Care Standards*, April 2015

How NHS Organisations in Wales are Structured and Run

For the NHS in Wales, governance is defined as 'A system of accountability to citizens, service users, stakeholders and the wider community, within which healthcare organisations work, take decisions and lead their people to achieve their objectives.'

As in England, all NHS organisations have a board which is the pre-eminent governing body and has some functions 'reserved' to it (including financial stewardship, strategy and appointing senior executives). However, they are also required to establish (as a minimum) a number of committees to cover the following aspects of board business:

- quality and safety
- audit
- information governance
- charitable funds
- remuneration and terms of service
- Mental Health Act requirements.

As in England, NHS bodies must have an 'Accountable Officer' (the chief executive) who is accountable to the Welsh Government for the proper stewardship of public money and assets and for the organisation's performance. Chief executives are also accountable to their own board for meeting its objectives and the day-to-day running of the organisation.

Following extensive consultation, the Welsh Government has issued two documents outlining expectations relating to the behaviour of NHS employers and employees: the *Code of Conduct for Healthcare Support Workers* and the *Code of Practice for NHS Wales Employers*. Both codes support the basic principles of service user safety and public protection and should underpin the day-to-day working practices of NHS Wales.

Shared services in Wales

The NHS Wales shared services partnership (NWSSP) is an independent organisation, owned and directed by NHS Wales that supports NHS Wales through the provision of a range of 'back office' functions and services including internal audit, procurement, counter-fraud services and employment services (including payroll and payment of expenses).

Commissioning

LHBs are responsible for deciding how to use their funding to meet the health needs of their population including hospital, community, GP and other primary care services. LHBs also fund services provided by the private and independent sectors although the Welsh Government is committed to eliminating the use of private sector hospitals.

LHBs also contribute to the WHSSC, which plans and funds specialised services on behalf of the boards. The WHSSC decides how to use its funding to meet the specialist health needs of the whole Welsh population.

Patient flows between LHBs are funded through healthcare agreements between the boards. These are currently based on historic costs, but consideration is being given to introducing an all-Wales standard price for activity.

Although LHBs have a large amount of discretion in relation to how they use their funding, they must meet the priorities set out in the *Delivery and Outcomes Framework* issued by the Welsh Government, and they must develop their plans together with local authorities.

Costing

Since 2009/10, costs have been based on HRG version 4 and costing of provider services has been a requirement for LHBs. LHBs are also required to analyse costs over the 23 programme budget categories, based on version 10 of the *International Classification of Diseases*.

The Welsh Government has encouraged all LHBs and Velindre NHS Trust to produce patient level costing information and NHS Wales has declared a long-term goal to move to the collection of patient-level cost data.

The development of costing and benchmarking in NHS Wales is overseen by a Financial Information Costing and Benchmarking Group – a sub-group of the NHS Wales Directors of Finance Group.

How Services are Paid for

As mentioned above, patient flows between LHBs are funded through healthcare agreements between the boards. These are based on historic costs. Work is expected to be undertaken to review current inter-LHB commissioning arrangements in Wales, which will be led by the Welsh Health Collaborative. Healthcare agreements also cover funding allocated by the WHSSC to specialised services health board providers.

Treatment for some Welsh residents, particularly for specialised services and patients living in North Wales and Powys, is delivered by English NHS providers. These treatments are funded through contracts with the English provider. Where applicable, payment is based on the English tariff (see chapter 18).

Charitable Funds

Charitable funds are held by NHS trusts and LHBs in Wales under the same legislative framework as exists in England. All funds are registered with the Charity Commission and accounts must be submitted to the Charity Commission.

See chapter 19 for more about charitable funds in England and Wales.

References and Further Reading

Welsh Government health and social care web pages:
http://new.wales.gov.uk/topics/health/?lang=en

Health in Wales Information Service: www.wales.nhs.uk

All legislation referred to is available via: http://www.legislation.gov.uk/

Final budget main expenditure group, components of the Welsh budget, March 2016
gov.wales/docs/caecd/publications/160301-meg-en.pdf

Details of the 2016/17 allocations: gov.wales/topics/health/nhswales/circulars/finance/?lang=en

Public sector business cases using the five case model HM Treasury, 2013: www.gov.uk/government/publications/the-green-book-appraisal-and-evaluation-in-central-governent

Better Payment Practice Code: www.payontime.co.uk/

NHS Wales Governance e-Manual (including the NHS Wales Act 2006 and Citizen Centred Governance Principles): www.wales.nhs.uk/governance-emanual/home

LHB and Trust Manuals for Accounts:
http://www.wales.nhs.uk/governance-emanual/local-health-board-and-nhs-trust-annual-

Wales Audit Office: www.wao.gov.uk/

Healthcare Inspectorate Wales: www.hiw.org.uk/

Together for Health, 2012:
http://gov.wales/topics/health/publications/health/reports/together/?lang=en

Prudent Healthcare: Securing Health and Well-being for Future Generations, Welsh Government and NHS Wales, 2016: http://www.prudenthealthcare.org.uk/wp-content/uploads/2016/02/Securing-Health-and-Wellbeing-for-Future-Generations1.pdf

NHS Outcomes Framework, 2015: http://gov.wales/docs/dhss/publications/150417whc017en.pdf

Health and Care Standards, 2015:
gov.wales/topics/health/publications/health/guidance/care-standards/?lang=en

Code of Conduct for Healthcare Support Workers and The Code of Practice for NHS Wales Employers: http://www.wales.nhs.uk/nhswalescodeofconductandcodeofpractice

Appendix
Glossary of Terms

> This listing includes a brief explanation of some of the terms used in the Guide but is not exhaustive. If you are planning to study any of the HFMA's e-learning modules you will have access to an extensive on-line glossary. In addition, the Association has produced a number of briefings that list key financial and governance terms. These can be downloaded (free of charge) from the publications section of our website – type in 'glossary' to the search function: https://www.hfma.org.uk/publications

Accountability	Demonstrating on an ongoing basis that public money is being used wisely and effectively.
Accountable/Accounting Officer	Responsible for ensuring that his or her organisation operates effectively, economically and with probity; makes good use of resources and keeps proper accounts.
Accounts direction	Sets out detailed rules about the preparation, approval and publication of the annual report and accounts.
Accrual	An accounting concept that is designed to ensure that the accounts and budget reports show all the income and expenditure that relate to the financial year.
Activity-based budgeting	Produces a budget for a defined activity level. As activity levels change, so do costs and income.
Administration income/expenditure	Income/expenditure that is not for the direct provision of healthcare or healthcare related services.
Allocation	The annual amount of money made available to deliver/purchase healthcare for local people.
Amortisation	Follows the same underlying principle as depreciation but is the term used in relation to intangible assets such as patents, intellectual property and software licences.
Audit	The process of validating the accuracy, completeness and adequacy of disclosure in financial records.
Audit committee	A statutory committee of the governing body/board of all NHS organisations. Its role is to review and report on the relevance and rigour of the governance structures in place and the assurances the board receives.
Balanced budget	A budget that delivers break-even or a surplus.
Benchmarking	The process of measuring and comparing performance against other similar organisations to obtain information that helps to identify areas for potential improvement.
Best practice tariffs	Reflect the costs of delivering treatments in line with NICE guidance. They financially incentivise the clinically appropriate model against other treatments for the same condition.

Better care fund (BCF)	CCGs and local authorities in England contribute an agreed level of resource into a single 'pot' that is then used to commission health and social care services enabling patients to experience a seamless service with a single point of access for their health and social care needs.
Block contract	Allows a healthcare provider to receive a 'lump sum' payment to provide a service irrespective of the number of patients treated or the type of treatment provided.
Board assurance framework (BAF)	Records the key processes used to manage the organisation and the principle risks to meeting its strategic objectives.
Break-even	Income equals expenditure. All NHS bodies are expected to operate a balanced budget ensuring that total expenditure does not exceed total income.
Budget	A financial and/or quantitative statement that is prepared and agreed for a specific future period. It translates aims into a statement of the resources needed to fulfil them and has either a monetary or non-monetary value.
Budget manager	The single named individual responsible for ensuring that the budget is met and highlighting when the budget is likely to be under or over spent.
Budget monitoring	A continuous process of reviewing actual income and expenditure or non-financial data – for example, patient activity against the budget.
Business case	A formal process for identifying the financial and qualitative implications of options for changing services and/or making investments.
Business plan	The written end product of a process that identifies the aims, objectives and resource requirements of an organisation over the next three to five year period.
Capital	An asset (or group of functionally interdependent assets) with a useful life expectancy of greater than one year, whose cost exceeds a minimum threshold, normally £5,000.
Capital resource limit (CRL)	A limit on the amount that may be spent on capital purchases. It takes account of money owed by and to the organisation in relation to capital as well as the sale or disposal of assets. If net capital expenditure is less than the limit, the target has been achieved.
Code of accountability	This defines the public service values that must underpin the work of NHS governing bodies, sets out accountability regimes and describes the basis on which NHS organisations should fulfil their statutory duties.
Commissioning for quality and innovation (CQUIN)	Payments designed to ensure that a proportion of providers' income in England is conditional on quality and innovation and is linked to service improvement.

Consolidation	The requirement for individual NHS bodies' accounts to be included in a consolidated set of accounts with other bodies under common control.
Constitution and/or standing orders	Translate an organisation's statutory powers into a series of practical rules designed to protect the interests of the organisation, its staff and 'customers'. They specify how functions will be carried out and how decisions will be made.
Cost improvement plan/programme (CIP)	Sets out the savings that an NHS organisation plans to make to reduce its expenditure/increase efficiency. It is used to close the gap between the funding received and the expenditure incurred in any one year.
Cost pressures	A generic cost pressure is an increase in cost that is generally beyond the control of an individual organisation. A local cost pressure is an increase in cost that, although it may or may not be geographically widespread, is considered to be within the control of an individual organisation.
Costing	Quantifying, in financial terms, the value of resources consumed in carrying out a particular activity/service or producing a certain unit of output.
Currency	A defined unit of output activity or healthcare that is paid for by commissioners.
Deferred income	Income received in advance for goods or services that have not yet been delivered or provided.
Depreciation	A non-cash expense that recognises that assets are 'used up' during their useful life. The term relates to tangible assets such as property, plant and equipment, as well as some intangible assets such as software development.
Direct costs	Costs that can be directly attributed to a particular activity or output.
Discretionary capital	The element of Welsh NHS organisations' capital resource allocations that is intended for meeting statutory obligations.
Drawdown	The amount of cash that a CCG can access. Cash cannot be accessed in advance of when it is needed.
External financing limit (EFL)	External financing limit (EFL) is one of the performance targets against which financial performance is measured. It is a control on net cash flows and trusts must not overshoot their EFL.
Financial model	A mechanism used for illustrating what the income and costs for different scenarios will be, when they will be received and incurred and what tolerances there are for each.
Five case model	The HM Treasury approach used to develop public sector business cases for spending proposals. It requires consideration of five 'cases': strategic, economic, commercial, financial and management.

Fixed costs	Costs that do not increase or decrease with changes in levels of activity.
Forecast	A prediction of future financial performance.
Full business case (FBC)	A written document that brings together the arguments for a preferred planned investment including current and future service requirements, affordability, the organisation's competitive service position and the ability to complete the project within the specified budget and time scale.
Governance	The system by which organisations are directed and controlled. It is concerned with how an organisation is run – how it structures itself and how it is led.
Governance statement (GS)	A key component of the annual report and accounts and is signed by the Accountable Officer (on behalf of the governing body). It is designed to provide assurance in relation to the system of internal control that has been operating throughout the preceding year.
Governing body/board	The organisation's pre-eminent group that takes corporate responsibility for the strategies and actions of the organisation and is accountable to the public for the services provided.
Gross Domestic Product (GDP)	The total money value of all final goods and services produced in an economy. GDP is the most commonly used indicator of national income and measures the sum of incomes received by the various wealth creating sectors of the economy: manufacturing, agriculture, service industries. It is 'gross' because GDP does not allow for the depreciation of physical capital – wear and tear on factory machines, office equipment becoming outdated, etc.
Healthcare agreements	Contracts agreed between two local health boards or a local health board and an NHS trust.
Healthcare resource groups (HRGs)	The currency used to collate the costs of procedures/diagnoses into common groupings.
Incremental/historical budget/base budget	The previous year's budget adjusted for all known changes and developments.
Indirect costs	Costs that cannot be attributed directly to a particular activity or cost centre.
Liquidity	A measure of how long an organisation could continue if it collected no more cash from debtors.
Local modification	An increase to a national price agreed between a commissioner and provider in England if local circumstances make it uneconomic to continue to provide a particular service at the national price.
Local price	A price for a healthcare activity that is negotiated and agreed between a commissioner and provider in England.

Glossary of Terms

Local variation	An increase or decrease in a national price or a change in currency agreed between a commissioner and a provider in England if the national price is not appropriate for local circumstances.
Manual for accounts	Sets out how health bodies should apply international financial reporting standards (IFRS) when preparing their accounts. It includes sector specific disclosures required in their annual report and accounts.
Market forces factor (MFF)	A payment index applied to all NHS bodies in England providing services under the national tariff to account for geographical variations in the cost of providing healthcare in different parts of the country.
National price	The price set by NHS Improvement for a defined unit of healthcare. It is the amount paid by a commissioner in England to reimburse a provider of NHS funded healthcare.
National tariff	The system of financial flows to move funds around the health service. It enables healthcare providers in England to be reimbursed for the costs of providing treatment.
National tariff document (NTD)	The document jointly published each year by NHS Improvement and NHS England outlining the payment mechanism for the NHS in England.
Nolan principles	The key principles for how individuals and organisations in the public sector should conduct themselves.
Non-executive director/non-officer member/lay member	Normally appointed by the organisation's nominations committee, they are key members of the organisation's governing body/board. Appointed based on their individual skills and what they will bring to the overall composition of the board, they are expected to challenge decisions and strategies.
Non-recurrent	One-off income, expenditure or savings.
Outline business case (OBC)	A written document that evaluates different investment options using economic appraisals to identify the preferred option in financial terms.
Overhead costs	Those costs that contribute to the general running of the organisation but cannot be directly related to an activity or service.
Patient level costing	Allocating costs to an individual patient.
Patient level costing and information system (PLICS)	Computer software that enables an organisation to determine and analyse patient-level costs.
Personal health budget (PHB)	The support a person purchases or arranges, to meet agreed health and/or social care outcomes.
Pooled budget	A local authority and an NHS body combine resources and jointly commission or manage an integrated service.

Prime financial policies/standing financial instructions (SFIs)	Set out the organisation's detailed financial procedures and responsibilities. They are designed to ensure that NHS organisations account fully and openly for all that they do.
Programme income or expenditure	Any income spent or expenditure incurred on the direct provision of healthcare or healthcare related services.
Public dividend capital (PDC)	Represents the Department of Health's equity interest in defined public assets across the NHS. The Department is required to make a return on its net assets of 3.5%. For NHS providers this is paid as a PDC dividend.
Quality, innovation, productivity and prevention (QIPP)	A programme in England designed to identify savings that can be reinvested in the health service and improve the quality of care. Responsibility for achievement lies with CCGs.
Recurrent	On-going income, expenditure or savings.
Reference costs	NHS organisations are required to submit a schedule of costs of delivered healthcare resource groups/activities to allow direct comparison of the relative costs of different providers. The results are published each year in the national schedule of reference costs.
Reserves	Monies that are set aside for a specific purpose, often on receipt of specific or ring-fenced income.
Resource limit (RL) or revenue resource limit (RRL)	One of the financial performance targets used to determine whether or not operational financial balance has been met.
Revenue costs	The day-to-day costs of running an organisation.
Revenue funding	The funding received by an NHS organisation to meet the costs of its day-to-day activities.
Scheme of reservation and delegation	A detailed listing of who the governing body/board empowers to take actions or make decisions on its behalf.
Semi fixed/step costs	Costs that tend to remain fixed for a given level of activity but change in steps when activity levels exceed or fall below given levels.
Service line management (SLM)	An 'organisation structure and management framework' where specialist clinical areas are identified and managed as distinct operational units.
Service line reporting (SLR)	Looking in detail at the profitability and financial contribution of services in much the same way as a private sector company analyses its business units.
Standards of business conduct	The strict ethical standards to be applied by all staff when conducting NHS business.
Transformation programmes	Enable an NHS organisation or number of organisations to fundamentally change the way that a service is provided/delivered.
Underlying deficit	A recurrent, ongoing mismatch between an organisation's revenue and expenditure.

Value for money (VFM)	The maximum benefit has been obtained from the goods or services bought or investment made.
Variable costs	Those costs that increase/decrease in line with changes in the level of activity.
Variance	The difference between what was planned and what actually happens in financial terms.
Virement	The process of transferring money from one budget heading/line to another.
Working capital	The money and assets (owned resources) that an organisation can call upon to finance its day-to-day operations.
Zero-based budgeting (ZBB)	An approach to budgeting that involves starting with a blank sheet of paper and building up the budget, working out all figures based on the agreed objectives and what it will cost to meet them.